Suddenly we were in the hornets' nest.

There were 109s and 190s all around. I saw three 190s screaming down on Blakeslee to take him off the tail of their two buddies. "Horseback Blue One to Horseback Leader; three coming in on you at 3 o'clock high. I'm trying to cut them off."

I tried to pull out of my thundering dive, but the controls were rigid. All my strength wouldn't move the stick and I knew I was in the so-called "terminal dive" from which many P-47 pilots never were able to pull out. I reached for the small winder that set the trim of the plane for take-off and landing, hoping that the little servo edge on the tail-plane would ease it up, but not fast enough to buckle the wings.

I blacked out and felt as if my back was broken, but when my vision cleared I saw the 190s ahead of me, much closer, but still out of range. I was gaining on them thanks to the terrible speed I'd built up, but they were gaining on Blakeslee, and he was doggedly pursuing his prey.

I pressed my mike button. "Break, Horseback Leader, break hard right!"

TUMULT IN THE CLOUDS

Lt. Col. JAMES A. GOODSON

ST. MARTIN'S PAPERBACKS

TUMULT IN THE CLOUDS

Copyright © 1983 by James A. Goodson.

Library of Congress Catalog Card Number: 83-24422

ISBN: 0-312-90477-0

Printed in the United States of America

St. Martin's Press hardcover edition/June 1984
St. Martin's Paperbacks edition/November 1986

10 9 8 7 6 5 4 3 2

DEDICATION

This book is dedicated to the Happy Warriors: those of the RAF who were the inspiration; those of the Eagle Squadrons who led the way; and those of the Fourth Fighter Group, who wore the wings of two great Air Forces with pride and honour.

Acknowledgements

I would like to express my sincere thanks to all my friends who have given help and encouragement in the preparation of this book; and particularly to Danny Morris, author of *Aces and Wingmen*, Roger Freeman, author of *The Mighty Eighth* and to Leroy Nitschke, of the Association of the Fourth Fighter Group for putting their photographic collections at my disposal; to Colonel Richard Uppstrom and his staff at the Air Force Museum, Wright Field, and particularly to Charles Worman of the Research Division; to William Hess of the American Fighter Aces Association, Barrett Tillman of the Champlin Fighter Museum in Mesa, Arizona; Garry Fry, Keith Braybrooke, Harry Holmes, Thomas Foxworth and Len Morgan, for their help with research and photographs. And, of course, to the late Grover Hall, for his careful record of the life and times of the Fourth Fighter Group.

J.A.G.

Contents

An Irish Airman Foresees his Death (1917)

I know that I shall meet my fate
Somewhere among the clouds above;
Those that I fight I do not hate
Those that I guard I do not love;
My country is Kiltartan Cross
My countrymen Kiltartan's poor
No likely end could bring them loss
Or leave them happier than before.
Nor law, nor duty bade me fight
Nor public men, nor cheering crowds,
A lonely impulse of delight
Drove to this tumult in the clouds
I balanced all, brought all to mind,
The years to come seemed waste of breath
A waste of breath the years behind
In balance with this life, this death.

W.B. YEATS

(By kind permission of M.B. Yeats, Anne Yeats,
and MacMillan London Limited.)

CHAPTER ONE

The King's Enemies

'This morning the British Ambassador in Berlin handed the German Government a final note stating that, unless we heard from them by 11 o'clock that they were prepared at once to withdraw their troops from Poland, a state of war would exist between us.

'I have to tell you now that no such undertaking has been received, and that consequently this country is at war with Germany ...

'Now may God bless you all. May He defend the right. It is the evil things that we shall be fighting against — brute force, bad faith, injustice, oppression and persecution — and against them I am certain that right will prevail.'

The voice sounded clipped and pedantic, even politely bored.

There was silence in the Third Class Lounge. Finally I said: 'This is the way the world ends: not with a bang but a whimper!'

'Who said that?'

'T.S. Eliot.'

'Well, we're well out of it!' That was the feeling of most of the passengers. We had left old Europe only hours before she slid into the abyss. It was 3rd September 1939. The ship was the SS *Athenia*.

The loudspeaker announced the lifeboat drill. I dutifully went back to my cabin to pick up my life-jacket and made my way to the deck and lifeboat station. The boat was large, and I calculated that there would perhaps be just enough space for us all, but it would be crowded. The normal capacity of the ship was about 1,000, but with returning American and Canadian tourists, English, Scottish and Irish emigrants and Eastern European refugees, there were at least 1,300 passengers.

In the lounge, there was laughter and singing. It may have been because they'd had more to drink, but the English-speaking nationalities were leading the entertainments. The young Americans launched into a sing-song, accompanied by a piano, and by the Canadians, English, Scots, Irish and Welsh. There was 'Home on the Range', 'Shenandoah'. 'My Old Kentucky Home', 'Mammy', and the rest of them. The English came up with 'Ilkley Moor Baht 'at', 'Knees up Mother Brown', and of course 'Land of Hope and Glory'. From the Irish, we had 'The Mountains of Mourne' and 'Danny Boy'; from the Welsh, 'Men of Harlech', 'We'll keep a Welcome in the Hillsides' and 'Land of my Fathers' sung beautifully by bass, tenor, contralto, and soprano voices, with descant thrown in; from the Scots, we had 'Scotland The Brave', 'Roamin' in the Gloamin' ' and 'I belong to Glasgow'.

Then a young boy was persuaded to sing solo. He was about seventeen, like me, but he seemed younger, with dark hair, but blue eyes. He was small and slight and almost feminine. His voice was a beautiful high tenor and every note was as true as a bell. He held his audience completely. There was no sound from them. The beer was left untouched. He sang 'Oh where, tell me where has my highland laddie gone', 'The Bonnie, Bonnie Banks of Loch Lomond' and 'The Road to the Isles', and each of the well-known songs was given a new pathos and yearning, reflecting his own sadness and touching the homesickness of all those who were leaving home and family, probably never to see them again. There were tears in their eyes, and in the blue eyes of the singer, and even in the eyes of the Canadians and Americans as they shared the great sense of nostalgia for old places and beloved faces. That was the mood of the *Athenia* on the last full day of her life.

By the evening we were off the Hebrides. The strong west wind was cold, the sky cloudy, and the ship was pitching and rolling slightly on the ocean swells.

I had just mounted the staircase and was moving forward to the dining room when it struck. It was a powerful explosion quickly followed by a loud crack and whistle. The ship shuddered under the blow. The lights went out. There were women's screams. The movement of the ship changed strangely as she slewed to a stop. People were running in all directions, calling desperately to one another.

We all knew the ship was mortally stricken; she was beginning to list.

The emergency lights were turned on. I went back to the companionway I had just come up. I gazed down at a sort of Dante's Inferno; a gaping hole at the bottom of which was a churning mass of water on which there were broken bits of wooden stairway, flooring and furniture. Terrified people were clinging to this flotsam, and to the wreckage of the rest of the stairway which was cascading down the side of the gaping hole. The blast must have come up through here from the engine room below, past the cabin decks, and the third class restaurant and galley. I clambered and slithered down to the level of the restaurant. I started by reaching for the outstretched arms and pulling the weeping shaking, frightened women to safety; but I soon saw that the most urgent danger was to those who were floundering in the water, or clinging to the wreckage lower down. Many were screaming that they couldn't swim. Some were already close to drowning.

I slithered down the shattered stairway, slipped off my jacket and shoes, and plunged into the surging water. One by one, I dragged them to the foot of the broken companionway, and left them to clamber up to the other rescuers above.

When there were no more bodies floundering in the water, I turned to those who were cowering in the openings of the corridors which led from the cabins to what had been the landing at the foot of the stairs and which was now a seething, lurching mass of water. Most of them were women, many were children and some were men. I went first to the children. They left their mothers, put their small arms around my neck and clung to me. They clung as we slipped into the water; they clung as I swam to the foot of the dangling steps; they clung as I climbed the slippery wreckage; and they clung as I prised their little arms from around me and passed them to those at the top. These were members of the crew. A few stewards and stewardesses, and even some seamen. The *Athenia* was a Glasgow ship and so was her crew. They knew their jobs, they rose to the challenge, and above all, they kept their heads. One seaman had climbed halfway down to take the women and children from me and pass them on to those waiting above. With a strong Glasgow accent, he soothed and comforted the mothers and children, and shouted praise and encouragement to me.

'Bloody guid, mon! Keep 'em coming!'

I looked up out of the water.

'I could do with some help down here.'

The seaman shook his head sadly.

'Ah wish the hell ah cuid, but ah canna swum!'

I looked up at the others. They shook their heads too. It had never occurred to me that members of a ship's crew would not be able to swim. Finally there were no more left either in the water, or waiting at the openings of the corridors. I was at the base of the broken stairs. For the first time, I was able to pause and look around. By now, the ship had listed much more. The water had slopped into the corridors on the down side until it was waist-high. The corridors on the upper side were out of the water. Two seamen were crawling down to help.

'We've got to make sure there's no one left in the cabins. We'll take this upper passageway. Can you swim to the lower one? There's not many of them. The emergency watertight doors have been closed at the next bulkhead, so we just have to check the ones in this section.'

I pushed off into the lurching water and swam to the opening of one of the half-flooded gangways. I was able to swim right to it, get to my feet and splash my way into darkness, walking half on the floor and half on the bulkheads. The water in most of the cabins was too deep and the light was too dim to conduct any kind of a search. What was worse as I stumbled through the water and darkness, there was a movement of the ship as it listed further. The water sloshed higher, and there were deep rumblings in the bowels of the sinking ship.

I yelled out through the dark, ghostly gangways and cabins. 'Anyone there? Anyone there?'

There wasn't. The feeling grew in me that this deck was already at the bottom of the sea, as it would be for hundreds of years.

As I felt my way through the flooded, dark cabins and gangways, I stumbled across mysterious objects moving under the shifting water. I stumbled into what seemed to be a half-submerged bundle of clothing. It seemed to follow me as I returned towards the open shaft. In the dim light, I turned it over. Then I saw the innocent face, gashed and bloodied, and the dark, curly hair, and the blue eyes, which would never weep again for the bonnie banks of Loch Lomond. Now other lips would be asking where their highland laddie had gone.

I realised it was useless to search any longer. I struggled back to the light, and left the lower decks to the dead, the darkness and the sea.

The crew members were waiting to help me up the wreckage, up past the smashed dining-rooms to the upper decks.

'Thanks!' I said when we got to the top. I shook both seamen by the hand.

The ship was listing quite a bit now. We headed up the sloping deck to the higher side. We found them launching one of the last lifeboats. It was crowded. Members of the crew were holding back those for whom there was no more room and telling them to go to another boat. Meanwhile, the two seamen fore and aft in the boat were desperately trying to lower it. But as the heavy boat lurched unevenly down as the ropes slid through the pulleys of the davits, a problem arose which was apparently not foreseen by the designers of lifeboat launching systems. Because of the listing of the ship, when the lifeboat was lowered from its davits, and, as it swayed with the slight rolling, it fouled the side. Although the seamen were playing out their ropes as evenly as possible, the forward part got caught against the side of the ship. The seaman continued to play out his rope. Suddenly it slid free and dropped. But the after rope hadn't played out as much as the one forward. The front of the boat dropped, but the rear was caught by its rope. Soon the boat was hanging by the after rope. The screaming passengers were tumbling out of the boat like rag dolls, and falling down to the surface of the sea far below.

There was nothing we could do. I helped the crew to shepherd the remaining group of passengers to the other side of the ship.

We made our way to what seemed to be the last lifeboat, at least on that deck. Here there was another problem caused by the same list and the same swell; the boat was hanging on its davits, but swinging in and out. On its outer swing, there was a yawning gap between the lifeboat and the ship. Most of the passengers were women or elderly, or both. The responsible crew members were trying to persuade them to make their leap into the boat when it was close to the ship, but many of them waited too long, and the boat swung out again.

We pushed our way through the waiting crowd to help. As I reached the boat, the seaman in the bow shouted to an elderly lady: 'Jump! Now!'

But she hesitated. Perhaps she was pushed and the push badly timed. As the boat swung away, she lurched out towards it, the gap was already too wide. Her arms reached the gunwale, but her body fell through the space between lifeboat and ship, wrenching her arms away from the boat and those who were trying to drag her into it. I gazed after the falling body, dazed and speechless, until it hit the waves far below.

Finally the lifeboat could take no more passengers, and was lowered away, leaving a small group of us on the deserted, sloping deck. One of the ship's officers took command.

'That was the last of the boats, but the Captain's launch will be back for us soon; it's distributing the passengers evenly between the boats. Some of the ones that got away weren't quite full!'

'Aye, but how much time do we have before she goes?'

'There's no immediate danger. There was only one torpedo which hit midships and blew up through that compartment. The watertight doors were closed before other compartments were flooded, so they should keep her afloat awhile.'

Now that there was nothing to do, I felt depressed. Suddenly I thought of my money and papers I'd left with the Purser. I ran back to the companionway, and made my way to the Purser's office. There was the large safe still firmly locked shut. The state of the papers on the desk indicated a hurried departure. I tried in vain to open the safe, then turned and clambered back to the upper deck. Somehow I didn't feel like waiting for the Captain's launch; I wanted to be doing something, anything.

I went to the higher side of the ship and looked down the sloping side to the dark, rolling sea. There, just about 100 yards from the ship, I saw a lifeboat. Hanging from the davits, and making down the steel side of the ship were the ropes which had launched the boats.

In the dark, I couldn't see if they reached all the way to the sea, but they went far enough for me. Soon I was going down a rope hand over hand, fending myself off the side with my feet as the ship rolled. It was further than I had thought. Halfway down, my arms were aching. Long before I reached the bottom, I couldn't hold on any longer. As the rope slipped through my hands, I kicked away from the side and fell. It seemed a long time before I hit the water. I went in feet first. I started to struggle to the surface right away, but it seemed to take a long time. I thought I was a good under-water swimmer, but soon I desperately needed to breathe. In the darkness, there was no sign of the surface. For the first time I wished I'd been able to get to my life-jacket. If I passed out, it would at least have brought me to the surface. Just as I felt I could hold out no longer, I got to the surface. I gasped for breath. The sea was choppy, and I got a mouthful of water. It was colder, rougher and more brutal than I had expected. I looked for the lifeboat I had seen from the deck. I could only see it when I was lifted by a wave, and it looked much further away now.

I struck out in the direction of the boat, but it was a struggle. At times I felt I was making no headway at all. Eventually I got close enough to see one of the reasons. They had a few oars out, and were trying to row away from the ship. I knew that was in line with instructions, because of the danger of being sucked down with the ship when she sank; but, as I struggled to keep going, I did feel they could at least stop rowing until I caught up with them.

Fortunately, their efforts were badly co-ordinated and I finally reached them, and grabbed the gunwale, I tried to pull myself up, expecting helping hands to lift me into the boat; instead a dark young man, screaming in a foreign language put his hand in my face to push me away. A frantic middle-aged woman was prising my fingers off the side of the boat and banging on my knuckles. Dimly I realised they were panicking because they felt the boat was already over-crowded. I heard the voices of the seaman in charge down in the stern yelling to them to stop, but help came from another direction, and it was much more effective. The diminutive figure of a girl appeared. In a flash, she had landed a sharp right to the face of the young man, and sent him sprawling back off his seat. In the next second, my other tormentor was hauled away, and the strong young arms were reaching down to me. Other hands helped to haul me over the gunwale.

I collapsed in a wet heap on the bottom of the boat and gasped my thanks to my rescuers.

Amid peals of young female laughter I heard: 'Hey! You're an American!'

'So are you!' I mumbled in surprise.

'My God! You're half-drowned and freezing cold! Here!'

A blanket was being wrapped around my shoulders. I struggled to sit up, and opened my eyes to look at my guardian angel. She was a small, slim brunette, about nineteen or twenty, with an elfin face, full of life and humour. She was wearing a bra and pants and nothing else. I realised she had been wrapped in the blanket she was now trying to put around me.

'No! No! You need it more than I do,' and I took it off my shoulders and put it around hers.

'OK. We'll share it. That way we'll keep each other warm!' and she snuggled into my arms as I wrapped the blanket around us.

'What happened to the rest of your clothes?' I asked.

'We were dressing for dinner when the torpedo struck. We grabbed what we could and ran.'

I looked around and saw we were surrounded by young girls in various stages of undress. Some had borrowed sweaters and jackets from members of the crew. Others were huddled in blankets. At least most of them had life-jackets. As they snuggled together around us, I showed my surprise.

'Who are you?'

The little brunette laughed. 'We're college kids. We've been touring Europe after graduation. I guess our timing could have been better. I'm Jenny. This is Kay. That's Dodie.'

They were a wonderful, cheery bunch, cracking jokes and singing songs. We were an oasis of fun in the lifeboat. Most of the others were frightened or seasick or both. Many were refugees, mostly from Poland. Many were Jewish, but by no means all.

I was surprised at how large the boat seemed, even as it rolled and pitched on the North Atlantic swells. Up in the bow was a member of the ship's crew, and another in the stern. In spite of the crowd in the boat, they had been able to get some of the oars out, and had got some of the men to start rowing. After getting warmed up, I felt guilty at not pulling my weight. I got up and picked my way carefully to within shouting distance of the seaman in the stern.

'Do you want me to help out on the oars?'

He was surprised to find a volunteer. 'Ay! These two here are having a struggle. Maybe you could help them out. All we need to do is to keep away from the *Athenia* and head into the waves.'

I took the place of a young Jewish boy who was more of a hindrance than a help to his partner on the oar. He didn't speak English, but was delighted to find I spoke German, which meant he could communicate with me in Yiddish. He was even happier to be relieved of his task. The other man on the oar was also young. He didn't speak Yiddish or German, but he spoke a little English. He seemed to be somewhat handicapped by something hanging out of his mouth. At first I thought it was saliva or spittle, but when he saw me looking at it, he took it out of his mouth, and I saw that it was a St Christopher medallion on a silver chain around his neck.

'He save us!' he said and put the medal back in his mouth, clamped between his teeth.

I nodded, but I sincerely hoped that St Christopher was being helped by the last messages of the *Athenia*'s wireless operator. I knew that the crack of the second explosion had been a shell from the U-Boat, but I had seen that although it had killed a few people on the upper deck, it hadn't hit the radio mast or superstructure.

After an hour or so on the oars I suggested that we could stop rowing. We were far enough from the ship to be out of danger, but shouldn't get too far from her, because the rescue ships would be heading for her last reported position.

I went back to Jenny and my friendly college girls. Through the night, we clung together, chatted, sang and slept fitfully. At one point, I remember the Jews joining in singing that beautiful plaintiff dirge which became the hymn of the Jewish refugees, oppressed, and martyred throughout the world.

Occasionally we looked across to the stricken *Athenia*. We were amazed at how long she was staying afloat. She was sinking lower in the water, and listing further, but during most of the night, she was still there. It was about 1.30 a.m. when everyone in our boat woke out of their fitful sleep and looked across at the dark hulk. There had probably been a noise of some kind; or perhaps a shift in her position, although I don't remember either. Anyway, we were all watching when the stern began to sink lower. Soon it seemed to me that most of the near half of the ship was under water. Everything was in slow motion. Gradually, as the stern disappeared, the bow began to rise. We could see the water cascading off as the great ship reared up; slowly, and with enormous dignity. It was frightening, unbelievable, awesome. Finally the entire forward half of the ship was towering above us. When it was absolutely vertical, it paused. Then she started her final dive; imperceptibly at first, but gaining in momentum until she plunged to her death. A column of water came up as she disappeared, then there was only a great turbulence, and then nothing but the rolling sea and some floating debris. We felt lonelier and sadder. There was no singing now. We were tired and shivering with cold.

It was 4.30 when I saw it looming up through the dark. It was a ship. It was even carrying lights. We were too numbed to cheer. There was just a stirring in the boat; a grateful murmuring. The rowers picked up their oars and started rowing slowly towards the ship.

Other lifeboats were doing the same. Soon we found ourselves close to the big rescue ship, surrounded by five or six other boats. The big ship had stopped as soon as she was close to the boats. Rope ladders were dropped over the side near the stern of the ship. She was a tanker and must have been empty. She towered above us and we could see the blades of her big propeller as we came around to her stern. I looked up and saw her name and home port: '*Knute Nelson* — CHRISTIANSAND'; a Norwegian tanker.

As we came close, I called on the seaman on the tiller of our boat to keep us away from the menacing propeller. It was not moving, but I knew it could windmill, or the Captain might call for some weigh, unaware of the boats under his stern. One lifeboat was being tossed by the waves ever closer to the propeller. I yelled across to them, but apparently there were not enough rowers to stop the drift. Then the great propeller started to turn, churning up the water, and sucking the lifeboat in under the stern. As we watched, they were drawn into the whirlpool. We saw one big propeller blade slash through the boat; but as the shattered bow went down, the rest of the boat was lifted by the next blade coming up. The rearing, shattered boat spilled its human cargo into the churning water.

I called to the man on our tiller and on the rowers to make for the spot where the survivors were floundering in the water. The screw was no longer turning, and the ship had moved forward slightly. Some of the strong swimmers were already making for the bottom of the rope and wooden ladder dangling down the side of the ship close to the stern; some were pulled into our boat; others clung to the gunwales or oars for the short distance to the ladder; but many just disappeared under the foaming water.

We got the survivors from the broken lifeboat onto the ladder first. Then it was the turn of the weakest from our own boat. It wasn't easy. The boat was rising and falling on the waves, smashing against the steel sides of the tanker. Sometimes we got someone onto the ladder only to have them fall back into the boat as the ladder swung, or the boat dropped away too soon. We had to get them to get onto the ladder when the boat was at the top of its rise.

Finally there was no one left in the boat but the two seamen, the American college girls and myself. One by one, the girls started up the twisting, writhing ladder. Even for lithe, young, athletic teenagers, clambering up the tricky rope ladder took all their strength and concentration. There was no way they could keep the blankets wrapped around them; even those who had huddled into seamen's jackets which were far too big for them, wriggled out of them before attempting to scale the towering side of the tanker.

When I finally reached the top of the ladder and was hauled over the rail by two large Norwegian sailors onto the deck. I saw the incredulous Captain of the *Knute Nelson* staring at a group of shivering girls, mostly dressed in pants and bras, and nothing else. He hurried them to a companionway.

'Go down! Down! Any door! Any room! Warm! You must have warm!'

I followed them down the iron stairs until we came to a lower deck, and into the first door. The cabin was dark, but warm! It smelt cosily of human sleep; there was the sound of heavy breathing.

The light came on. We saw a series of bunks, one above the other. In each bunk was a large Norwegian seaman. The girls had only one thing in mind: to get warm. They didn't hesitate. The seamen, who had been at sea for weeks, and didn't even know that war had been declared, awoke to find half-naked girls clambering into their bunks and snuggling up to their warm bodies under the rough blankets. I'll never forget the expressions on the faces of those big Norwegians. They knew they must be dreaming.

When we had explained what had happened to those who understood English, and they had translated it to the others, those magnificent gentle giants turned out of their bunks, made us coffee, served out hard-tack biscuits, lent us their sweaters, and blankets, showed us the way to the 'head', and made us feel that, in spite of what we had been through, life was good!

We slept the sleep of the exhausted for many hours. When we came to, we learned that, as a ship of a neutral country, the *Knute Nelson* was taking us to the nearest neutral port: Galway on the west coast of Eire. We heard that other rescue ships, including British destroyers, had picked up other survivors.

Yes, Ireland is as green as they say, and Galway is as Irish as it's possible to be. We saw the green of the fields from the deck of the *Knute Nelson* as we sailed into Galway Bay. We saw Galway when we glided up to the docks. The whole city must have been there. We said our fond goodbyes to our Norwegian Captain and his crew. They insisted that the girls keep the voluminous sweaters which reached to their knees, and were rewarded by enthusiastic kisses of gratitude. I thanked every member of the crew. For me they joined that long list of great Norwegians, a list out of all proportion to the size of the country. They were also the first of a long list of solid Norwegian friends who seemed to turn up when I needed help; Berndt Balchen, Harald Swenson, Brynyulf Evenson, Arne and Bengt Ramstad and many others. A very special people, the Norwegians.

But on the docks of Galway, a more tumultuous welcome was waiting for us. Galway was a centre of republicanism in the neutral Republic of Eire, and one would expect the citizens to be neutral or even anti-British, but there was nothing neutral about the weeping, cheering Galway crowd on that September day in 1939. They swamped us with their sympathy and generosity. They listened to every harrowing story, and hung on every word. They tried to unite husbands and wives, and help children find their parents, and they cried with them when hope gradually faded.

As we arrived on the quay, those survivors who had been brought to Galway by the British destroyers, besieged us to ask if we had seen or heard of the friends and relations from whom they had been separated. Many were desperate and gave way to their grief and anguish. Others just asked with a terrible quiet dignity. I remember a brother and sister about ten or twelve years old who asked in clear treble voices if we had seen their parents.

For the first time, I felt an overwhelming fury that was to sweep over me time and time again during the war. No one had the right to cause such suffering to innocent people. At first my rage was against the Germans, but later, when I saw the same suffering among their innocents, my fury was against those who used their power with such callous lack of responsibility to heap personal tragedy on the little people who wanted only to live; to cut down the young before they have had time to savour life; to deprive the old of the peace and fulfilment of age for which they had toiled throughout their lives; to tear away from parents the sons and daughters without whom life has no meaning; to inflict on a young woman the loss of a husband and condemn her to a life of loneliness and mourning; to sentence to cruel death those who are killed; to sentence to a crueller life those who are bereaved. No one had the right to cause such suffering, and those who assumed that right had to be stopped and punished. That was the vow; simple and profound; corny and devout. That was the way we were; no doubts; we knew what was right and wrong, and we knew what we had to do.

Meanwhile we were swept up by the Irish of Galway, who literally gave us the clothes off their backs. I remember being overwhelmed by sympathetic citizens who almost carried me off to a nearby pub. I was dressed only in slacks and a shirt. As we went into the bar, one of the crowd selected a raincoat from those hanging from pegs in the entrance and insisted on putting it on me.

'But is this yours?' I protested.

'Of course not! It's yours! Fits you to a tee!'

'But it belongs to someone!'

'Sure, he'd want you to have it!' The others agreed, and slapped a cloth cap on my head to complete the outfit.

The emotional reception was not reserved for the Canadians and Americans, but was just as warm for the English. Among the sympathetic crowd in the pub were a number of Irishmen wearing in their lapel a simple gold circlet. When I asked what it was, they explained that they were members of a movement devoted to the promotion of everything Irish, and opposed to everything English. The gold ring emblem meant that they had made a vow to speak only Irish and never speak English.

'But you're not speaking Irish now,' I said.

'Well, we have to learn it first! That's why we're here in Galway.'

It wasn't easy, but I finally slipped away from my exuberant friends. The other survivors were being allocated to various hotels or billets. By the time I arrived, there wasn't much left. In any case, as a third class passenger with no cash, and no hope of getting any, I wasn't expecting much.

As I waited patiently, I recognised one of the girls from our lifeboat, and joined her. She was a striking girl, as tall as I, with golden blonde hair and a magnificent athletic figure.

'Remember me? We spent last night together.'

'Of course, but I don't remember your name.'

'Jim Goodson. What's yours?'

'Katerina Versveldt, — but wait a minute, I think they were looking for you. I think that was the name they called out on the loudspeaker.'

We went up to the survivors' centre, and, sure enough, to my surprise, it was my name that had been called. Even more amazing, a well-dressed businessman came up and greeted me with obvious enthusiasm and a welcoming smile.

'Mr Goodson, I'm Jack Warren. Thank God you're safe! We've got a room ready for you in our home, and you can stay as long as you like!'

'That's very nice of you, but I don't understand. How did you know about me?'

'Your uncle knew you were on the *Athenia*, and that most of the survivors were being brought to Galway. He got in touch with his friend Joe Boyle who's with Shell Oil, and they got in touch with me. I'm the Shell manager here.'

'Well, I can't imagine why Shell should go to all this trouble just for me; and I'm afraid I'll be imposing on you.'

'Nonsense, this is the least we can do. And how about your friend? Can we put you up too? Let's go!'

The Warrens opened their house and their hearts to us. They used their precious petrol to take us through the West Irish countryside. They showed us the wild rocky coast, the little fields surrounded by low stone walls of stones fitted together with no cement or mortar. They explained how many of these minute plots had been hewn out of the solid rock. First the rock had to be cracked by building a fire on it and then dousing it with cold water. Then a wedge of wood was pounded into the crack, and water poured over it to make it expand, thus extending the cracking process. Then followed the laborious process of pounding and prising, until the cracked pieces of rock could be lifted out and piled around the plot. Finally, baskets of seaweed, kelp, and what earth could be found were carried to the cavity, and, after years of care, there was a little plot capable of producing potatoes, or enough grazing for a cow or goat.

The Warrens lived between Galway and Connemara, where they showed us the Claddach, the old section, where the little white, thatched cottages had stood unchanged for over a century. They had wooden doors split across the middle like a stable, so that the top half could be opened to let in the light and air, while the bottom half stayed closed. Most of them had dirt or stone floors, and the chickens wandered in and out at will.

But we only had two days on peaceful Galway Bay. We were to be sent from neutral Ireland to Glasgow, presumably to be given passage from there back to Canada or The States.

The night ferry from Belfast to Glasgow brought back memories of the *Athenia*; the black heaving swell, the hissing along the sides of the ship as she cut her way through the salt sea; but uppermost in our minds were the scenes on the lower decks after the torpedo struck. It had left a claustrophobia from which I never recovered. Perhaps it had been there all along, but it made me realise that, if I were to play a part in the war, it couldn't be in the confined space of a submarine, or even a ship, or a tank. It had to be the open freedom of the air. There is a basic difference in the make-up of a flyer and others. I've often heard submariners say the thought of being miles high in the sky in a small plane filled them with fear, and confided to them that most pilots would hate to face hours of inactivity, but grave danger, in a small submarine in the depths of the ocean.

So Katerina and I sat close together on the deserted deck, clinging together to keep warm in the cold, damp September night, both thinking of lurking U-boats and not daring to mention them, until the next morning when we sailed down the Clyde to Glasgow.

We were expecting to be greeted warmly by the Donaldson-Atlantic Line and learn when we could sail home. It was explained to us that the small print on our tickets explicitly stated that the Line's responsibility to carry us across the Atlantic was null and void if 'Acts of God or the King's enemies' prevented them from carrying them out. Since 'the King's enemies' had sunk our ship, and since the others had been commandeered by His Majesty's Government, there was nothing they could do for us at present, but they would let us know. In the meantime, we would be billeted in the Beresford Hotel. I at least got something out of it. I was presented with a badly cut, cheap suit and shirt. I accepted it gratefully. Somehow clothes didn't seem to matter much in those days.

It was the next evening that Harry Lauder came. By now he was Sir Harry Lauder and almost seventy, but he was known to

Scots, and almost everyone else around the world. He epitomized the tough, cocky little Scotsman, and brought a nostalgic memory of home, humour and sentiment to every corner of the globe, when, in a world with no air travel, 'home' was very far away, and would probably never be seen again. It was typical of him that he would come out of his retirement to give freely of his time to the *Athenia* survivors, and he gave of his best! From the moment the short stocky figure with his kilt and Glengarry bonnet, and his gnarled black stick arrived, he had us laughing and crying. All the old, well-loved jokes and songs came out one after the other: 'Roamin' in the gloamin', 'There is somebody waiting for me, in a wee cottage down by the sea', 'On the bonny, bonny banks o' Loch Lomond', and ending with the song he wrote himself, when his only son was killed in the First World War: 'Keep right on to the End of the Road'. He left us all in tears, feeling a whole lot better!

The next day, walking down Sauchiehall Street, I saw three men in RAF uniforms putting the finishing touches on what was obviously going to be a recruiting station.

'Can I join your RAF?' I asked.

'Come back tomorrow when the sergeant's here.'

I was there at 9 a.m. At about ten the sergeant appeared, accompanied by two airman with their arms full of boxes of forms.

They had no shortage of volunteers, and a line soon formed behind me. Finally I was allowed in. The sergeant simply said, 'Can you write? Then fill in this form.'

But I had lots of questions: 'Can an American join the RAF? How long would I have to wait? . . .'

The sergeant sighed. 'Look, son, the Air Marshal's busy, so he's just asked me to stand in for him. Just fill in the form, and don't bother to apply for air crew.'

'But why not? I want to be a fighter pilot.'

'Of course you do, and so do a million others.'

'But somebody's got to be a fighter pilot, why not me?'

'Just fill in the form!'

I filled in the form.

The next day I was back to see if they had any news. Suddenly, only one thing in life mattered: to become a fighter pilot as soon as possible. I took to hanging around the recruiting station. Sergeant McLeod and I became good friends, but this didn't help my cause; on the contrary, I soon realised that, although the recruiting station religiously sent in their forms, it was a one-way street. They received no response from the Air Ministry, and it began to dawn on me how completely unprepared for war they were.

This was confirmed when Sergeant McLeod announced one day that an officer was going to turn up on a tour of inspection. I explained how essential it was for me to talk to him and McLeod promised to do his best.

Thus it was that I found myself in the presence of Flight Lieutenant Robinson. I was not only in awe of his rank, but also because he had actually served in the Royal Flying Corps at the end of the First World War. Talking to him made me feel that the war we were now starting was just a continuation of the last. He spoke of the Germans as 'Jerry', 'the Boche' or 'the Hun'. Planes were 'kites', men were 'types': It was a language I was to become very familiar with. The US Air Force picked it up from the RAF, who had preserved it from the RFC of World War I. It's not only in tactics and equipment that one war starts where the last leaves off. At least that applies to the victors. Only the vanquished seem to learn from the past, and prepare to take their revenge. And so it was that Germany was ready with a new concept of total war, based on air supremacy and perfect coordination between tactical air power and motorised infantry and armour, with the fleets of Me109's, Me110's, Stukas and Heinkels designed for the job. Meanwhile the Air Ministry contemplated the overwhelming problem of creating an air force to meet the threat, and processing my application form; and Flight Lieutenant Robinson expressed the pious hope that 'Now that the balloon's gone up, they'll pull out their fingers and get cracking!'

He also gave me practical advice. 'We can't possibly train enough pilots in England. Even if Jerry would leave us in peace, the bloody weather would put the lid on it. No, the training's going to take place in the Commonwealth, and mainly Canada. So even if the RAF get around to your application, and accept it, they've got to get you to Canada. On the other hand, the shipping

Johnnies have to get you back to Canada. Now, if we can add to your application that you are going to Canada under your own steam, that should help. At least, your case would stand out from the mass. There might even be a good piece of publicity: young American torpedoed on the *Athenia* volunteers for the RAF.'

I appreciated what he said, but I was sceptical about the liaison between the RAF in England and the RCAF in Canada.

'That's fine', I said, 'but when I turn up in Canada, they may not have any record of my application here. I wonder if I could ask you to write a letter confirming that I have volunteered here.'

'Jolly good! ' He was so willing, I decided to risk all.

'Perhaps you could suggest that they consider my application favourably?'

'Oh, I don't think I could commit the RAF to that!'

'It would simply be your personal opinion.'

'Yes! Why not. Jolly good show!'

I never knew if the letter helped, but it may well have done. In those days especially, lives were changed, and lives were lost, by even more insignificant happenstances.

In one respect, Robinson was right. After an initial reaction of non-committal pessimism, the Donaldson Line and the Admiralty were paying more attention to us. We were treated to bus trips to Loch Lomond, and were well looked after in our hotels. What's more, we were told, for the first time, that arrangements were being made to give us passage back to Canada. More important, they had given us some pocket money, which, together with a loan from my aunt, gave me enough for a trip to London. Along with the rest of the population, we had been issued with gas-masks. It was carried over the shoulder in a cardboard box, and this, with a tooth-brush, tooth-paste and a bar of soap, tucked into it, was my luggage. The almost immediate supply of gas-masks to the entire population of Britain was to me one of the many enigmas of that strange period, and one which has never been commented on. Against a background of general complacency and complete unpreparedness, the Government somehow produced some fifty million gas-masks almost overnight!

London in those first few days of World War II was in an unreal sort of daze. The war in Poland was drawing to its inevitable

tragic end; but Poland was far away, and most people thought
that when Germany came up against the combined might of
England and France, we would be 'hanging up our washing on the
Siegfried Line'. But behind the stoic good humour and jingoism,
there was uneasiness and fear, and business was not quite as
usual as they tried to make out.

The theatres were still putting a brave face on it, in spite of the
black-out, but it was a losing battle. John Gielgud, Edith Evans,
Peggy Ashcroft and Margaret Rutherford were playing in Oscar
Wilde's *The Importance of being Earnest* at the Globe theatre, and
I spent my last resources on what I thought would be a chance I
might never have again. In the theatre, I admired the ornate, gilded
cherubs and Edwardian decorations, but the large theatre was
practically empty. Scattered through the empty seats was a
handful of people; but the cast gave a brilliant, polished performance. I suppose Gielgud was in his late thirties at that time,
tall, thin and elegant. He was so perfect in the leading role that it
was impossible to imagine it being played by anyone else. He
belonged in the precious, prim, well-ordered world of Victorian
England, as did Edith Evans as Lady Bracknell, and all the rest of
the cast. The play ended with polite curtain calls, and 'God Save
the King'.

We went out into the blacked-out, bewildered, frightened world
of pending doom and horror. Not for the last time, I felt that
most of the English were as unprepared for it as John Worthing,
Dr Chasuble, Miss Prism and Lady Bracknell.

Back in Liverpool, the liner, *The Duchess of Athol*, was preparing
to sail for Montreal, carrying, in third class, those refugees from
Eastern Europe lucky enough to have scraped together enough
money to allow them to leave behind the grimness of Europe at
war to start a new life in the new world. In second and third
class were the remaining Canadian and American tourists, who had
delayed their departure too long. There were also British officers
and training personnel, the first of the many who would work
with the Canadians in the formation of, and training of, the Air
Force under the Commonwealth Air Training Scheme. Somehow,
the Admiralty also found room for the *Athenia* survivors.

Soon, once again we were sailing down the Mersey; once again waving goodbye to the Liver birds perched on top of the Liver Building, passing Birkenhead, New Brighton, Wallasey and Bootle, and then out to the open sea.

The ship lived up to her reputation for rolling, which had earned her the nickname of *The Drunken Duchess*.

We sailed alone, zig-zagging, and blacked-out at night. The theory was that the speed of the large liners, combined with constant changes in course, would give them a better chance against the slower U-boats than if they were part of a convoy where they would be held down to the speed of the slowest freighter.

It seemed to work. In a week, we were sailing down the broad St Lawrence, looking out at the brilliant scarlets, yellows and browns of the trees in the late autumn in a bright new world.

CHAPTER TWO

The Pole

Finally, I found myself in one of the vast halls of the Canadian National Exhibition in Toronto. This whole complex had been turned over to the Royal Canadian Air Force as the only accommodation large enough to process the thousands of airmen involved in the Commonwealth Air Training Scheme. We would be herded into one of the exhibition halls, clutching our process documents, and be called out for the next stage.

'All those who have had their interview, had their medical, but not their dental inspection, follow me.' And a mass of humanity would surge forward. It was the start of a system of classification and elimination which continued throughout the whole training period, until the chosen élite emerged as fighter pilot candidates. The slightly less fortunate became bomber pilots, or observers, or were obliged to become ground crew. The greatest catastrophe, and a terrible fear that dominated a would-be airman's entire training career, was the constant threat of being 'washed-out'. Out of those thousands of eager young airmen, probably less than five percent would become fighter pilots, and of them, far less than one percent would ever score a victory.

In that crowd of uniform humanity, one figure stood out. Taller than the others, with a thin handsome face, he had a strong, sober dignity, which distinguished him from the nervous, jabbering youngsters around him. His good looks were enhanced by a scar on the side of his aquiline nose, which also gave him a slightly disdainful look. He would have been ideal in a Basil Rathbone part in a Shakespearian tragedy. This was the first time I set eyes on Mike Sobanski. It was on the medical parade that I got talking to him. He was having trouble understanding what was being said to him. I thought he was probably French-Canadian, and offered to help; but his French was far from perfect, so I tried German. This went much better, and, after the medical, we

stayed together and chatted. I learned that he and I were probably the only ones in all those thousands of enthusiastic youngsters who had any taste of war. While I was splashing around in
the bowels of the stricken *Athenia*, Mike was crouching in the
rubble of Warsaw, as the German bombers pounded the dying
city.

He had been a university student, and had tried to join the
Polish Air Force when the Germans attacked; but it was too late
for the Air Force to take on young men for training. They knew
the war would either be won or lost long before a long training
course could be completed. In any case, their shortage was in planes,
rather than in pilots.

So Mike found himself, a private soldier in the infantry, in-
adequately trained, riding a train to the Vistula River to reinforce
a battle front which, like the whole of Poland, was crumbling
before a German army, and a German air force, which blasted
everything that stood in the army's way, and destroyed the
vitals of the whole country. Even the train carrying Mike and the
rest of the last desperate, hopeless young recruits came under
attack from the Stukas. They didn't even need the protection of
the Me109's. They had already done their job of annihilating the
Polish Air Force, much of it on the ground. Even in the air, the
slow, obsolete high-winged PZL fighter planes would have been no
match for the 109's, even if they had not been hopelessly outnumbered. The Italian General Douet had said in 1921, 'A decision
in the air must precede a decision on the ground,' and General
Billy Mitchell had preached the theory of subjugating an enemy by
air attack. If other nations only paid lip service to the idea, the
Germans had learned the lesson, and learned it well. Kalinowski,
then a major in the Polish Air Force, and later a wing commander
in the RAF, put the number of operational planes in the Polish Air
Force at the time of the German invasion at 150 fighters and
about the same number of bombers. Against these, the Germans
threw in about 1,500 modern front line aircraft, backed up by at
least the same number in reserve in Germany. Colonel Litynski
wrote: 'Already by the second day the telephone and teleprinter
systems had broken down ... As a result, there was virtually no
effective military command from the start.'

Mike Sobanski was becoming increasingly aware of the in-
equality of the battle. The train crawling towards the crumbling
front was as helpless as a worm about to be pounced on by a
bird. At 5,000 feet above, the Stuka pilots went through the
drill which was now so familiar to them: 'Close radiator flap.
Turn off super-charger. Tip over to port. Set angle of dive to 70
degrees. Accelerate to 300 mph. Apply air brakes. (which also
caused the high-pitched wail, a fore-warning of the destruction to
come to the terrified victims). Take aim on the target. At 3,500
feet, press the release button on the control column.'

With the same deadly accuracy which had paved the way for
the advance of the panzers across Poland, the bombs blasted the
railway tracks, and the train itself.

Mike heard the dull drone of the planes turn into the rising
roar of the engines in the dive, and then the banshee scream of
the air brakes. There was a sudden flash of flame and wind like a
body blow, as the bombs exploded.

Mike came to, numbed and confused, coughing blood and
dust out of his throat as rescuers tried to free him from the
debris. The shattered glass had lacerated his face and slashed
through his nose. His legs were pinned by something heavy; bombs
were still falling; and there was nothing Mike or anyone else
could do about it. The feeling of helplessness gave way to angry
frustration. Then a furious, determined rage took over; a hatred
for the grinning, wailing Stukas, smashing Polish trains, troops and
men, women and children; a hatred for the efficient panzers
riding down the Polish cavalry; a hatred for the self-confident
Germans, making a graveyard out of Poland.

And out of the hatred, came a solemn vow; a vow never again to
lie helpless in the rubble and dirt; a vow to be up there in the free
air, in the driver's seat, looking down on the pathetic ants on the
ground, calling the shots, holding the power — like a god!

Mike lay in hospital in Warsaw while his country was being destroyed. On 17th September the remaining serviceable Polish Air
Force planes flew out to Rumania to surrender before they too
ran out of spares. The pilots made their way to France, and then
to England, where they formed the Polish squadrons in the RAF,

which became the highest scorers in the Battle of Britain. On 25th September a massive unopposed Luftwaffe air raid on Warsaw forced the final capitulation.

That night, Mike crept out of his hospital bed. He found that he could only hobble on one good leg, but he knew this was the time to move. They didn't know he could walk, and, in the general confusion, he made his painful way out of the rear of the hospital. Near the back exit, there was a row of hooks where the porters and male nurses left their coats. Mike found one that he could get into, even if it was short, and limped out into the smoking, defeated city. German military vehicles and marching infantry were everywhere, but they were too busy to pay attention to the huddled, crippled creature hobbling through the debris.

He was making for the family house. There, perhaps, there would be some news of his mother and father, if only from the neighbours. His father was a colonel in the infantry. He'd had no news from any of the family or friends for two weeks.

He had hoped that the area, being residential, would have escaped the bombing, but, as he turned into his street, his ideals of chivalry took another knock. In the determination to shock the population and Government into capitulation, the bombing had been indiscriminate. His street was no different from the others he had dragged himself through: burning buildings, pathetic piles of personal belongings, rescued from the rubble; dazed and bewildered people moving aimlessly among the chaos; a few firemen trying to cope with rescue work; a few ambulance men caring for the wounded. It was a scene which was to become hideously familiar across Europe. It was the start of a virulent plague which would spread to almost every city and town, leaving death and destruction: destruction of a whole era.

Mike found himself staring dumbly at the ruined house. Some of the walls were standing, but it had been gutted by fire. Slowly he stumbled into the rubble, not knowing what he was looking for, nor why. Lying shattered on the floor, was the grand piano on which his mother had accompanied herself as she sang so beautifully one glorious operatic aria after another in those unbelievable, idyllic days a month — a million years ago. It was all dead now, like the smashed, yellowing photographs of old

family grandparents still in their silver frames, or the broken
porcelain in the broken cabinet, which had been his mother's
love and pride, or the scattered toys, which she had treasured
because he had treasured them.

Then he became aware of the approaching figure. The straight
back was now slumped, and the eagle eye was dimmed, but Mike
knew him almost before he saw him.

'Father!'

Mike took him in his arms, as his father had taken him so often
as a child. They stayed in each other's arms, not wanting to show
their tears. Finally, Mike asked the questions he hadn't dared to
ask.

To each of them, the old man could only shake his head. 'Gone!
All gone! Everything gone!'

They sat among the ruins of their home, their country, their
world. Finally Mike said, 'We must go!'

'Go? Go where?'

'I'm going to join the Air Force.'

'But there is no Air Force any more. The war is over.'

'No,' said Mike, 'The war is just beginning. England and France
are at war now. They'll need pilots. Our pilots will have to leave
their planes in Rumania, but they should be able to get to France,
and that's what I intend to do.'

The old man shook his head. 'I doubt if the French and British
want untrained volunteers, but there is another possibility. You
were born in New York, while your mother was visiting her
sister. You don't have an American passport, but anyone born in
the United States has the right to be an American citizen. The
problem is that you are also a Polish soldier, and before you
could get a passport, the Germans would have you as a prisoner
of war. One thing we have always kept is this.'

He took a black folded paper from his pocket. 'It's a photocopy of your American birth certificate. It might help. No one
wants to offend the Americans! If you get into real trouble,
insist on seeing the American Ambassador. Take this too, it's
the address of your Aunt Nydia and her husband, Harry Bruno
in New York. He could help you. He has connections in aviation.'

Mike took the precious papers. 'And you?' he asked.

The older man shook his head. 'You have a chance. I don't. Your life is just beginning. Mine is over.'

'No!' said Mike, 'Now that France and England are fighting Germany, the war will soon be over. I'll be back before you know it!'

The old man nodded. He didn't believe it. Neither did Mike.

When Mike told me the story, I said: 'God knows how you got from Warsaw to New York!'

He looked at me solemnly. 'What makes you think God knows?'

It took months. He got through Poland, Czechoslovakia, Hungary, Rumania and Istanbul, that age-old gateway for refugees, and finally, against all odds, he found himself standing outside the door of Harry Bruno's apartment at 400 East 57th Street, New York City.

Harry Bruno had spent his life in aviation. At the age of seventeen, he and his brother had built a glider, at eighteen, he volunteered for the Royal Flying Corps to fly for the British in World War I. The war was over before he flew in combat, but, back in the States, he became the first aviation public relations consultant. He was an intimate friend of every important aviation figure in the world, and wrote about them in his classic book, *Wings Over America*. I met him when I got back from the war. He was organising a hero's tour, and explained that he was a public relations consultant.

'I'm sorry,' I said. 'I'm just a simple fly-boy. I don't think I know what that means.'

'Who do you think was the first man to fly the Atlantic?' he asked.

'Charles Lindbergh.'

'That's what nearly everyone would say. Lindy was about the twenty-sixth man to fly the Atlantic. The difference is that I handled his public relations.'

Mike couldn't have had a better uncle, and he was in the right place, at the right time. Within weeks, Mike was in the Royal Canadian Air Force.

But Mike had to call on Harry again. We had survived primary training on the wonderful little Fleet biplanes. Our instructor had been Sparks, a jolly American, who taught us flying, but, much more, he injected us with his own joy of flying. We got to know and love the little Fleets, and felt we could do anything with them.

So we moved on to advanced training; but this was a different story. When we saw the shining American Harvard Advanced trainers, they looked enormous. When we climbed into the cockpit and gazed at the mass of instruments, we realised the big leap forward we had to make. The sweet smell of the high octane fuel, and the new paint added to the sick feeling in the pit of our stomachs.

The instructor was different too. Young Gerry Fuller was also one of the American instructors, but his methods were those of a man who probably realised how tough the war was going to be, and how ill-prepared were the kids going into it. He believed the slogan often repeated to those who asked for more time and patience: 'Given time, we could teach monkeys to fly, but we don't have time.' He played it tough because he knew only the tough would survive. He shouted and barked his orders from the back cockpit, and had no patience with any mistakes. This worked with pilots like our friend Ray Fuchs, who had had some training in the US Air Force and been washed out, or like Pappy Dunn who had some civilian flying time, or Phil Gofton, the Canadian from Winnipeg who paid no attention to his ranting and raving. But with Mike and me, it only made matters worse. He was only a sergeant, so couldn't wash us out before we'd had a final check flight with a senior officer. Mike's turn came first.

I waited in the empty pilots' locker room for him to come back. He came in. I looked at him. He shook his head. He had been washed out. I put my hand on his shoulder. He shook it off.

'Let's go!' he said.

'Where?'

'To call Harry Bruno!' he said.

Canada's greatest pilot was Billy Bishop, the First World War ace, and a close friend of Harry's. The next day Harry was on the phone to him. He told him Mike's story. He explained Mike's problem understanding and speaking English. Most of all, he told him of Mike's vow.

Billy Bishop understood. The next day Mike was back in training.

My turn came next. The checking officer was the CO himself. He was a young English fighter pilot who had been shot down and wounded early in the war. Over his RAF wings he wore one purple and white ribbon, the DFC. To us he was God.

He said nothing as he climbed into the rear cockpit. After that the instructions were short and sweet. 'Take off.'

I taxied out, turning to right and left to make sure the way was clear ahead. I stopped at the runway to go through a meticulous check-list. I looked right and left to make sure no planes were landing, pulled onto the runway and opened the throttle. I let the plane lift gradually on its own, and raised the undercarriage. As I turned left at five hundred feet, the engine suddenly stopped. Nothing but silence and the swish of the wind. Automatically I put the nose down. Then I realised he had cut the switch to force me to do a practice forced landing. I picked out a likely looking field, kept the plane at the proper gliding speed, and waited for him to tell me to switch on the engine again. He didn't. As we got down close to the field, I turned into wind. I dropped flap, but was still a little high and to the right. I banked to the left and applied opposite rudder to put it into a side-slip, and straightened out. I could see the leaves on the trees. Still no order to restart the engine. I was desperate, so I waited. At the last minute, as I was flattening out, it came.

'Restart the engine!'

I still think we were lucky that the engine roared into life. I waited a bit before raising the flaps, then climbed to fifteen thousand feet.

'Want to try some aerobatics?' he asked laconically.

'Slow roll,' I said. I looked around, put the nose down to pick up speed, pulled it up again and applied rudder. Slowly we rolled over. As we got on our back, I gradually pushed the stick forward to keep the nose well up. The dust and dirt came down from the floor. Then opposite rudder and we were back straight and level again.

'Loop!' I said.

More speed this time, then stick back slowly to keep the loop perfect, easing off at the top and bringing it back again as the horizon appeared again above us, and cutting the engine back as we came around.

'Roll off the top!'

This was the trickiest. We needed just enough speed at the top of the loop to roll out without stalling upside down. It was OK.

'Let's go home,' he said.

I headed for the base. Suddenly he shouted: 'Break right!'

I whipped the stick over right and back into my stomach, stomping right rudder. I was forced into my seat, thrown to the left, and nearly blacked out. I continued the tight turn, and then straightened out, still at full throttle.

'What are you doing now?' he asked.

'We were just jumped by an Me109. We out-turned him. He's now diving away, and we're on his tail.'

'Land,' he said.

Back on the ground, we climbed down from the cockpit. 'Did you enjoy that?' he asked.

I showed my surprise, then answered enthusiastically. 'Yes, sir!'

'So did I,' he said.

He walked away, then turned around. 'It's OK. You're a fighter pilot.'

Much later I met Gerry Fuller again. As commander of 336 Squadron of the Fourth Fighter Group, I flew into Atcham to interview replacement pilots. The Fourth got the pick of the pack, and most of them gave the Fourth as their preference. This time, I was God, and the eager but anxious candidates came in to the office one by one and stood in a rigid brace. I went through the files, and recognised a name.

'I'd like to interview this one,' I said.

He was in a US uniform now, but wore the RCAF wings over his left breast pocket. It was Gerry Fuller.

'Why do you want to join our squadron?' I asked.

'I know it's the best, sir,' he said.

'Any other reason?'

'I know its Commander is the best, sir.'

'Well, Lieutenant, he had a good instructor.'

I put him on the next mission. He had more flying hours than most of our pilots, and, after all that time as an instructor, he couldn't wait to get into combat. It was an easy mission, but, as we came in to pick up the bombers, I spotted a gaggle of Me109's at two o'clock high and told the squadron to watch them. I knew they would probably try to break us up so the others could attack the bombers.

When I saw four of them peel off and dive down on our Yellow section, I ordered them to break right. Yellow One, Yellow Two and Yellow Three broke violently into the attack. Yellow Four turned more slowly. 'Yellow Four, break hard!' I called. It still wasn't hard enough or fast enough. It was his undoing. The leading 109 got on his tail and out-turned him. It was all over in seconds. Yellow Four was Gerry Fuller. I blamed myself, I should have yelled at him harder.

After Pearl Harbour, the three Eagle Squadrons transferred in September 1942 to the US Army Air Force. We painted the US star over the red, white and blue roundels of the RAF and continued to fly our beloved Spits; but eventually came the day when we had to turn them back to the RAF, and take over the huge American long-range P-47 Thunderbolts. We gazed up at these great, solid aircraft in amazement. They looked like whales and the nimble little Spitfires, like darting minnows.

No one, least of all Mike, liked the change. In vain I talked about the advantage the 'Thunderjugs' would give us and the bombers with their longer range, speed in the dive, and the invulnerability of their great air-cooled radial engines.

Gradually, the pilots learned to love and appreciate the new planes, but Mike was the last to give up. The day came when the last two Spitfires were due to leave. Mike and Bob Messenger took off for one last flight. Before they landed, every police force in Essex had phoned the base. They thought at least fifty planes had gone wild and were attacking everything in sight. In fact it was Sobanski and Messenger saying goodbye to their beloved Spitfires in the only way they considered befitting; by taking them on a 'beat-up' to end all 'beat-ups'. They came screaming down in vertical dives, levelling off at the last minute to flash past farm houses at less than roof-top height, missing them by inches. They screamed under bridges; they clipped the tops off trees; they flattened the wheat in the fields; they shattered the glass in windows and the greenhouses around Bishop's Stortford; they scattered cattle, chickens, men, women and children; and then they zoomed up into a loop, and came thundering down to start all over again.

Normally such conduct would have been considered childish, dangerous, and, above all, an offence against the friendly, long-suffering locals; and therefore subject to the most severe punishment. In this case it was different. Dusty Miller was their flight commander. He confined them to the base for a month, and assured them that their irresponsibility would be duly entered in their records. I doubt if it was. Years later Dusty and I met again at Debden to unveil a memorial which the British presented to honour the fallen Eagles. He talked about 'the Great Beat-up'.

'Yeah, you can laugh about it now!' I said.

'Hell! I laughed about it then!'

At the time, I saw nothing funny about it. 'Why don't you save all that for the Germans?'

'Don't worry!' he said. 'That was just a rehearsal!'

'Great rehearsal if you'd flown into the ground! Come on! I'll check you out in the Thunderjug.'

Later, Mike and I shared a room in well-built officers' mess. The first night I was awakened by what I thought was a dribbling tap in the wash basin. I went over to turn it off, to find that the sibilant sounds came from Mike talking Polish in his sleep. I got to like the soft 's' and 'sh' sounds. He even taught me a Polish version of 'She sells sea-shells', which concerned seventy-seven partridges, and consisted of a series of 's', 'sh', 'strps' and 'z' sounds and no vowels.

Each night after a mission, without fail, Mike performed a solemn rite. He would take out a large black-paged photograph album and painstakingly print in white ink, the events of the day. Whenever possible the narrative was illustrated by photographs, which covered every phase of his service life: the planes he had flown, people he had known, and missions he had accomplished. Each time he had destroyed an enemy aircraft, either on the ground or in the air, he included a combat report, culminating in his fifth, when he wrote in large letters: 'To-day I am an Ace!'

One night, he seemed to be taking longer than usual.

'For God's sake come to bed. We've got an early briefing tomorrow. You can do that any time!'

'No,' he said in his slow deep voice. 'This is important.'

'What the hell is important about it?'

'My family and friends in Poland don't know where I am, or what I'm doing. It's OK for you guys. Every time you shoot one down, or get promoted or decorated, it's in your local newspaper. As far as my people know, I just ran away. That's why this is important. I'll show it to them after the war!'

'I'm sure your family don't think you goofed off!'

'No, but they don't know I'm a captain in the leading fighter group in the US Air Force.'

Then, after a pause, 'Besides, there's the girl I'm going to marry. I want her to see all this!'

'If it's that important to you, maybe you'd better give me her name and address, just in case.'

'No,' he said with conviction. 'I know I'm going to survive this war. I know!'

Not long before D-Day, I was cursing Mike and his diary. In Holland, directly on the route the bombers took to the Ruhr and Berlin, was the Luftwaffe fighter base at Gilze-Rijn. It was so strategically placed that the Germans could get up to attack, and return to base for refuelling and rearming three times during one of our missions. It was therefore decided that the Fourth Group would attack the base, with 334 Squadron using the new dive-bombing techniques introduced by General Kepner. 335 and 336 Squadrons were to fly cover for 334, while they were bombing and strafing, and then dive down themselves to strafe and destroy what was left. It was an outstanding success. We left a trail of burned-out aircraft on the ground, and great black clouds of smoke from burning fuel stores; but we had stirred up a hornets' nest, and we had to fight our way out as we climbed back up. 334 and 335 had used up most of their ammunition and we in 336 were not much better off. We were covering the other two squadrons as best we could as they headed for home, when I heard Mike's deep, slow Polish accent.

'I tink I go back and take some pictures!'

I saw the lone Mustang diving back down into the smoke and wheeled 336 around to cover him. We picked him up as he climbed back out.

That night, he carefully penned his combat report into his album, and three days later he stuck two photographs into the spaces he had left for them. They showed wrecked German fighters on the ground, and the columns of black smoke rising into the air.

It was in the dark morning hours of 6 June 1944 that Mike and I dressed for our part in the invasion. As I waited for Mike at the door, he put his precious album on my bed, and handed me a scrap of paper: It contained a name and an address in Cracow, Poland.

I looked at him. He shrugged his shoulders and smiled. It was the last time I saw him. We had told Eisenhower and his staff that we could prevent the German air force and army from moving up to the beach-head during the hours of daylight, and we spent the day proving it. We attacked everything that moved on the roads and rails of Normandy leading to the landing area. The destruction was terrible. We strafed columns of trucks and light tanks, while the Germans leapt from their vehicles and drove into what cover they could find at the side of the roads, or desperately tried to set up flak guns before we could mow them down. We sprayed the columns of marching men and watched them fall as our eight machine-guns cut them down. The heavy tanks of the élite 'Panzer Lehr' based around Le Mans were not given the order to advance, apparently because Hitler thought the Normandy landings were not the main invasion force. In the early hours, we would have had difficulty in stopping them, but, by the time they finally moved, the roads were choked with wrecked vehicles, and the beach-head was already secured.

We flew non-stop that day from 3 a.m. till after midnight, returning to base three times for refuelling and rearming. On each mission, the Group, the squadrons and sections were split up as they went down to strafe or bomb. There was no time to reform; there was too much to be done. Anyway, to try to reform out of range of the murderous flak would have taken us up into the cloud cover. The Group lost six pilots that day, but because each pilot was fighting his own battle, we don't know exactly what happened in every case.

We know what happened to three of them. It has been stated that only two Luftwaffe planes came up on D-Day, one of which was piloted by 'Pips' Priller, then *Kommodore* of Galland's old JG26, 'Schlageter' Squadron, known to us as the 'Abbeville Boys'. It's true that only two got through to the beach-head, but that was because of the intervention of Allied fighters south, east and west of the landings.

'Kid' Hofer was leading a section of 334 Squadron when they were attacked by fifteen German fighters. Flying with him was someone who shouldn't have been there: big handsome Captain Bernard McGrattan had his bags packed to go back to the States for a well-deserved rest after a year in combat, and nine victories. He was determined not to miss D-Day but he was due to leave that afternoon. He figured he could sneak in one mission and still catch his afternoon transport.

He didn't make it.

Hal Ross was shot out of the sky by a 109 while he was attacking another German plane which was strafing a Canadian pilot parachuting down. His last combat was watched by the villagers of the town of Bacquepuis, who buried him in their cemetery.

From that section, only Hofer survived.

Mike was also flying with 334, so must have been in the same area. I heard him tell his wingman, Ed Heppe, he had flown through some electric cables while attacking a train. When the wingman reported little damage, Mike reported he was going after a second train. Some minutes later we heard Ed say: 'Watch those behind you, White Leader!'

That was the last we heard of either of them.

When the Battle of Normandy was over, through friends in British Intelligence, I arranged to talk with German officer prisoners taken south of the beach-head. When they learned I could speak German, and had been above them on D-Day, they looked at me in wonder. 'We couldn't believe the ferocity of the attacks, nor the tenacity of the pilots. They ignored the flak completely, and came in time and time again almost touching the ground.'

One officer in particular interested me. 'We know about Japanese Kamikaze and Russian desperate attacks, and German ram fighters, but they were all fighting with their backs to the wall. We never expected you Americans to fly like that, especially when you were winning. Do you know, I saw two Mustangs destroy two trains completely. The leader must have been mad. He flew through walls of flak and small arms fire and even electric cables. I know he was hit many times, but he kept coming back. On his last dive, German fighters were after them, adding their fire to the ground fire. The leader crashed into the train, and it was all over. Now why should an American do that? He must have been mad!'

'He just might have been a Pole!' I said. A Pole on a beat-up to end all beat-ups.

Right after the war, all of Europe was partly in ruins, short of food, clothing and housing, and almost everything else; but, at least in the West, there was relief that the war was over, and, even if there wasn't much optimism, there was something which could be called hope. Even in West Germany and West Berlin, the basic energy and drive of those irrepressible people had not been killed. But the Germans who had just seen the barbed wire and watch towers of the POW and concentration camps destroyed as symbols of an intolerable regime, now saw them surrounding a concentration camp covering most of Europe. And the barrier was no artificial line of demarcation. Those on the other side were already different. The East Berliners had already lost the cheeky exuberance for which Berliners were famous, and which West Berliners had somehow managed to preserve. The *joie de vivre* of the Hungarians, the subtle humour of the Czechs, the towering strength of the Poles, the open friendliness of the Bulgarians and Rumanians, the liberty of the hardy Latvians, Lithuanians and Estonians, and the greatness of the soulful Russians; all submerged under a vast, dismal, grey blanket of fear and despair.

It had been difficult obtaining the visas to get through East Germany and into Poland, and even more difficult changing trains in railway stations which were in complete confusion.

Millions of Germans were being moved out of what had been
Eastern Germany, and had now become part of Poland. Millions of
Poles were being moved in. Every vestige of Germanism was being
eradicated, by force if necessary. Millions of Poles were being
moved out of what had been Eastern Poland to make room for
Russians, and the streams of refugees, which should have ended
with the war, were as massive and as tragic as ever.

There was another, even more sinister deportation. There were
the same freight wagons, with barbed wire over their windows,
which I had seen on their way to the concentration camps during
the war. Now they were transporting those thousands of Russians
and others who had changed allegiance during the war, and fought
on the German side. They had been turned over to the Russians
by the Western Allies, who naively believed they would be treated
humanely. They have not been heard of since. Even Poles were
not sure what their fate would be. Certainly the Russians, and
the new Polish Government were highly suspicious of Poles who
had fought for independence in Poland, or had had contact with
the West. Those Poles who had been fighting so valiantly in
England for the liberation of Poland had got the message. There
was no heroes' welcome for them to come home to; no joyful
reunions with wives, children and loved ones. The best a grateful,
victorious nation could offer them was the right to stay in England.

I thought of what Mike had once said to me when I talked of
the success of the Russian army. 'Poland,' he said, 'has always
been attacked by Russia to the east or Germany from the west.
Both aggressions have been brutal and vicious, but we Poles know
that, of the two, the eastern enemy is by far the worst.'

As I looked around at the confusion, misery and fear pervading
post-war Poland, I understood.

I felt it as I sat in the drab cafe in Cracow. The girl had been
hard to trace and harder still to persuade to come to a meeting.
When she finally came into the cafe, she was ill at ease. She
recognised me easily by my clothes, and came to my table. She
shook hands coolly, and didn't return my warm smile. Her English
was poor, so we spoke in German. Almost her only comment was:
'Don't speak German so loud.'

She may have been nervous, but she showed little emotion of

any kind. I told her Mike's story. I explained his desire for her to know about it, and went through his album page by page. Before I had finished, I saw her looking around. She obviously wanted to leave. I closed the book, stood up and handed it to her. She shook her head. *'Es ist alles vorbei*! — It's all over!'

'Yes, and we won!'

'No,' she said. 'You won your war, we lost ours!'

She handed the book back to me and turned and left.

The next day, I crossed the border into West Germany. As soon as the police control, passport control, currency control and customs control were finished, I went to the dining-car. A great load seemed to roll off my back. I realised I had caught the mood of the Iron Curtain and had been worried, depressed and nervous all the time I had been behind it. Now I knew we were back in the West. The dining-car steward was smiling.

CHAPTER THREE

The Boss

But no doubts or worries about what would happen after the war bothered Mike, or any of us in those heady days in 1940. We were going to win, and everything was going to be fine.

Yet when we finally set sail for England, we were in for one let-down after another. It started with the old P&O liner which took us across the Atlantic. The over-crowding was unbelievable. The lower decks, presumably allocated to third class and steerage in pre-war days, and now crammed full of 'other ranks', reminded me of descriptions of the Black Hole of Calcutta. All facilities were hopelessly overloaded: the sanitary conditions were indescribable, particularly when the sea-sickness set in; and the catering arrangements were not much better. In the nether regions, it was impossible to move the troops to an eating area, so some sort of slop was delivered to the crowded masses where they squatted or lay on the filthy decks. Some of the pilots immersed themselves in a poker game which started as the convoy assembled in the great harbour of Halifax, Nova Scotia, and continued non-stop until we docked in Southampton. Others drowned their sensitivities in smuggled liquor. Our friend Duffy only came to when we arrived in Southampton. He staggered to the port-hole, peered out at the land, and said: 'Hell, we haven't even left yet.'

We looked down from the deck at the little trains and cars, so much smaller than anything the Canadians and Americans had ever seen. Ray Fuchs said: 'It's Toyland!' In a way he was right.

Now, we thought, we would soon be leaping into our Spitfires, and dog-fighting with the Hun. But, if the RAF were desperately in need of new pilots, they didn't show it. First we went to a reception centre in Bournemouth where we fretted and fumed for weeks until we were sent to Advanced Training on Miles 'Master' trainers. They weren't much more advanced than the AT-6 Harvards we'd been flying in Canada, but we certainly needed the additional flying time.

The frustrations of being stuck in training while history was being made in the busy skies of southern England, were partially compensated for by the beautiful countryside of Cumberland. The airfield was a few miles west of Carlisle, almost on the Solway Firth, on the other side of which was Dumfrieshire in Scotland. The base took its name from the nearest village: Crosby-on-Eden. And Eden it was. If you've never strolled out of The Dog and Gun into a glorious summer evening, hand in hand with a doe-eyed WAAF through the beautiful lush countryside of Crosby-on-Eden, then, my poor friend, you have never really lived!

But I suppose my memories of Crosby-on-Eden are clouded by nostalgia. At the time, all other thoughts were dominated by the desperate eagerness to get into combat. We could only console ourselves by hoping that 'they also serve who only stand and wait'.

Finally the great day came, and we were posted to an operational squadron; but our dreams of daily duels between Spitfires and Me109's remained unfulfilled. To begin with, we flew Hurricanes, not Spits; but we learned to love the rugged, solid old 'Hurry', which was really the mainstay of the Battle of Britain. Also, in the beginning we were not in 11 or 12 Group which were taking the brunt of the Luftwaffe attack. We were further north, and Air Marshal Dowding was reluctant to commit these reserves to the battle. My logbook for those days shows endless convoy patrols, and scrambles after high-level reconnaissance planes, and sneak raiders; but any German attack on coastal convoys was easily chased away; our Hurricanes couldn't reach the altitudes of most of the recco planes; and the intruders used bad weather and cloud cover so effectively, that, even with radar, which in any case was only really effective over the sea, they were seldom caught.

I wrote polite but persistent requests for transfer to 11 Group. I would like to think it was due to my eloquence, or the glowing reports from my CO that did it, but I suspect the RAF were thinking more of the public relations angle in the States. In any case, I was posted to a front line squadron in 11 Group.

True, as an unblooded youngster, I was pretty much ignored, and still consigned to patrols and standing readiness. A typical chore for new pilots was to fly at dawn to forward bases like Hawkinge, Lympne and Manston, which were so easy for Jerry to hit, no planes were based there overnight. One sat in the cockpit waiting to be scrambled and hoping to be able to get off before being clobbered by a hit-and-run 109.

Of course we flew operations with the squadron too, but always in the tail-end Charlie position under strict orders to stick to your number one, under pain of death, or worse. RAF Fighter Command was on the defensive, trying to keep up its strength for the expected German invasion. It was during that period that we learned the strict RAF discipline: staying in formation, sticking to your leader, only acting on orders, no 'swanning about' on your own. They were lessons the RAF had learned the hard way. Their losses had been heavy, not only in combat, but even more through bombing and strafing attacks on the ground, and, above all, accidents in training and as a result of bad weather.

The Luftwaffe had been switched from attacking fighter bases to bombing cities just when they had almost destroyed RAF Fighter Command. It was a fatal decision, and now the scales were tipping the other way, but the RAF still had to build up its strength.

The German daylight raids had to be abandoned for night raids. Although we had done night flying training at the cost of many accidents, it was only late in the game, and then very seldom, that we were allowed to take off at night. As the bomber stream droned over our bases on its way to London, we had to leave the defence to the night fighters and anti-aircraft guns. I couldn't help feeling that launching a massive attack by day fighters against the night bombers would have stopped the blitz much sooner. They were undoubtedly afraid of accidents and collisions, but years later when the tables were turned, Hajo Herrmann's 'Wild Boar' tactics showed that day fighters could shoot down 123 British bombers in three nights for virtually no losses of their own.

I think the situation was that the Battle of Britain had been won, but it took the RAF some time to realise it. Indeed I'm not sure that we knew there had been a Battle of Britain. I never heard the term used until it was all over.

But, if there were a few Americans in the Battle of Britain, and the Eagle Squadrons were getting organised, the part they played was a modest one, and they were the first to give all the honours to the glorious Few. It was their show.

We were happy and proud to idolise them and try to emulate them. It was enough to be in their team, even if unnoticed. To be with the Command that was to produce Johnny Johnson, Sailor Malan, Pierre Clostermann, 'Paddy' Finucane, Bob Stanford Tuck, Doug Bader, Al Deere, Bluey Truscott, Cobber Caine. It was enough to be there, even on the fringe, at Tangmere, Biggin Hill, Kenley, West Malling: the names never lose their magic.

It was also the show of the English people. I remember when we were based at Tangmere with 43 Squadron. We were frustrated and weary; a frame of mind popularly known in the RAF as being 'browned off'. Probably because I was rated the most expendable, I was sent to pick up a replacement aircraft. The train journey gave me a chance to catch up on some sleep. When I came to, I found myself under the solemn gaze of a distinguished looking elderly gentleman sitting opposite me.

'Excuse me', he said, 'I couldn't help noticing that you're a pilot.'

'Yes, Hurricanes.' I said.

'I was in the last show, 14—18. Too old for this one. Gammy legs, too. Somme, you know. Home Guard now.' He spoke in short sharp phrases, and was obviously forcing himself to overcome a natural reticence.

I mumbled something about the importance of the Home Guard.

'Wish my chaps could hear you say that. Damned difficult keeping up morale when there's no action!'

I sympathised with him, and considered the conversation ended. But I sensed that he was trying desperately to bring himself to say something.

'I live in Goring. Goring-by-Sea. Don't suppose you've ever heard of it.'

'Sure,' I said, 'I fly over it almost every day. It's only a few miles down the coast from us.'

It was the opening he had been looking for.

'I don't suppose you could drop over to see us. Mean everything to the men. No, of course not. Damned stupid of me. Much too busy of course.'

I was about to seize the excuse he'd given me to get out of an embarrassing situation, but something stopped me. The craggy face showed no emotion, but the grey eyes which had gazed on the slaughter of the Somme were too earnest — almost pleading. I said I'd go, and immediately regretted it.

I cursed my foolishness even more on the fine Sunday afternoon I had to give up. Even if there wasn't much chance of action, I might have been able to get in some flying time. He met me at the railway station, looking quite different in his uniform with two rows of ribbons. He had even organised transport in the form of a diminutive bull-nosed Morris, driven by a middle-aged man in khaki battle dress, who was obviously the owner of the car and had been persuaded to use his precious petrol ration to do me honour. We pulled up next to a stretch of green which in happier days had boasted tennis courts, a croquet lawn and a bowling green. Beyond it was the sea-front, now covered in barbed wire.

The sergeant had the men drawn up on parade. They had battledress and World War I rifles. They were all ages and sizes, but they stood as rigidly to attention as any Guards regiment at the Trooping of the Colour, as the CO and I solemnly passed down the ranks in review. Afterwards, they marched, formed fours, presented arms and generally showed off their paces. They were not good, but were better than I had expected. The old man had obviously drilled them thoroughly, and afterwards, when they were stood at ease, I congratulated them, and their CO, and told them that we in the RAF appreciated their backing, and could fight better in the knowledge that the defence of the country was in such good hands. I didn't believe a word of it, and neither did they, but the fact that we both knew it bound us together in a mutual conspiracy.

I also shamelessly committed President Roosevelt and the United States Congress to entering the war, which compounded the conspiracy by putting it on an international level.

There was no way to avoid having tea with the old man and

his wife in a small cottage with a large, beautiful garden. The photographs in the crowded house told the story of an army life, from army forebears through military college, the regiment, the 14—18 war, the investiture at Buckingham Palace. It was all there.

His wife was very much in his shadow, but, although he seemed to ignore her most of the time, an occasional pat on the hand indicated a deep understanding, forged over the years.

Tea in the garden was difficult. I was impatient to get away and back to the squadron. We were all painfully aware of the contrast between the very English, ageing lieutenant-colonel and the brash young American fighter pilot.

I took my leave as politely — and as quickly — as I could. He walked with me to the garden gate. Again I had the feeling that he desperately wanted to say something and didn't know how.

'Damned decent of you to come! Meant a lot to the men.' We shook hands. 'Meant a lot to me!' he added awkwardly.

'It was a pleasure! You have a fine unit. I was most impressed.'

'No,' he said. 'We both know it's damned pathetic!' He paused, struggling to express his feelings, after a lifetime spent concealing them.

'There's just one thing,' he said gruffly. 'If the Hun lands — and he probably will; if he goes through here — and he probably will, not one of those men will be alive to tell the tale. I just wanted you to know that.'

'I know that, sir,' I said. I stepped back and saluted. 'That's why it's not so pathetic!'

Back at base, I found I hadn't missed anything but frustrating scrambles and uneventful patrols. After dinner I was having a drink with my New Zealand Maori friend, Kempton Werohija.

'Where were you, to-day?' he asked. The others at the bar turned around and said, 'Yeah, where did you goof off to?'

I couldn't tell them. It was part of the RAF tradition that nothing serious or corny should be discussed in the Mess. There could be no hint that the tragedy of war was anything but a farcical comedy.

'I've been with Drake on Plymouth Ho!' I said.

'I thought you said you were going to visit the Home Guard.' said Ray.

'Same thing!' I said.

We were not to know it then, but in spite of our frustrations, or perhaps because of them, we were absorbing the savvy and the spirit that formed the basis of the Fourth Fighter Group.

Gradually, we went over to the offensive. Unfortunately, in my opinion both then and now, the first big effort was a tragic waste. We were thrilled when we were briefed for the Dieppe Raid in August 1942 — until we learned that, after risking their lives in capturing their objectives in Dieppe, the troops were simply going to turn around and leave. They explained that it was a dress rehearsal for the invasion. I only hoped there would be enough left after the rehearsal to take part in the main event. I felt so strongly about it, I wrote a suggestion through the CO that the target be switched to the Channel Islands. That would have given the Canadians their training, but they could have stayed and held them, liberating an occupied part of Great Britain, giving the RAF airfields from which they could better gain air supremacy over Northern France, and providing a possible jump-off base for the invasion. The RAF, Royal Navy, and Army were strong enough even by then: they could have held them.

We were flying Hurricanes in close cover to the landing. Stacked up above us were most of the fighter squadrons in England. They held their own against the Luftwaffe, but were neither prepared, nor expected, to give much help to the struggling troops. We came in with the first wave, duly strafed the targets we had been given; but we were up against some of the heaviest fortifications in the Atlantic Wall. As we turned for home, most of the Canadians were still pinned down on the beach. We refuelled at Tangmere and went back. At first it looked as if they were still pinned down on the beach, but as we roared in low, we saw no movement from those prostrate bodies.

We went back again to cover the withdrawal, but for a lot of them, there was no withdrawal. The last to leave were the first to have landed, and I believe the only unit to have taken all their objectives dead on time: Lord Lovat's Commandos. They seemed in no hurry to leave. As we twisted and turned we saw them drawn up in front of their CO and his piper. Something was burning and smoking. I was told afterwards it was part of their Scottish tradition. They were cremating their dead.

As we finally turned for home over the deserted beaches strewn with dead, I shook my head and murmured: 'They should have taken the Channel Islands.'

By now we were carrying the air war to the Luftwaffe over France in the form of fighter sweeps. We now had Spitfires. It was a whole new kind of flying: we were one with the machine, and, more important, we had new confidence. For the first time we felt we had a plane that could out-perform the Me109 and FW190.

It may have been true in a turn, but not in a dive. I remember one sweep over St Omer. The squadron was flying in perfect formation, when a Me109 came down in a vertical dive behind us, pulled up behind the last plane in the last flight, shot him down, continued through the squadron, pulled up in front of the squadron leader, did a slow roll and then split-essed, and dived for the ground.

It must have been on one of the early sweeps that I shot down my first enemy plane. I'd chased them before, and even dog-fought with them, but always as wingman, protecting my number one. I was still flying wingman, and last man in the flight. I knew it was the most dangerous position in the squadron, so when the gaggle of 109's came down on us and the flight leader yelled, 'Break,' I hauled back so hard on the stick, I blacked out temporarily. When my vision cleared I saw the last 109 turning in front of me. I could see the black crosses! I pulled tighter in the turn and was easily gaining on him. I peered through my lighted gun-sight and saw it moving up the fuselage as I tried to lay off the right deflection. The correct procedure was to give short bursts, but I was too eager for such niceties. I pressed the firing button on the spade grip on the stick, and held it, simply hosing the target from stem to stern. I pulled right on through until he disappeared under the long nose of my Spitfire. I kept in the turn and looked back to clear my tail. Suddenly I was totally alone. There were no Germans, and no squadron. It said a lot for the sense of discipline instilled by the RAF that the pride in gaining my first victory was obliterated by the horror of having lost my number one. I went into a dive for the coast, twisting and jinking to clear my tail. As I approached the home base, I heard the others landing. I followed them in and hoped no one would notice I'd come home alone. At the debriefing, I was relieved to learn that everyone had returned safely.

I knew that Buzz Beurling, the Canadian sergeant-pilot had been disciplined for being too independent and attacking on his own by being posted to Malta; but when they saw my combat film with the flashes along the fuselage and the cockpit, I learned that success could make up for breaches in squadron discipline. Beurling learned the same thing. In Malta he became Canada's leading ace by shooting down thirty-one enemy planes!

Those of us who had flown with other RAF squadrons left them with sadness when we were posted to join the Eagle Squadrons in the autumn of 1942. Ray Fuchs, 'Whitey' White and I said good-bye to 416 Canadian Squadron with some sadness.

It had become our home; and its CO, Lloyd Chadburn, and all of its pilots were our family. We knew that 133 was one of the three Eagle Squadrons composed entirely of Americans in the RAF. It was based up in Essex in 12 Group. With 416, and before that, with 43, we had been at the front-line stations of 11 Group: — Kenley, Biggin Hill, Tangmere.

The train chuffed off, leaving us alone except for the station-master making his way back to the small station-house. We asked him if there was transport waiting for us.

'No,' he said. 'That'll be at Saffron Walden. All aboard!'

He indicated a small train on another track. He seemed to find it hard to believe that everyone was not aware of the fact that Audley End was not a town or even a village, but simply a stop on the main line where passengers could change trains for the four-mile ride to the town of Saffron Walden. We never learned why the original Victorian builders of the line didn't run it through the town. It could hardly have been for the convenience of the owners of the beautiful stately home of Audley End. They were probably powerful enough at the time, but would they have cared that much to be on a main-line railway? Over the next few years, hundreds of Americans puzzled over the apparent inefficiency of the change at Audley End, but they never got an answer. It never occurred to the English to question the situation. The only thing they found strange was the reaction of the 'Yanks', which they accepted as another peculiarity of their unsophisticated, but likable country cousins.

'You mean we're supposed to take this lil ol' Toonerville Trolley to Saffron Walden?' Thanks to Whitey's Tennessee accent, as far as the Stationmaster was concerned, he might have been talking Greek.

'Don't knock it', said Ray. 'If it wasn't for this we'd probably have to walk. They run this train system like we run street-cars. It's convenient and cheap, so sit down and relax. The secret of enjoying life in this country is never to be in a hurry. If you push them they resent it. It's kind of like an Old Folks Home.'

When we got out of the little train at Saffron Walden station, it was getting dark, there was still a chill in the air, and it was raining. We found a small camouflaged van outside, eventually located the driver, and were driven out to the base of Debden. It had been a pre-war base and we were impressed with its solid brick buildings; but they were not for us. They gave us a meal, but then we had to move on again. For reasons of defence and security, the squadrons had been 'dispersed'. 133 was based at a satellite airfield at Great Sampford. It was just down the road about two miles, through Wimbish Green and Radwinter, which were not really villages but collections of five or six houses. The airfield was only a grass field, with wooden huts dispersed around the edge for sleeping accommodation. There was nothing great about Great Sampford. We were dumped off in front of the barracks reserved for officers, and the van immediately headed back for the civilization of the main base at Debden. We couldn't blame it.

Dragging our gear with us, we opened the wooden door, and gazed down a dark corridor with doors on either side. There wasn't a sound or a light. We opened a door. The neat little room was deserted. There were two beds, two little desks, two little wooden chairs and two wooden lockers. On the desks were photographs of girl-friends or wives. It looked well lived-in, but somehow that made it all the more desolate.

'Guess they're at chow or out on the town!' said Ray, but he knew, and we knew, it wasn't that.

We closed the door behind us and walked on down the corridor. Suddenly a door at the end opened. A young, worried looking pilot came out. He was tall, with jet-black curly hair, and his good-looking Italian appearance reminded me of a film actor; either Cesar Romero or Victor Mature. Right now, he looked shaken and nervous.

'Hi! I'm Don Gentile. I sure am glad to see you. I'm all alone here.'

'Where are the others?' I asked.

'Don't you know?'

We didn't answer.

'None of them came back.'

We still didn't understand. 'Came back from where?'

'From the mission. They were escorting the first Fortress raid to Brest. There was a lot of cloud, and maybe the wind changed. I guess the Forts kept going, and our guys stayed with them. On the way back they were already short of gas when they were bounced by Jerries. Then they couldn't get back across the Channel. I've heard Beaty made it back to the South Coast, but he's the only one.'

We didn't answer. There was nothing to be said. We went back to our kit and looked at Gentile.

'I guess you can take any room. They're all empty.' He made a dash for his door and slammed it behind him.

Ray and I moved into the next room. I opened a locker. Inside was his overcoat and best uniform; his shaving brush, razor, soap, toothpaste and toothbrush were neatly lined up on the shelf. There were well-thumbed letters, and the beginning of a reply on a fresh sheet of paper: 'Dear Mum —'.

'I don't think I'll unpack to-night. They'll come and pack this stuff up tomorrow.'

'Yeah!' said Ray. 'I feel like an intruder.' He was looking at the photograph of a good-looking girl beside his bed. Across it was written: 'For ever, yours, Doll.'

I think it was a day or so later. We had been flying formation

under the command of Red McColpin, the CO of 133 Squadron,
until dusk. After dinner, we found our way by bicycle to Saffron
Walden and The Rose and Crown, the old pub on the market
square. We weaved our way back to Great Sampford, parked
the bikes and approached the barracks.

Suddenly the wooden door of the hut was shattered as if by
an explosion. A body came hurtling through, closely followed
by another. They were followed by two kit bags. A six foot
figure appeared in the doorway. His open-necked shirt and unbuttoned blue tunic made his shoulders seem even broader than
they obviously were. His head was lowered like a bull about to
charge showing his short-cropped hair, and broad forehead over
blue eyes. His powerful chin added to the overall impression of
forcefulness and drive.

The two sprawled figures began to pick themselves up slowly
and painfully. They were RAF administration officers. Ray,
Whitey and I moved towards the door but it was still blocked
by the glowering figure.

'You pilots?' he asked.

We nodded and he let us in.

'I'm Don Blakeslee.' He said it as if no other explanation was
necessary. He was right.

Apart from a few like Red McColphin, Spike Miley, Dusty
Miller and Dixie Alexander, 133's most experienced pilots were
lost on the last mission or were eligible for rotation to the States,
where they needed instructors with European combat behind
them; so that those of us who had been brought in from RAF
and RCAF Squadrons to fill the gaps had more hours of flying
and combat than the survivors. This was particularly true of
Blakeslee so, when McColphin went back home, it was natural
that Don should take over as CO.

But, while no one questioned his talents in the air, many in
the top command had less confidence in his behaviour on the
ground. He had established his reputation at the time of transfer,
by choosing the very night before General Hunter's visit to the
base to entertain two female officers in his barrack room. The
General started his tour early the next morning. Warned of the
approaching danger, the two WAAF officers just had time to

cover some of their embarrassment, and scramble out of the barracks window right into the path of the General and his staff.

Told that Blakeslee would be demoted and transferred as a first lieutenant, 'Monk' Hunter remarked: 'For one, maybe; but for *two*! He should be promoted!'

Maybe that was why he was a captain again within a few weeks, and given command of the squadron.

Most newly appointed squadron CO's made a speech; sincere, patriotic, sentimental, amusing, profane, bawdy, blasphemous, or any mixture thereof. Blakeslee simply stood on the bar and announced that the drinks were on him. It was well after one a.m. when he announced to those who were still at least semi-conscious that all pilots would report ready for take-off at 6 a.m.

Somehow the faithful batmen and the more abstemious pilots were able to get most of us to the briefing, in body, if not in spirit. Blakeslee was in fine form. He was a great believer in the RAF tradition of hard drinking and high living, and never permitting either of them to interfere with constant readiness to fly, and fly well, at any time.

There was no enthusiasm on the part of the pilots. The loss of most of the squadron, the thought of flying with pilots we didn't know, the depressing facilities at Great Sampford, and the fact that we were stuck off there, while the other two Eagle Squadrons relaxed in the luxury of the main station at Debden, all combined to create an atmosphere of depression and cynicism. There was no *esprit de corps*; most of us had had to leave the squadrons we loved, and the few 133 survivors saw their squadron taken over by brash strangers. There was no enthusiasm or spirit; and, without these, no fighter squadron could survive. In short, we were not a true squadron, and we knew it.

Apart from the poor amenities at Great Sampford, there was the problem of the grass airfield itself. It was small, irregular in shape, with an uneven surface. By the time you got the Spitfire's tail up, and could see over the long nose, you were often practically on top of the boundary fence.

Normally, fighter planes took off in two's, a leader with his wingman. On a very good field, I had seen a section of four scrambled off at the same time. Only twice had I ever seen a whole squadron of sixteen aircraft take off in formation; once on the huge grass airfield at Martlesham Heath, and once at the big main airfield at Tangmere.

As Blakeslee put names to the planes outlined on the board, we all presumed that, as usual, those were the positions we would take up once we were airborne. Then, incredulously, we heard him say almost casually: 'We'll form up this way on the east perimeter. When I give the signal, the squadron will take off in formation!' There was a gasp of disbelief. It was cut short by a bellow from Blakeslee: 'Move!'

It wasn't quite daylight as we started to taxi into position. To add to the confusion, there was a slight, patchy ground fog. It was a miracle that everyone got into position without chewing the tail off anyone else, with their prop, as we zig-zagged from side to side to try to see around the long nose. Blakeslee was standing up in his cockpit. The Spit's in-line engine heated up if it had to taxi too long, so the minute every plane was more or less in position, he brought his arm forward like John Wayne leading the US Cavalry, flopped down into his seat, and started to roll.

The engines' splutter built up to a roaring crescendo. We were soon bumping over the rough grass surface. The frightening thing was to have to pull back on the throttle on the ground to keep formation when we knew we needed every bit of power and speed to get off. It was worst for us in the last section. We had to be jockeying our throttle violently to stay in position. But when we saw the fence and the trees looming up, we pushed the throttle to the gate and kept it there. We resisted the temptation to haul the nose up — and risk a stall — and cleared the fence by inches. We had to swerve to miss the trees, which were higher than us.

'Tighten it up. Let's show these bastards!'

It was Blakeslee on the RT, and I realized we were already flying over the centre of the main airfield at Debden. We knew what he meant. The other squadrons were watching, and we were going to show them the best formation flying they'd ever seen at under 500 feet. They said afterwards that the effect was dramatic: a whole squadron rising out of the ground and sweeping across the middle of the base in perfect formation in a roar of sound which shattered the windows.

To them it looked like a perfect precision exercise; but in those planes we were sweating, swearing and working as we'd never worked before; straining desperately to fly as close formation as possible without colliding with the next plane, or crashing into the ground.

The formation was even better when we came back over the base at Debden, peeled off and landed at Great Sampford. It was when we climbed out of the planes that I understood. There was excitement, enthusiasm, boasting, and pride. Everyone was babbling about how, against all odds, they faced and overcame catastrophe and gave a show fit for heroes. That evening Blakeslee wasn't the only 133 pilot with the belligerent swagger as we arrived in the officers' mess at Debden. It had become a squadron characteristic, and the other squadrons accepted it. Next day we left Great Sampford and moved into the main base at Debden.

It was about this time that King George VI came to Debden. He probably knew that we were going to be transferred to the US Army Air Force, and wanted to express Britain's appreciation to its adopted 'Yanks'. He presented British decorations to some of us, and in simple sincere words, told us our being there was appreciated. He made one mistake. I think it was Snuffy Smith he asked if everything was all right. Snuffy was a Texan, and shocked all of us by asking if it couldn't be made official for Texans to wear Texas boots with the RAF uniform. Politely the King agreed. Everyone thought that was the end of it, until, some weeks later, King's Rules and Regulations officially approved the wearing of Texas boots with RAF officers' uniform by Texan pilots, providing they were black and without decoration.

But it came a little late. By now we were being transferred to the US Army Air Force. 71, 121 and 133 Eagle Squadrons were to become 334, 335 and 336 Squadrons of the US Eighth Army Air Force, forming the Fourth Fighter Group. The Eagle Squadrons had shot down seventy-three German aircraft. As the Fourth, they would shoot down over 1,000 more making them the leading Allied fighter group of the war.

The US Army Air Force and the American Government needed

ready-made pilots already in combat, and we were proud and happy to be able to fight in the uniform of our own country. But we had been through too much with England not to have a split loyalty. We loved and respected the country, its people, the RAF and, strangely enough, its Royal Family. We couldn't give up everything; so we had the impertinence to make our demands: we had earned our RAF wings, and we wanted to wear them on our US Air Force uniform. To our great surprise, and to the everlasting credit of the US Army Air Force and its top brass, they agreed, providing they were miniature RAF wings worn over the right breast pocket, while the US full-sized wings were to be worn over the left breast pocket over our ribbons, including our foreign decorations. If the double wings were more highly respected by the British, and, incidentally by the Germans, than by the Americans, that was OK by us. The main thing was, *we* were proud of them.

We never stopped flying. We went to London by ones and twos during our precious 24-hour passes to transfer, and pick up US uniforms. We had no American planes, so the RAF turned the Spitfires over to us, and we painted US Air Force stars over the red, white and blue roundels of the RAF.

The first two Spits to be repainted belonged to Dixie Alexander and myself. We started badgering Blakeslee to let us go on a mission — a US mission — the first US fighter mission. Don liked the idea, and was able to sell it to General Monk Hunter, who understood Blakeslee and the spirit of the Fourth.

What I had in mind was what we called a 'Rhubarb' in the RAF. When the weather was too bad for normal 'Ops', two or four fighters were sometimes authorised to make sneak strafing raids over France and Belgium, very low level, to avoid being picked up by radar or hit by flak. Presumably the code-name Rhubarb was meant to indicate that they flew so low the propellers clipped the rhubarb. Their targets were shipping, rail transport, and any other strategic ground targets. Apart from the destruction of transportation and shipping, it was felt that it would be discouraging for the Germans, and a morale-booster for the occupied French and Belgians. It certainly did wonders for the fighter pilots, frustrated by inactivity, when bad weather kept them grounded.

We went out on the deck under the low, grey clouds, skimming the waves; Dixie leading and I keeping a few lengths out to the side and slightly behind. We made a perfect landfall as planned where the canal goes straight in from the coast to the town of Gravelines. As we flashed over the sand dunes, the flak opened up; bright tracer like fiery golf-balls, deceptively slow and harmless-looking, as it lobbed up at us, but blindingly fast when it passed near. But we had surprised them, and the shots were arcing over us and behind us. We hit a few boats on the way up the canal and more where it opened up into a small port on the west side of the town. The wrecks of the boats we hit could be seen in Gravelines harbour for many years after the war.

Behind Gravelines, we turned east, and were almost immediately over Dunkirk. We hurtled down the big canal, firing on a large barge which we knew would be carrying coal or oil.

Then we saw Ostende on our left, but kept going until we saw the distinctive outline of Bruges. Like Gravelines, it had its canal coming into the town from Zeebrugge on the coast; but it also had a large railway marshalling yard on the south side of the town. The historic and picturesque city of Bruges was ringed in red on our maps as off-limits for bombing, but low-flying fighter planes could pick out individual targets for strafing with deadly accuracy, and it was the locomotives in the marshalling yards which were our targets.

We each picked out an engine with steam up. The flak was more accurate now and we did a lot of jinking and stomping of rudder as we lined up on our targets. They were both belching steam, as we flashed over them. We didn't pull up, but hugged the ground, as the flak arched over us, behind us, and all around us.

Suddenly, we were out in the country and there was no more flak. We turned north, to hit the coast of Knokke. As we roared over the coast road, a lone cyclist was directly in front of me. I had to pull up a bit to be sure the prop didn't hit him. As I flashed over, only a few feet above him, I was surprised to see he was bent over the handlebars not even looking up. I'm sure he hadn't seen me. I kicked rudder to dodge the flak coming up from the defences on the coast, and caught sight of the look of amazement on his upturned face, just as the bike swerved and fell, probably hit by the blast of air from my propeller.

In a flash we were over the sea, setting course for home. The total time over enemy territory had been about fifteen minutes. We had accomplished our mission as planned, but had no illusions about its importance. We considered it more of a training exercise, and our report to the Intelligence officer was duly modest, if not laconic.

But we overlooked the fact that this was probably the first purely US fighter mission over France and Belgium and the newly arrived public relations corps were hungry for news. It only took about twenty-four hours for it to hit the fan. *The Stars and Stripes* army newspaper led the parade, with the others sounding the same clarion call. It read as if thousands of planes had spread destruction and fear throughout northern Europe, leaving the transportation system in disarray, and Hitler himself chewing the carpet. Dixie and I destroyed all the news items we could find, so I can't be sure of the exact wording, but one of them went something like this: 'At dawn today fighter planes of the US Eighth Army Air Force carried out daring low-level attacks on rail, road, and water transport in Northern France and Belgium, leaving behind them a trail of destruction . . .'.

That evening, I heard Blakeslee bellowing long before he burst into the mess. We had been steeped in the RAF tradition that any exaggeration or line-shooting was intolerable, and, worse still, 'bad form'; so I knew what was coming. As he bore down on me he bellowed, 'All right! Where's the other half of the Eighth Air Force?'

'He's taking a pee,' I said.

When Dixie reappeared, he held up his hand and said: 'Let me show you what happened.'

He peeled off his tunic, his shirt and his undershirt, and turned around. There was a gasp. In the middle of his back was a lurid red bleeding gash, from which protruded the blue handle of a dagger. It was so perfectly done, it was only when we moved closer that we saw that it was a beautifully executed tattoo.

'I was stabbed in the back!' he said.

Blakeslee turned to me. 'What's your excuse?'

'All I claimed was one bicycle damaged. I blew the guy off on the way out!'

Blakeslee was calming down. He saw from the reaction of the others that, if it had done nothing else, the mission had helped build up squadron morale and pride, and that was desperately needed at that time. 'Well,' he said grudgingly, 'I've just seen your combat film, so I'll buy you a drink. From then on, the drinks are on you!'

The first commanding officer of the newly formed Fourth Group was loaned by the RAF. Wing Commander Duke-Woolley turned up in a midget green, open MG sports car. We marvelled at the leather belt around the engine, the gas-tank perched on the rear, and especially its minute size. To us it was like a toy. Forty years later I met Duke-Woolley and reminded him of his car. 'Yes,' he said in his matter-of-fact way, 'I'm still driving it.'

Duke-Woolley was soon succeeded by Chesley Peterson, the most experienced and respected pilot in the Eagle squadrons. Like many of the most successful fighter pilots of the Fourth, he had been washed out of training in the USAAF for lack of inherent flying ability. He was one of the few CO's of whom I have never heard anything but praise and affection.

As soon as we had transferred, we knew that sooner or later we would lose our beloved Spitfires and be equipped with the new long-range P-47 Thunderbolt, but we put the thought out of our minds, and flew our Spitfires as often and as hard as we could. This meant joining the RAF on fighter sweeps sometimes escorting medium bombers, or escorting heavy US bombers on the first leg of their mission, or picking them up again as they came out. It was a continuation of what we had been doing in the RAF, with the same restriction of range which limited us to Northern France and Belgium. Paris and Brussels were at the extreme limit of our range. Of course, it never became boring. We gained more knowledge and respect for the yellow-nosed 109's which came up from St Omer and Abbeville. We called them the 'Abbeville Boys'. Not many of us knew that this was Jagdgeschwader 26, which had produced most of the great German fighter pilots, including Adolf Galland himself. JG52 had more victories, but the Luftwaffe made a very clear distinction between the Russian front and the Western front. 'Macky' Steinhoff said of fighting the Russians: 'It was like shooting ducks.' Our pilots confused JG26 'Schlageter' Squadron with the 'Richthofen' Squadron, JG2 in which both the Red Baron and Hermann Göring had fought in World War I. They were in Northern France too, but it was JG26, first under Galland, then under Schoepfel and then under 'Pips' Priller, that defended the Western front from the beginning to the end of the war, and even the aces of the Russian front rated Galland's 103 victories and Priller's 101 in the same category as 'Bubi' Hartmann's 352 and Barkhorn's 301 on the Russian front.

Personally, I felt frustrated at our inability to protect our bombers into Germany, and, almost alone among the pilots, looked forward to getting longer range fighters. The valiant Spitfire which had performed so well in the defence of Britain had been overtaken by events. It was now time for us to go over to the offensive. A new chapter in aviation and in warfare was starting.

If most of the pilots of the Fourth didn't welcome the prospect of long-range fighters, there was one group of pilots who did. These were the US Army Air Force generals, Toohey Spaatz, Jimmy Doolittle, Monk Hunter, Ira Eaker, Jesse Auton, Bill Kepner and others. They had foreseen the way air warfare would develop back in the 1920's when they backed Billy Mitchell in his battle for recognition of the potential of future air power. They had shared Mitchell's frustration when he was court-martialled and dismissed from the service, but they had battled on and won. Now they had learned that their long-range bombing offensive could only be continued if the bombers had fighter escort all the way, and they were determined that they would have it.

When the first Thunderbolts turned up in England, they asked for volunteers from the Fourth to check them out, and then introduce them to the rest of the Group. They only got three, one from each squadron, 'Hoppy' Hopson, Snuffy Smith and myself. We joined Cass Hough in the Air Technical Service, a small but highly effective unit which was already working on the development of droppable external fuel tanks, which would, within a year, stretch the combat radius of the Thunderbolt from 280 miles to 575 miles, and that of the Mustang from its original formidable 350 miles to a staggering 750 miles.

Back at Debden, I checked Blakeslee out on the P-47. Of course he didn't like it. It was daunting to haul seven tons of plane around the sky after the finger-tip touch needed for the Spit. I tried to sell Blakeslee on the opportunities this plane could open up for us.

'For one thing,' I said, 'they'll never be able to dive away from us again.'

He must have been listening. On 15th April 1943, Blakeslee was leading us over Belgium when we spotted a couple of FW190's. We attacked: as usual they dived away, and we followed. Admittedly it took a while. We jumped them at a little over 20,000 feet and Blakeslee was at 500 feet before he finally blew his victim out of the sky and into a suburb of Ostend. It was the first victory for a P-47.

Back at Debden, I caught up with Blakeslee at debriefing. 'I told you the jug could out-dive them!'

Grudgingly he conceded, 'Well it damn well ought to be able to dive; it sure as hell can't climb!'

It was unfair. The P-47, in spite of its weight and size, was an amazing aircraft, and we continued to build up our score, almost in spite of ourselves. If we'd had as much fanatical loyalty and faith in the P-47 as the 56th Group under Hub Zemke, we would have kept our lead over them; as it was, the 56th probably flew more aggressively and were rivalling our scores, but then, as we used to say in the Fourth: 'They don't know any better; the poor bastards never flew Spits.'

In the meantime, Pete Peterson had been taken off combat for a rest. Blakeslee had more experience than any other pilot in the group, if not more rank. Don was still a captain, although some less experienced pilots were majors. A little diplomacy would probably have corrected the injustice sooner, but diplomacy was one thing Don Blakeslee could never be accused of.

Peterson was succeeded by a regular career officer, Colonel Anderson, who won our respect by allowing others to lead missions while he would lead one of the sections; but, above all, by flying missions at all at his advanced age. He was thirty-nine.

Nevertheless, in spite of everything, finally, to the delight of the pilots, and to the everlasting credit of the commanding generals, Blakeslee took over as CO of the Fourth.

Major General Monk Hunter, Commanding General of the Eighth Fighter Command was very much a fighter pilot's general, and must have understood the spirit of the Fourth, and what Blakeslee could do for it. In August 1943, Hunter turned the Eighth Fighter Command over to Major General William Kepner. Hunter said to us: '... I came here when the first group of you were transferred to Eighth Fighter Command. You will never know what it meant to us to receive a group of fully trained operational pilots. It has formed a nucleus around which we have built our fighting machine.'

Kepner added, 'The Fourth Fighter Group has been the stem whence fighter command doctrine has sprung.'

Yet on 16th August 1943 the Eighth Fighter Command came within a hairsbreadth of losing their most promising group leader. It was a short mission for those days. 170 B-17's were to hit the aircraft repair depot at Le Bourget, the main Paris airfield. The target was within our range even without external belly tanks, so with the 4th, 56th, 78th and 353rd P-47 Groups covering the bombers at 23,000 feet and Spitfires sweeping the area at about 15,000, the Fortresses would have strong fighter cover all the way in and all the way back.

At morning briefing, Blakeslee explained that 334 would fly top cover, 335 would fly below them and Blakeslee would lead with 336 from the lowest position. I therefore moved over to lead the second section just behind and to the left of Blakeslee's lead section. Coming out of the briefing I said to Don, 'With all that mob around the bombers, we should be able to do a little free hunting on our own.'

I knew he was as frustrated as I was at having to let German fighters dive away to safety because we had to return to our main task of escorting the bombers.

'Right!' he said, 'That's why I'm flying where I am, and that's why you're flying where you are; to give me cover!'

The weather was perfectly clear, and on the climb out, the south coast of England and the north coast of France spread out below us like a map.

I looked across at my wingman. It was Lieutenant Bob Wehrmann's first mission. I figured it was an easy, short mission to break him in on. I had told him it was a milk-run, and all he had to do was stick with me like glue. I gave him a thumbs up gesture and waved him to spread out; we were crossing in over the French coast just east of Dieppe and I flicked on my gunsight and fire button. I was looking all around, but my gaze was constantly drawn down to our left where I could see the river Somme winding out to the Channel. A few miles up the river was Abbeville, and, a little further east, St Omer, and, to the south, Poix, near Amiens. These were the home bases of the 'Richthofen' Geschwader, JG2 led by Egon Mayer, and the yellow-nosed JG26, 'Schlageter' Geschwader, made famous by Adolf Galland, now led by Gerd Schoepfel. Both Geschwader had produced most of the leading aces of the Luftwaffe. These two Geschwader were responsible for the defence of the Western front after most of the other Geschwader had been transferred to the Russian front.

It should be remembered that Luftwaffe Geschwader were composed of three or more Gruppen, and it was the Gruppen which corresponded to the US fighter squadron, while the Geschwader was more like a large American fighter group.

It was a few seconds after we sighted the airfield at Abbeville that we saw our bombers ahead, and almost at the same time, the first FW190's.

I heard Blakeslee on the RT. 'There's a million of them, 190's . . . down there. Horseback Leader to Horseback; continue to join up with the bombers. I'm going down. Goody, give me top cover!' 'Horseback' was the Fourth's call sign at the time.

Blakeslee started his diving turn as he started to speak. By the time his brief message was over, his P-47 was in an almost vertical dive. He wanted to get down to attack the 190's before he lost them, and he needed the speed. I knew immediately that, if I was to stay with him, I had to move as fast and dive as steeply as he had. The rest of Don's flight hadn't reacted as fast, and a gap opened up between them and their leader. I realised I had to try to catch Blakeslee or he would be on his own. I went into a vertical dive, glancing behind, every so often, but never losing sight of the leader.

I saw him pull out of his almost vertical dive to come up under

two 190's. I pulled out of my dive as hard as I could to cut the
corner, almost blacking out. He was closing on one of the 190's.
I knew he wouldn't fire until the last moment. He admitted to
being a poor shot. But he left it too late. They had spotted him,
and flipped over onto their backs and dived away in their classic
evasive manoeuvre. But Blakeslee was after them, and me after
Blakeslee, and Wehrmann after me. Our speed had hardly slackened
in the few seconds we had levelled off, and now I was diving
vertically again. The speed was building up well over 500 mph
as I tried to catch up, and the plane was shaking violently. We
flashed through a squadron of Spitfires, but there was nothing
they could do but watch. They could never follow us at our
diving speeds.

Suddenly we were in the hornets' nest; there were 109's and
190's all around. We still had more diving speed, but I saw that
Blakeslee's two 190's were easing out of their dive, and he was
following them. At the same time, I saw three 190's screaming
down on Blaskeslee and cutting in behind him to take him off
the tail of their two buddies. 'Horseback Blue One to Horseback
Leader; three coming in on you at 3 o'clock high. I'm trying to
cut them off.'

I tried to pull out of my thundering dive, but the controls
were rigid. All my strength wouldn't move the stick and I knew
I was in the so-called 'terminal' dive from which many P-47's
pilots never were able to pull out. I dare not pull back on the
throttle in case the nose went under in the start of an outside
loop. I reached for the small winder that set the trim of the
plane for take-off and landing, hoping that the little servo edge
on the tail-plane would ease it up, but not fast enough to buckle
the wings.

It worked. I blacked out, and felt as if my back was broken,
but when my vision cleared I saw the 190's ahead of me, much
closer, but still out of range. I was gaining on them thanks to the
terrible speed I'd built up, but they were gaining on Blakeslee,
and he was doggedly pursuing his prey.

I pressed my mike button. 'Break, Horseback Leader, break
hard right!'

It was just in time. Don broke into a tight right turn, but the

190's turned with him. We were well under 10,000 feet by now, where the FW190 could out-turn a Thunderbolt. But it gave me the chance to cut the corner, and zoom up under the last 190. He was intent on what was going on ahead of him and it was easy for me to close to where I could see the yellow nose and the black crosses on the fuselage and wings.

My first burst scored hits, so I gave him three more in quick succession. I was hitting him mostly around the starboard wing root. Suddenly there was a flash and a puff of smoke and his wing came fluttering off. The wing and the wildly spinning plane tumbled past me. I took a quick glance behind. Incredibly Wehrmann was still there, and I blessed him for it. There were other German planes above, but not dangerous — yet.

The danger was up ahead. Blakeslee was twisting and turning in a desperate effort to shake the leading 190, but the German was sticking with him like glue and he was scoring a few hits. The second FW was pulling up to close the trap on what he still must have thought was a lone Thunderbolt; but I was closing on him fast. My attention was on the lead German and Blakeslee in their deadly duel. 'Hang on, Horseback, I'm gaining on him!'

I had plunged the stick forward to pick up more speed. Soon I was right under the second 190. I pulled up, laid off deflection aiming in front of his engine, and fired. I was too close to miss. The fire was concentrated. Flashes appeared on the engine and continued down the under-belly in four long bursts. The engine must have stopped, because I hurtled past him. The FW went straight into a vertical dive, trailing smoke, and exploded in a field not far below.

Now I could concentrate on taking the last 190 off Blakeslee's tail. 'I'm coming up, Don, hang on!' He was too busy to answer. I wasn't quite in range, but I was gaining. Each second like an hour. I saw more flashes on Don's Thunderbolt. I had to try to hit his attacker even if I was out of range. I took careful aim and fired from dead astern. There were no hits. I tried two more bursts. Nothing. Then, on the fourth burst, I saw a flash!

'I've got him, Don!' I said.

'The hell you've got him. He's got me!' was Blakeslee's breathless reply.

Now I hit the 190 again, and was closing fast. He slewed around to see what was behind him, but then continued his attack on Blakeslee. He was either a very cool guy, or he mistook the two radial engined P-47's behind him for his own wingmen.

I pushed the firing button again to finish him off. There was the start of the juddering burst of the machine-guns, then a sudden silence. At first I couldn't figure it out; then I realised with a shock I was out of ammunition!

I looked back at Wehrmann, he was too far behind to be in range, and could never catch up in time. By now I was gaining fast on the 190, but he was still on Blakeslee's tail, and Don wasn't taking enough evasive action. Then I knew why.

'I can't see a damn thing! I'm covered in oil!'

I had to do something fast. I had no ammo, but I had speed, and was close behind the 190 now. I pushed the stick forward, dived under him, turned out to the side and up, to come up beside and a little ahead of him. I then turned straight into him. He must have been amazed to see a P-47 coming in on him at such close range, and the bluff worked. Probably almost by reflex action, he turned into the attack, rolled right on over, and split-essed for the deck. The ground was only a few hundred feet below us now, and I lost sight of him.

It was over, at least for the moment. It had seemed like a lifetime, but the whole action had lasted less than five minutes.

I pulled up alongside Blakeslee. His canopy was wide open, his goggles were on, and at times he peered out from behind his windscreen which was completely covered by black oil. The whole fuselage was streaked with oil. The big white letters WD-C on the side of his plane were practically obliterated.

'Can you make it, Don?' I asked.

'I don't think so,' he said. 'Oil is spewing all over the place, and I have to keep the throttle wide open just to keep altitude. How far do we have to go? I don't even know where we are.'

'We're about twenty miles from the coast and from there it's another thirty miles across the Channel.' What I didn't mention was that we were almost in the traffic pattern of the Luftwaffe airfield of St Omer.

I took a good look at his plane and said, 'I think you'll make it. These jugs can absorb a lot of punishment. Steer five degrees further to the right.'

That way he'd avoid Calais and its flak, and cross out between Calais and Gravelines, and he'd be heading straight for the long emergency-runway at Manston on the south-east tip of England. The bad news was that that heading would take us closer to St Omer.

I was now weaving about and behind Blakeslee, straining my eyes to make sure no German fighters were following us out. The faithful Wehrmann had now caught up with us.

Suddenly I saw them. Two FW190's coming in low from the direction of St Omer. They would probably have been able to see us from the ground. Quickly I turned to meet the two 190's before they could attack Blakeslee. Wehrmann was on my wing. As we attacked the 190's broke and turned. That was good enough. I didn't think they would be able to catch us again from their low altitude before we were across the Channel. In any case number one priority was to protect Blakeslee. Also, I was really worried about fuel now; the needle was flicking against zero.

We swung back to catch up to Blakeslee again. Soon I saw the coast and picked out his plane just as he crossed out. We were pulling up to join him when I saw what I thought was another P-47 coming in at Blakeslee's level, but the next second, I knew the slim little stubby silhouette could only be an FW190. Once more Wehrmann and I wheeled down in a frontal attack; once more, he flipped over and dived for home. Once more we broke off and came back to escort our charge.

I pulled up alongside Blakeslee to lead him as straight as I could to the long Manston runway. It wasn't only that he had no forward visibility, but I thought there was a good chance he'd been hit in the hydraulics, which would mean no flaps and no brakes. He'd need all the runway he could get.

Right after leaving the French coast we saw those welcome white cliffs of Dover. I'd done a lot of flying over this tip of England, over which most of the Battle of Britain had been fought. Its airfields, Lympne, Hawkinge, West Malling and Manston had been home to me in the early days.

I heard Blakeslee say, 'Where the hell are you taking me?'

We had passed Dover and I could see St Margaret's Bay on our left. 'We're dead on course. The longest runway in England is about ten miles ahead of you. You can go straight in.'

When we were passed Deal and were coming in over Pegwell Bay, I pulled out a Very pistol, pulled back my cockpit canopy, and shot off a red flare to make sure Manston was ready for an emergency landing. Ramsgate was on our right, Sandwich and its golf courses on our left and, dead ahead, the long runway.

'Drop your wheels, Don!' I was flying right on his wing now, and he was watching me, as I was watching him. Both of our undercarriages came down at the same time.

'OK! They're down.'

I waited till I knew he could reach the end of the runway before saying;

'Flaps.'

I put mine down, and he started pulling ahead of me. No flaps!

'No problem, Don, we're in good shape!' I raised my flaps, caught up to him, eased back the throttle and flattened the approach.

'OK, Don, cut your throttle, you're almost on the end of the runway.'

I was a few feet from the grass at the side of the runway. I opened the throttle, poured on the power, raised the wheels, pulled up to go around again, and prayed there was enough juice for a tight circuit. As I pulled around, I saw Wehrmann coming in on his approach. He probably had even less gas than I had.

I made a tight Spitfire circuit, dropped the Jug on the start of the runway, and let her roll down to the end where Blakeslee and Wehrmann had stopped. I pulled up beside them, cut the engine, and clambered out.

Blakeslee was walking around his plane inspecting the damage. Both of them were covered in black oil.

'You OK?' I asked.

'Yeah, but I don't know how they missed me. Look!'

The sturdy old P-47 was riddled all down one side. He turned to me 'That was real good shooting.'

'Thanks,' I said.

'I don't mean you; I mean that bloody 190! What the hell took you so long? I thought I'd had it.'

'Oh, I took the scenic route. Anyway, I knew the old bastard could take it,' I said.

'Yeah!' he said patting the oil-streaked side of the P-47. 'This old gal can sure take it!'

'I don't mean the plane; I mean you!'

I walked over to where Bob Wehrmann's plane had pulled up. He was still sitting in the cockpit in a daze. I climbed up on the wing, clapped him on the shoulder, and said: 'Damn good! I don't know how you stayed with me!'

The sweat was still running down his face, as he said with feeling, 'Neither do I!'

'Thanks!' I said as I turned away.

He nodded, then called after me: 'Say, Goody, let me know when you're planning the next milk-run.'

Blakeslee was looking over my plane. 'Do you want to fly her back to Debden?' I asked.

'Not on your life! Do you know you've bent the wings?' I had noticed the wrinkles in the skin of the wing-roots. It wasn't surprising considering the velocity of that dive and the terrific strain on pulling out.

'Yeah, but it still flies all right. You take Wehrmann's kite.'

'My God!' he said, shaking his head. 'I'll see you back at the Mess, if you make it — I want to buy you a drink. After all, you saved my ass!'

'Everyone's entitled to one mistake!' I said.

I got my drink; and, some time later, the Silver Star — the third highest decoration for valour!

So we gradually earned respect and a grudging affection for the P-47; but, from the very moment we transferred, every man in the group had one fervent wish: to get the 'Mustang'. They were joined in their prayers by the bomber crews who were taking horrible losses as soon as their escorting fighters had to turn back, so that only ten percent were surviving their twenty-five prescribed missions. Their bitter comment on the need for fighter escort all the way to the target and back was: 'Hell, we've got it now:

Spitfires and P-47's to the German border and FW190's and Me109's the rest of the way!'

Most experts now agree that the P-51 Mustang was the most successful fighter plane of World War II. Those of us who flew Spitfires, Thunderbolts and Mustangs loved the Spit for its manoeuvrability and tight turns, but when the defensive air war of the Battle of Britain was over, and it was time to carry the war to the enemy, we knew that the short-ranged Spit had been overtaken by events. The P-51 could catch up with the Me109 straight and level, or in a dive, and it could hold its own in a dog-fight where I would say the best pilot would win; but, most important, the P-51 had this superior performances from 30,000 feet down to the deck, and 750 miles from its base. The Luftwaffe fighter pilots rated it the best, and most agreed with Hermann Göring that when Mustangs escorted bombers over Berlin, they knew the war was over.

Yet this remarkable plane came into being almost by chance and might easily not have been developed at all. As soon as England found itself at war, a purchasing commission headed by Sir Henry Self was sent to the United States to buy planes. Because of the urgency, they originally considered only those designs which were already in production or close to it. The only fighter, or 'pursuit' plane, available to them was the Curtiss P-40. Although this plane was manoeuvrable and relatively fast, its top speed of 340 mph could only be achieved between 12,000 and 15,000 feet. Its Allison engine was not supercharged, and, since it was common to the P-38, P-39 and P-40, was in short supply. The P-40 itself was in short supply, and Curtiss was having trouble meeting the requirements of the US Army Air Corps and the British and French who had ordered some 1700 by early 1940. A sub-contractor was needed, and the British Purchasing Commission contacted their old friends at North American, who had a good record supplying them with the AT.6 Harvard advanced trainer. James 'Dutch' Kindelberger, who headed North American, agreed, but the more he studied the problem, the more he became convinced that his company could design a better plane of their own. The British finally agreed on condition that it would meet their specifications, and entail no delays. The prototype was to be ready in four months. North American accepted this daunting challenge, and the P-51 was born. They boldly designed a slim, low-drag airframe, incorporating the relatively untried laminar flow airfoil wing. The large radiator necessary to cool the glycol coolant of the in-line engine was placed as far to the rear as possible to preserve the streamlining of the engine.

Even with the Allison engine, the new plane could attain 375 mph at 15,000 feet, 35 mph faster than the Spitfire V and, with its four hour endurance, twice the range. Not only had North American designed a revolutionary, successful design, but they met their almost impossible time schedule. Strangely enough, the Assistant Chief Engineer at North American, and chief of the preliminary design group on the Mustang was Edgar Schmued who had started his career in aeronautics in his native Bavaria.

The weak spot remained the Allison engine which limited the Mustang to an effective ceiling of 15,000 feet, but the plane continued to be improved. In April 1942, Rolls-Royce test pilot Ronald Harker flew a Mustang at Duxford at the Air Fighting Development Unit and the idea of fitting a Rolls-Royce Merlin engine was born. This engine was already being manufactured under licence by Packard in Detriot. He had an enthusiastic backer in Major 'Tommy' Hitchcock, assistant air attaché at the US Embassy in London, World War I pilot in the Lafayette Escadrille, and, incidentally, uncle of Jim Clark, a leading pilot in the Fourth Group. Hitchcock was backed by ambassador John Winant. Again in record time the Mustang had a Packard-Merlin engine, a top speed of 433 mph and a ceiling of over 30,000 feet, and became the longest range highest performing fighter plane in the world.

Mustangs with Allison engines had been in service with the RAF, mostly on photo-reconnaissance for some time, but in December 1943 the 354th Group of the Ninth Air Force arrived in England equipped with P-51 Mustangs. Since they needed an experienced leader for their first combat missions, Kepner gave the temporary assignment to Blakeslee. He probably reasoned that this would give him a good appraisal of the relative merits of the P-47 and the P-51. If so, he got more than he bargained for. The few missions Blakeslee flew with the 354th confirmed his previous gut feeling. This was the plane!

He immediately stepped up his pressure on General Kepner to get Mustangs for the Fourth. He was backed by the entire group, who clambered over and around the sleek plane when Blakeslee flew it back to Debden after his missions with the 354th.

Kepner was opposed to the idea for only one reason. We were in the midst of an aggressive bomber offensive, and he could not afford to take the Fourth out of combat long enough for the pilots and mechanics to check out the new aircraft.

Blakeslee's solution was simple — and typical. 'How much time can you give us to switch, sir?'

'If the Fourth is out of action more than 24 hours, we're in trouble,' was Kepner's reply.

'General, give me the Mustangs and I give you my word. I'll have them in combat in 24 hours. I promise!'

It was a hell of a promise, and a hell of a risk, but both men knew each other, and they knew the Fourth, and its pilots. They also knew that there were still enough pilots with hundreds of combat hours in Hurricanes and Spitfires to make up a full complement for a mission; and they knew that the mechanics had worked on Rolls Royce engines when we had our Spitfires.

So Kepner got us our P-51's and in 24 hours we were on our first mission. Most pilots have about 200 hours in a front-line fighter before taking it into combat. We had about thirty minutes!

The Mustang gave a new impetus to the Fourth. While flying Thunderbolts, their only rivals, the 56th Fighter Group, under 'Hub' Zemke, had forged ahead, and soon had 300 destroyed against the 150 of the Fourth. Having flown only P-47's in combat, the 56th had no other love. Most of their pilots had hundreds of hours in the plane, knew its every whim, and knew how to get the most out of it. They also had an aggressive, intelligent leader who was a great strategist, but still encouraged individual flair among his star pilots like Bob Johnson, Gabby Gabreski, Dave Schilling and Bud Mahurin. When the 56th Group's score soared past that of the Fourth, I heard mumbled complaints that the 56th were not adhering to the strict orders to give top priority to protecting the bombers. I'm sure that was not true. What they did do was to organise a free-ranging sweep as soon as they were relieved on their escort, a strategy which the Fourth adopted later, but then more on an ad hoc basis by squadron leaders or section leaders, rather than on an organised group basis.

When the long range fighters of the Eighth Air Force had gained air superiority and the bombers were no longer taking the terrible losses of the days before total fighter cover, General Kepner cautiously authorised more aggressive tactics in attacking and destroying enemy fighters; always providing the bombers were adequately protected.

Once again, I think the 56th Group took advantage of this new approach faster and more aggressively than the Fourth. I don't remember Blakeslee ever telling us of any change in strategy, but then I never remember Blakeslee ever discussing strategy. Talk wasn't his style; with him it was action. He motivated us by example, not by instruction. He disliked words and mistrusted those who used them glibly.

As for strategy, I remember one evening in the mess, when Don had just come back from a session at headquarters. He was always ill-at-ease in those meetings, and bad-tempered afterwards. 'Goody,' he said, 'why do they talk so much about strategy and tactics? Hell, what you do depends on what's happening at that moment. What good's a strategy when you've got three 109's on your ass?'

It was a typical fighter pilot's reaction, and therefore typical Blakeslee. 'What the hell *is* our strategy?' he asked.

I knew he wanted an answer. 'In 1917 when von Richthofen was asked that question, he said: "Find the enemy and shoot him down — anything else is nonsense." I guess it still holds.'

It held for Blakeslee, and probably all successful fighter pilots.

The old argument as to whether fighters should give first priority to protecting the bombers or pursuing and destroying the enemy whenever sighted raged throughout the war on both sides. During the Battle of Britain, German bomber losses became so heavy that Göring ordered his fighter commanders to fly close cover on the bombers and stay with them as long as their fuel permitted. It cut bomber losses, but Moelders, Galland, and the other Luftwaffe fighter leaders were furious. They knew they could only eliminate the RAF by destroying their planes either in the air or on the ground. What was worse, they knew that for fighters, the best defence is offence. The aggressive spirit of attack must be maintained. A purely defensive fighter force is a contradiction of terms.

When the American air generals found themselves faced with the same problem at the beginning of the daylight bombing offensive, they avoided the typical extreme decision of Göring, and settled on a compromise, which left a certain amount of flexibility to the commanders, and even to individual section leaders. As the number of long-range fighters increased, more freedom was given to, and taken by, the pilots.

I always felt that fighter commanders could be compared to cavalry commanders in the days when cavalry were the deciding factor in warfare. Captain Nolan, the cavalry expert who played such a key role in carrying Lord Raglan's order for the charge of the Light Brigade to Lord Lucan, wrote: 'The tactics of cavalry are not capable of being reduced to rule. ... With the cavalry officer almost everything depends on the clearness of his *coup d'oeil* and the felicity with which he seizes the happy moment of action.' Had Raglan, Lucan and Cardigan understood this, there would have been no tragic charge, and the British cavalry would have won the Crimean War.

In the air war, ninety years later, the generals, Hunter, Auton, Kepner, Eaker, Doolittle, Spaatz, all experienced pilots themselves, understood, and so did we.

In early 1943, when less than ten percent of the bomber crews completed their twenty-five missions, and there was a real question as to whether the offensive could be continued, we didn't need to be told that protection of the bombers had top priority. Since the Fourth provided cover on the last lap of the fighter relay, usually over the target area, we were in on the hottest battles, when the Luftwaffe pilots hurled themselves at the bombers when they were most vulnerable. None of us could ever forget those nightmare scenes; a great bomber tumbling out of the air like a crazy toy; another spiralling down almost vertically; another somehow staying straight and level, but losing speed and altitude while smoke and flame licked the entire fuselage; yet another disappearing in a bright explosion, leaving a cloud of smoke and a wing and other pieces of debris fluttering down.

In those days, no one was going to goof off looking for Hun fighters. They were there!

Our generals were quick to react as the situation changed, and more long-range fighters became available, but it was that very availability that made the difference. They had quickly recognised the need for the long-range fighters, and insisted we got them fast, even if, as in the case of the Mustang, the original idea was someone else's.

But their real genius was in encouraging their wing, group, and squadron leaders to take the initiative and play it as they saw it. The German fighter leaders had brilliance, experience, and incredible bravery, but they were defeated by the lack of understanding and backing of Göring and Hitler.

The generals of the Eighth Air Force needed all the understanding they could muster in backing Blakeslee, but he never let them down. Probably the event that underlined the final complete air superiority of the long-range fighter, and represented the peak of Blakeslee's combat career was the England-Russia-Italy shuttle. The plan was to escort bombers from England 1,600 miles across Europe to Poltava in Russia.

From Russia, the bombers would take off for Italy, bombing an oil refinery in Southern Poland on the way, escorted by the Fourth as far as the Yugoslav coast where Mustangs from the Fifteenth Air Force based in Italy would take over. From Italy, the bombers and their escort would fly from Italy back to England, bombing railroad yards in France en route.

The 1,600 miles from England to Russia would be the longest leg, but it should take only seven and a half hours, and we had already been airborne for eight hours before. Nevertheless, every precaution was taken to assure success. Only 104 bombers were to be escorted to Russia and 1,000 bombers and their escort were to act as a diversion by bombing Berlin. The fighters were ordered not to engage in combat, nor to drop their wing-tanks until crossing the Polish-Russian border.

The group was to fly at only 15,000 feet across Europe to the Russian border and then drop to below 6,000 feet. As Blakeslee said at the end of the briefing: 'This whole thing is for show!'

Blakeslee was armed with sixteen maps, but those covering Russia showed very little. In the event, none of them were necessary: there was cloud cover over the whole route. This meant that everything would depend on Blakeslee's ability to fly an accurate compass heading. He always maintained he was lousy at instrument flying, and flatly refused instrument practice in the Link trainer.

There were only two incidents on the flight to Russia, each resulting in the loss of a plane. Flying straight and level on one heading gave the German flak an excellent opportunity to line up their guns. South of Berlin a sudden intense barrage came up through the undercast. In spite of the accuracy only one Mustang was hit.

The other loss was a bomber, but a special bomber as far as I was concerned. Some of our crew chiefs and mechanics went along on the mission as gunners in the bombers so that they could service the Mustangs in Russia. East of Warsaw, they were hit head-on by ten to fifteen 109's. The B-17 which went down was the one in which my crew chief, Staff-Sergeant Bob Gilbert, was flying as waist-gunner. They were able to bale out and eventually joined up with a group of Russian partisans with whom they lived and fought for some weeks before finally getting back to England.

Estimated Arrival Time was 7.35 p.m. At 7.35 exactly the Russian flares floated up from the base. Blakeslee had hit it on the nose!

However, if the Eighth Air Force had shown the Germans that they had air superiority over Germany, the Luftwaffe showed that they didn't have it over Russia. German planes had shadowed the American fighters and bombers to the Russian airfields. On the second night, Luftwaffe bombers attacked Poltava where most of the B-17's had landed. Although it was never reported, forty-three bombers were destroyed. A few Ju88's bombed and strafed the bases where the Mustangs were parked, and put fifteen Mustangs out of action. One 88 was shot down by a Russian YAK. A section of P-51's scrambled into the air. They didn't get any hits, but may have driven the raiders off.

In the meantime, Blakeslee had been taken to Moscow to be

wined and dined, and to make a radio broadcast to America. He hated anything to do with public relations, but acquitted himself nobly. Asked how he enjoyed it, he said, 'It was tougher than the trip over.'

The flight from Russia to Lucrera near Foggia in Italy was uneventful, but it was then arranged that the Fourth would join the Fifteenth Air Force on a bombing mission to Budapest. That was a different story. Lack of dust filters, and different sized nozzles on the drop tanks, led to many abortions, and the group arrived over Budapest with only twenty planes. 334 Squadron had only eight. The Fourth were flying top cover at 30,000 feet while the Fifteenth Air Force were flying some 10,000 feet lower.

Suddenly fifty to sixty 109's were screaming in to attack the bombers. Blakeslee called for the Fifteenth Air Force to come up and help, but in the event, the Fourth's twenty pilots were on their own. What they didn't know was that they were up against the unique squadron of aces, Jagdgeschwader 52, just transferred from Russia to Czechoslovakia. It included most of the top aces of all time: 'Bubi' Hartmann with 352 victories; Barkhorn, 301 victories; Rall 275; Batz, 237; Graf, the *Kommandant*, 212; Lipfert, 203; Krupinski ('Graf Punski') 197; and many others. Fifty or sixty of them now faced twenty of the Fourth, or, perhaps eight of 334 Squadron, since they were mainly involved. The best of the Luftwaffe against the best of the US Air Force.

In what was probably the last great dog-fight of the war the Fourth shot down seven, of which Blakeslee got one, and Deacon Hively got three, but they lost Hofer, and George Standford, who ended up a POW. Hively and Siems were wounded, but managed to get back to Foggia.

It would be unfair to give the Fourth a score of 7 to 2. The Luftwaffe's priority was obviously to shoot down the bombers, and, in doing so, they took the risk of exposing themselves to fighter attack.

The fact that the Fifteenth Air Force didn't come up to help the out-numbered Fourth came in for some criticism, but not from Blakeslee. Most of us have often had the experience of being in the thick of the battle while other units, even in close vicinity,

neither heard nor saw anything, and didn't become involved. The
first reaction is to jump to the wrong conclusions. In my experience, this overlooks three important factors. First, radio contact
could not be relied on; volume and clarity dropped off dramatical-
ly with distance, and short, shouted transmission from another
group would probably be garbled, or so weak as to be drowned
out, by other, closer signals.

With radio contact unreliable, reaction depended on visibility,
but, when one was flying in formation, escorting bombers, calculating speeds and times, it took a cool, and , above all, experienced,
fighter leader to spot, and identify as hostile, the minute specks
far above or far below, against a dazzling sun, or a background too
bright, or too dark.

But by far the most important factor in this sort of situation
was one of time. When one was attacking or being attacked, it
seemed like an eternity. In reality, the whole action was over in
seconds, rather than minutes; and, in those few seconds, enormous
distances were covered, in all directions and altitudes, particularly
in relation to planes flying on a different course. Therefore, even
if the leader of a distant group caught sight of the brief action,
and recognised the need for assistance, the chances that he could
bring his group up in time to be of any help, especially if he
didn't have the advantage of superior altitude, were nil.

But the shuttle shouldn't be judged by the number of bombs
dropped, or 109's shot down. Blakeslee was right when he said:
'This whole thing is for show!' And it showed a lot. It showed
that no corner of Germany's world was safe from the air. In 1944,
Churchill said: 'Hitler did make Europe into a fortress, but he
forgot the roof.' Quite independently, Lieutenant-General Adolf
Galland took 'Fortress Without a Roof' as the title of a chapter
of his book, and Lieutenant-General 'Macky' Steinhoff's book is
entitled *They Had Forgotten the Roof*. All three saw this air
supremacy as the basis of the Allied victory. The shuttle raid
underlined the fact that Allied air supremacy was complete, and
the end of the war only a question of months.

The Russian shuttle was the last big show for Blakeslee. For it,
he was awarded the Distinguished Service Cross for the second
time, which must be some kind of record. But there were other

records. Blakeslee had been in combat continually for three years — over 1,000 combat hours. He dreaded the day when he'd have to go home, and did everything to avoid it, but the day came when, if he had been poetic, which he definitely was not, he would have thought of Thomas Moore's poem:

> When I remember all
> The friends, so linked together,
> I've seen around me fall
> Like leaves in wintry weather,
> I feel like one
> Who treads alone
> Some banquet-hall deserted,
> Whose lights are fled,
> Whose garlands dead,
> And all but he departed!

Most of his old squadron were prisoners of war, or killed in action. A few, like Deacon Hively, had finally gone back to the States. He knew they were ganging up on him. It might have made it a little easier to take to know that Hub Zemke, his rival CO of the 56th 'Wolfpack' Group, would be going back to the States at the same time, but on his last mission, Zemke's plane iced up and he had to bale out and spend the rest of the war as a POW.

The same day, Blakeslee was grounded.

The two leaders were almost opposites: Zemke, conservative, level-headed, intelligent, self-disciplined, every inch an officer and a gentleman; Blakeslee, every inch a flyer and a man.

But they had one thing in common: the ability to motivate everyone in their command. Like most good fighter leaders, including their Luftwaffe counterparts like Moelders, Galland, Trautloft, Hrabak and Priller, in spite of having more opportunities, they were not among the highest scorers, but their groups produced most of the war's aces.

The Fourth Group ended the war with more than 1,000 enemy aircraft destroyed, but their contribution far exceeded the number of swastikas on the sides of their planes. They were only a symptom of the spirit of the Fourth. It was a spirit born during the Battle of Britain, incorporating the best traditions of the RAF and the USAAF. It was a maverick unit, with a maverick commander. They were happy warriors; happy to be flying; happy to risk their lives for each other. It was a winning team.

CHAPTER FOUR

The Playboy

We were still flying with the RAF when I first met Vic France.
He was in 71 Eagle Squadron, but in those days we were always
being shifted from one base to another and never had time to get
to know everybody in the other squadrons. Mike Sobanski, Ray
Fuchs and I were on a rare 48 hour pass and sitting in the 'Salted
Almond' bar of the Trocadero Hotel. The more usual hang-out
for Americans in the RAF was the 'Crackers Club' which was
one good reason for not being there that evening. We had dates
with three girls from the Windmill Theatre, and we didn't need
any competition. Also the girls preferred the Troc. It was on
Shaftesbury Avenue, just down Great Windmill Street from the
theatre, so it was handy in those days of bombs and blackouts,
but more important, they considered it 'posh', with its wall-to-
wall carpeting, a coloured barman (rare in those days) and such
exotic concoctions as Planter's Punches.

And I guess they deserved something a little 'posh' once in a
while. Their little theatre had struggled on throughout the Blitz
proud of its boast that alone among London's theatres 'We Never
Closed', and from noon till the late evening they put on a prim,
genteel, somewhat 1920's version of a vaudeville show, ranging from
Ivor Novello scores, to corny comedian spots featuring struggling
young hopefuls who in later days included such famous names
as Kenneth More, Jimmy Edwards, Michael Bentine, Peter Sellers,
Spike Milligan, Alfred Marks and many others. The whole was
accompanied by a three-piece tinny, and very elderly, band.
Apart from the scantily-clad girls in the chorus and dance sequences,
glamour was provided by statuesque nudes in the background.
This was considered daring in the extreme in those days, and was
only permitted by the Lord Chamberlain's office on condition
that the pose was artistic, not very revealing, but, above all,
immobile. The girls were made so conscious of the dire consequences

of any movement that even the bombs falling were not considered
a valid excuse for flinching.

I remember being in the theatre when there was a very close
one just off Piccadilly Circus. The whole building shook and
seemed to move, the noise could be felt as well as heard, like an
enormous wave. The lights went out, and the air was full of dust
and plaster. But when the lights flickered on again, at the back
of the stage the young nude, probably about seventeen or eighteen,
was still in her statuesque pose, her hair covered in dust and
debris, which also covered her naked body and the pure white
child-like breasts, one of which was scratched by a piece of falling
plaster. After all these years I can still see that scene so vividly.
The contrast between the snow-white breast and the dirty plaster
and dust, and the angry red scratch was what I felt so often in
those early days of the war. Whether it was the Windmill girls, or
the eager young pilots arriving bright-eyed and innocent at the
squadron as they had a few months ago for their school cricket
match; or the Vicar's wife asking us for tea on the lawn while
above us our squadron mates twisted and turned, sweated and
swore, killed or were killed; or whether it was the bedraggled
Home Guard with pitch-forks and bread knives tied to broom-
sticks preparing to stop Hitler's invasion or die on their village
green; it was bombs in the nursery, massacre in toyland. It was
pathetic and noble, silly and magnificent, ludicrous and tragic.
But above all it was wonderful and we'll never be so innocent
again.

I was thinking of all this when Audrey, Joy and Joan came into
the pseudo luxury of the Salted Almond bar. It was always amazing how they managed to look so good, in spite of the hours of
hard work they did in the theatre, where they all squeezed into
one little corridor of a dressing-room; in spite of their long walks
and bus-rides to and from work, often at night; and in spite of
having to rely on revamped pre-war dresses of their mothers or
the meagre choice of rationed war-time 'utility' clothes. But to
us they were radiant, and when I look around, I think they still
would be today.

They were duly installed and were drinking their Planter's
Punches and gin-and-lime squashes when I became aware that a

few other members of the First Cast had come in. Since the
show was non-stop, they had two casts that worked in shifts,
but it was unusual that they came along to the Troc.

But it was then that Vic arrived, and then that it was evident
why the girls were there. Every female eye in the place turned to
look as all 6 feet 4 inches of him ambled in. There was something
very slow and relaxed about Vic. An early version of Robert
Mitchum and Elvis Presley. Although he wore the uniform of an
RAF pilot officer, you had to look twice before you realised it.
Clever tailoring had accentuated the broad shoulders, thin hips and
long frame, and when he reached in his pocket, you could see the
flash of a crimson silk lining. The pants were cut narrow and bore
little resemblance to the somewhat baggy trousers normally worn
by everyone else in those days. What's more, the impression of
length and slimness was highlighted by the fact that, peering dis-
creetly out from under the narrow cuffs were a pair of highly
polished, black, pointed-toe high-heeled Texas boots.

Vic had gone one better for Texas. On the shoulder of his
jacket where foreign volunteers in the RAF had their 'USA',
'Canada', 'New Zealand', 'Rhodesia', etc., Vic had a neat 'Texas'.
Since underneath, he also wore the official eagle emblem of the
Eagle Squadron, the whole ensemble managed to look as different
from the official RAF pilot officer's uniform as possible. And
yet it never flagrantly broke with the King's Rules and Regulations
for official dress.

Vic moved slowly but smoothly and extremely effectively. He
nodded to three girls who were obviously expecting him, and who
immediately got up and followed him. On his way out he saw us
and said 'Hi', peeled a pound note off a wad he had pulled from
his pocket and gave it to the barman. From the time he had first
appeared to the moment the door closed behind him and the three
girls, about half a minute had passed.

The next time I saw Vic was at Southend. I'd landed there in
the evening to refuel after a convoy patrol in the North Sea. 71
Eagle Squadron had been there for a few weeks, and when I
walked into the mess, I saw my friends Bud Care and Brewster
Morgan. They had organised some sort of transport to town and
wanted me to come along. I didn't have money or a complete

uniform, but 'Bruce' insisted he could arrange everything. He was
a big amiable blond from Honolulu where his father was a church
minister, and he'd give you the shirt off his back. Of course, I
guess, we were all pretty generous in those days. After all, even
if we thought we were going to be one of the lucky ones to
survive the war, we knew that the odds were dead against it. It
was only much later, when things eased up, and we realised that
there was a good chance of the war ending before we'd 'bought
it' that we started to worry about money and possessions and trying to collect old debts.

But all that was far in the future. At that time our thirteen
shillings and sixpence a day was more than enough, and as Bud,
Bruce and I sat in the bar of the Queen's Hotel, Southend, we
felt we had never been so rich before and never would be again.
How right we were.

There were a number of nice-looking girls in the bar, but they
all seemed to be very much in the company of officers of the
Guards Regiment based nearby. This seemed like heavy competition to me, particularly since it was getting on for the witching
hour of 10 p.m. when the barman's call of 'Time, Gentlemen,
please' would clear the room.

But at ten minutes to ten a vaguely familiar figure moved
through the bar; it was partly the height, partly the gait, but
mostly that uniform, which most men compared to a Greyhound
bus driver's, but which most women said made him look like a
Hollywood musical star. I knew it had to be Vic.

He ambled past a table where a truly beautiful girl was sitting
with a Guards captain, paused to say a few words then slowly
moved down the bar with an occasional 'Hi' to an occasional girl,
and then went out the door.

'Not like the Playboy of the West End to give up like that, is
it?' I asked.

'Wait!' said Bud.

The captain's gorgeous companion whispered something to
him and slowly got up and went towards the door. Two or three
girls at the bar excused themselves from their officer escorts and
sidled out.

I looked at Bruce who shrugged, 'The Guards buy them drinks

all evening, and then Vic comes through and takes over.'

At that moment the barman's stentorian voice announced 'Time, Gentlemen, please'.

So time went by and one morning we heard about Pearl Harbour and learned that our own country had declared war. The Texans were worried that the USA had taken on more than it could handle until they heard that Texas was joining in too.

We switched to Thunderbolts, and then to Mustangs, and carried the fight ever deeper into Germany. As we went farther and farther, the veterans who survived slowly built up their score of victories, but the casualties built up too, usually among the less experienced. Sometimes we hardly had time to get to know the new arrivals. Many were shot down on their first mission, and probably never even saw the plane that shot them down.

But Vic was still around. He was a brilliant pilot, and his plane 'Miss Dallas', with its emblem of a provocative nude holding a Texas ten-gallon hat to cover her most strategic areas, was always among those who straggled home. And Vic's victories were not confined to the pubs around Saffron Walden and the bars in London's West End. Behind Miss Dallas' left thigh were ten neat swastikas, and Vic had become a captain and was heading a flight. It was about that time that things were at their hottest. Our P-51's with their two droppable tanks slung under each wing meant we could cover the bombers wherever they went, and the red-noses of the Fourth Group Mustangs were always with the bombers on their bomb run or as they turned for home, and it was there at the far end of our range that the German fighters concentrated their attacks.

That's the way it was on one of our first Berlin raids. They were making head-on attacks on the lead bombers when we made rendezvous and Blakeslee took 335 Squadron down straight-away. I followed with 336 to give cover, and 334 who were flying top cover came down behind us. No sooner were 335 attacking the first waves of 109's when others were coming in to hit them from behind. I took our squadron in to cover 335 as close as possible, but had to yell to our own sections to break as more came in behind us.

Soon it was a whirling maelstrom of fighters flashing by, bombers ploughing through; puffs and flashes of flak; streams of tracers from both bombers and fighters; and over the earphones, the cries and curses of panic and victory, the screams and prayers of fear and death.

We had covered 335, and I'd shot a 109 off a Mustang who was getting hit, and we were climbing back up to join the fray behind the last box of bombers. Through the screaming, jarring, crackling of the RT I heard a breathless plea 'Shirtblue Yellow 4, I'm being hit', and an unhurried steady drawl which I couldn't quite recognise replying with confident authority: 'Break harder left, Yellow 4, I'll have him off you right quick'. A few seconds later, the same slow monotone ordered: 'Yellow 4 get stuck in on my wing. The rest of you guys follow me back up over the last box of bombers to cover them out.'

Back in the mess that night after dinner, I was heading down the corridor with Mike Sobanski when a new pilot I didn't know pushed past us to catch up with a tall figure slouching along, ahead of us.

'Vic,' he said, 'I've been trying to get to you to thank you for today.'

Vic looked at him and shifted his cigar to the other side of his mouth. 'Forget it', he said, and ambled out into the night.

'I'll be damned,' I said.

'What?' said Mike.

'I've just recognised a Texas accent.'

The new pilot held the door open for us, awkward and embarrassed. 'Who's that?' said Mike.

'That's Shirtblue Yellow 4,' I said.

The big Berlin raids had started for us in early 1944, and in a little over a month, we'd lost Freeburger, Brandenburg, Fiedler, Saunders, Richards, Lehman, Hobert, Davis, Hustwit, Barnes, Goetz, Vilhinger, Herter, Skilton, Siefert and a few others I can't remember. Looking at the names now, they seem bare as skeletons, but to us, each one was a warm, laughing, close 'Ol' buddy', so much alive we couldn't believe he wasn't. We were lucky. There weren't bodies or funerals, they just weren't around any more.

Maybe that's why we were still willing and eager to climb into
the cockpit once more, take off by two's, wheel into formation
and climb on out on the now familiar trail: out over Orfordness,
over the North Sea, crossing into Holland over the Hook, dodging
the flak on the coast, moving past the flat Dutch countryside,
stretching out below, with the sun flashing on the many glass
green-houses, then through the flak of the Ruhr, out over the
open, green fields of Westphalia, past the reliable check-point, the
perfect round Dummer Lake, and on past Hannover, Braunschweig,
Magdeburg, and finally the vast stretch of built-up area, 'Big B'
itself.

I don't know that we realised it at the time, but the Luftwaffe
fighters were giving their all to defend the cities of their homeland.
After that summer of 1944, the Luftwaffe would never be the
same. As 1940 had been the Battle of Britain, 1944 was the
Battle of Germany. Galland, who was then still General of the
German Fighter Command, wrote in a report to the German Air
Ministry: 'Between January and April 1944, our daytime fighters
lost over 1,000 pilots. They included our best squadron, *Gruppe*,
and *Geschwader* Commanders. Each incursion of the enemy is
costing us some fifty aircrew. The time has come when our weapon
is in sight of collapse.'

Albert Speer, Ministry for Armaments and War Production,
agreed that this was the period during which Germany lost the
war. In his interrogation under oath (18th July 1945) he said:
'The Allied air attacks remained without decisive success until
early 1944 ... The Americans' attacks which followed a definite
system of assault on industrial targets, were by far the most
dangerous. It was in fact these attacks which caused the break-
down of the German armaments industry. The attacks on the
chemical industry would have sufficed, without the impact of
purely military events, to render Germany defenceless.'

April 18th saw us on the familiar trail again. We had broken up
the German fighter attacks on the last group of bombers, but
they had taken their toll. There were a few gaps in the formations.
Somewhere over Magdeburg, I heard Blakeslee call, 'Everybody
out'. Then I heard a Texas drawl which this time I recognised:

'There's a bunch of 109's on the rear Fort, reckon we'll go back and help.'

I figured most of the Group were up ahead, but I could see that straggling B-17, so I wheeled and punched my RT button: 'I'll cover you, Vic, but we're low on ammo and damn low on gas, so break off as soon as you can, or you won't make it back.'

'Well, if I don't, tell my girl so-long for me.'

'Which one, Vic?' I asked.

'All of them!' he said.

Then all I heard were those disjointed snatches that come over the radio during a dog-fight. 'You got him, Vic,' 'Break right, there's one on your tail. . . . OK, I got him off . . . He's going in on the bomber again . . .'.

I was closer to the straggler now, and could see the fighters around him. Then I saw him peel off slowly and go into his death-dive. Vic hadn't been able to get to that one German fighter soon enough. He'd got one of them and saved his wingman, but when I heard him, I knew he was mad. 'The rest of you guys go home, I'm gonna get that bastard!'

'For God's sake, Vic, break off,' I said. 'Let him go.'

'Not this baby,' he said.

By now I could see the 109, split-essing and diving for the deck, and almost in unison behind him, a lone Mustang, which I knew carried the curves and ten-gallon hat of 'Miss Dallas'.

I watched as the two planes hurtled down in a screaming vertical dive, winding up to terminal velocity.

Even my own plane was shuddering as I followed them down. The controls were rigid and I had to ease it out by slowly winding the trim handle back a fraction. I yelled: 'Pull out, Vic, pull out. God damn it!'

But there was no stopping him now. 'I'm hitting him, I'm gonna git 'im.'

He got him all right. A great ball of flame flared on the ground where the German went in.

But almost immediately a second searing flash burst close to the first as 'Miss Dallas' followed her victim in.

I started back up to collect what was left of my scattered squadron: 'Goody here. I'm climbing back up to angels twenty-five on a heading of 268 — it's time to go home.'

I'd made a few phone calls, so when I walked into the Salted Almond bar, the girls were there. I ordered drinks.

Audrey said: 'Vic?'

I said: 'Yep.'

Someone said: 'When?'

I said, 'To-day.'

Jackie said: 'Cheers.'

And we raised our glasses.

After a while, more of the girls drifted off to do their shows — or whatever, and I was about to leave to get back to Debden, but Jackie stopped me. 'There's another one,' she said. 'The special one.'

She was special, all right. I knew she'd arrived because the bar went quiet and every eye was turned to the door. Sure, she was beautiful, with her English rose complexion and blonde hair. Yes, she was well-dressed, with her black velvet jacket and skirt, black pill-box hat to match and lace blouse. But it wasn't that. Jackie got it right when she said, almost with reverence, 'That's class!'

She declined a drink and didn't even sit down.

'It's Vic,' I said. 'He'd have wanted you to know.'

She sat down then. Her eyes got very big and she started straight ahead, and I knew this one was really hurt.

To ease the strain, I said: 'He went out in a blaze of glory!'

It was a mistake. The girl looked at me incomprehensibly. Women knew there's no glory in death. It takes men years to learn it.

The girl got up to go. Lamely I said: 'If I can be of any help.'

'Thanks', she said, 'but I can weep on my own,' and she turned and was gone.

Jean said: 'She shouldn't be so cut up, poor kid. I mean he wasn't exactly faithful to her.'

Rita turned on her and flashed her dark Spanish eyes. 'He *was* faithful,' she said defiantly. 'To *all* of us!'

We stepped out into the evening bustle of Piccadilly with its stream of soldiers, sailors and airmen of all nationalities outnumbering the drab civilians.

It was a starry night, and we looked up at the sky.

'Do you think Vic's gone to Heaven?' said Rita.

'If he has,' said Audrey, 'the angels won't know what's hit them!'

CHAPTER FIVE

The Swede

He wasn't what you'd call a big-time hero.

I suppose he'd have made his home town newspaper, if Red Bluff, California, had a newspaper. He'd probably be quite a hero around home if they knew about his war-career, but he wasn't much of a hand at talking about what he'd done.

In fact there wasn't much glamour and glory about the Swede, but he was a nice guy to have around — if you know what I mean. He wasn't one of those big Swedes. In fact, he was a bit of a runt, and he wasn't what you'd call beautiful. His face was kind of homely and puckered up.

The first night I saw him down at the end of the bar he looked like the original Gremlin. He had a grin on him that wouldn't quit. It was the kind of grin that makes you forget what the rest of the guy looks like because it's the first and last thing you notice.

Next morning I went up flying with him. We had only recently switched from our neat little Spitfires which we loved so much, to the massive P-47, 'Thunderbolts', and we treated them with great respect. I didn't waste any time starting up and taking off, but I hadn't got my wheels up before he was formating on me with his wing-tip stuck inside mine and his prop churning away a few inches from my wing tip. We climbed up through 2,000 feet of overcast, and broke out into the sunshine above. I racked up into a tight turn, but when I looked up there he was, right on my wing tip, and all the time grinning and looking around like a kid. I put him line astern, flipped over on my back, and split-essed down to the undercast. I hauled her back, just about blacking out, shot up and racked it into a tight Immelmann. When I got through I figured I'd lost him, I couldn't see another plane in the sky. I punched the button and asked if he could see me.

'Hell, yes, I'm still around. Six o'clock on you.'

I cocked up a wing, and stomped rudder to slew myself around

a bit, and there he was behind and below me, with his prop
chewing right under my tail.

After we'd landed I looked up the Swede's flying record and
found he'd rolled up over 1,000 hours partly as an instructor,
but mostly long before, flying people to Reno for quick divorces.

'How come you don't tell me about your flying time?' I wanted
to know.

He just kind of grinned. 'Hell, it doesn't mean anything; it's
combat that counts, and I don't know from nothing about that.'

'You will,' I said.

He did. The next day we went to Paris. Back in those days,
early in 1943, a raid to Paris was something big. We'd used our
long range drop tanks before, but we'd never used them to escort
the bombers all the way to a No 1 target like Paris. This was long
before we'd shoved the Jerry fighters back into Germany, so we
were looking for plenty of fun.

The Swede was on my wing, and after we'd got formed up and
set course I could look across at him grinning like a cat. That grin
wasn't just for his own benefit, it was for mine too. This was the
first time I'd led a section, and that grin was just to let me know
that I had a backer.

I was kept pretty busy on the climb out just keeping my section
in position on the rest of the squadron — and scanning up, down
and around. Round about 27,000 feet we levelled off and slid out
into combat formation. The weather was perfect — visibility
unlimited. When we crossed in over the French coast we could
see the Seine wriggling down past Rouen towards Paris. It looked
real pretty and peaceful, and it didn't seem possible there were
Germans running around down there.

They tossed up quite a mess of flak when we crossed in. It was
low and in front of our outfit, and the little black clouds slid by
underneath, but one of the planes in the squadron below peeled
off and headed for home, losing altitude and smoking a little.

Everyone was spread out now, weaving and dropping their wings,
searching the skies above, below, in front, and behind. I was
doing plenty of rubbernecking myself. We still had our belly tanks,
and it's embarrassing to get caught with those things still slung
underneath. When the leader gave the word and we dropped them,

it was like a big load rolling off my back.

Then I saw the bombers. They were hard to pick out, with no cloud background, but you could see the flak bursts around them. It was as if the massed formation was standing still, and the black puffs were floating through them, like when a swarm of minnows heads upstream and stays put, while the stream flows by. That's the way flying at altitude is — like staying very still, while the rest of the universe swings past.

By now we could see a hazy blotch ahead which was Paris, and I figured our timing was perfect. We'd converge on the bombers right on the bomb run, the way we were supposed to. They made their final turn on the target, and we came swinging in over the top of them and started our weaving. The flak was getting heavier now. There was a big round sudden flash down in the lead box of bombers, and where there had been a bomber there was a big smoke ring. The others didn't waver, just ploughed on toward the target.

So far, no enemy fighters had been reported. I couldn't figure that out, but I didn't like it. The Swede was the first to report them, but we all saw them about the same time. First they were little specks like flies. The next minute they were swinging in from dead ahead. About a hundred yellow-nosed FW190's. Someone yelled, 'Jesus — millions of 'em'. I rammed the throttle against the stop and held it there, and the first five 190's peeled off, and plummeted down in a head-on attack on the lead box of bombers. They drove in line abreast, all firing. The leading edge of their wings were winking and flashing. The tracers from the bombers were sailing out into them. Three streams of tracers converged into the leader. After the flash there were just pieces floating and tumbling into the air. The others kept coming.

Our low squadron had been able to turn in to cut them off. They were able to close on the last two. One rolled on his back slowly and fell away downwards, smoking. The other went into a spin and a wing fluttered off.

The three others had too much speed for our boys. They drove on through, head on at the bombers, closing with a combined speed of 700 mph. At the last minute they rolled on their backs, still firing, and flashed down through the bomber formation. The third one left it a split second too late. He started to roll, but the bomber was already on him. His wing hit the bomber in No 3 engine. The tangled, blazing mass went tumbling down through the formation.

Now our top squadron had piled into the main bunch, and there was one big dog-fight up there. Still gaggles of them were slipping through. A flight of ten followed after the first. In a vague kind of way I realised I could intercept them. I remember how big and dry my tongue was when I said, 'Red Section going down.' I remember the Swede saying, 'I'm with you.'

I felt the air-speed build up as I dove down. The plane bounced around when I jerked at the controls in my nervousness. All I did was stare at the Huns; everything else was automatic. It seemed like I was doing everything slow and lazy, other things were happening so fast. Then I was on the tail of a 190 and firing. My left foot on the rudder pedal was trembling and shaking. My sights were on, but still there were no strikes. I was closing fast.

Then there were flashes and something came tumbling past me. He fell away and as I swung past him I saw flame licking along the grey fuselage and over the black cross. The fire grew until there was just a long flame streaking down.

But as I watched the red and yellow flame against the grey and black fuselage, they were suddenly on me — the bombers: I threw the stick into one corner of the cockpit and tramped rudder and slid under the first bomber. Then ship after ship, element after element flashed past me, as I hurtled through the formation.

Suddenly I was clear, and pulled up. All I wanted was to get back up where I belonged. I screwed my head around to clear my tail. There was a radial-engined plane behind me. It looked like one of ours, but I couldn't believe that anyone could still be with me. I punched my radio-transmitter. 'Pin-up Red Leader here. I'm waggling my wings. Is anyone with me?'

'Yeah, I'm still around — right behind you.' It was the Swede.

We were climbing back up, past the bombers, when we spotted the straggler, one lone bomber, with one engine smoking, falling behind and losing altitude; and the Jerries were buzzing around him like flies.

He was dishing it out as well as taking it, but by the time we got there it was too late to help much. He had started into a dive and two white chutes had blossomed out. Still the tracers coming out from the tail position showed that the rear gunner was in there fighting. The Huns followed the bomber down, and we followed the Huns.

The big ship began to spin, but the rear gunner was still pumping lead into the Jerries. One of them spiralled away trailing smoke. That tailgunner's tracers kept coming until the bomber spun into the woods. Then there was a flash, and a tall, still column of smoke.

The Jerry started circling the crash, and I was able to close. He wouldn't be expecting any of us to be so low, so I waited until I got close, and then clobbered him well. I was watching him crash, when I heard the Swede yell, 'Break! Break left!'

I hauled back on the stick, and my head went down, and my eyes dimmed as I started to black out. I heard a 'crump'. The plane shuddered and started to stall. I eased up on the stick and looked back. He was close behind me. I could see the round yellow nose and the grey body with the black crosses, but most of all I could see the flashes that lit up the leading edge of his wing. He wasn't allowing enough deflection, and his shots were sailing past under my tail. But his nose was creeping up, as he out-turned me. Soon his shots would be thudding into my fuselage.

I tightened my turn, and fought the plane with stick and rudder as it shuddered and bucked on the point of the stall. My mouth was so dry that it burned. My oxygen mask was soaking wet as I swore and gasped and spat into it. It had fallen down my nose with the force of my break. My head and neck ached as I screwed around to watch the Hun. And still he was out-turning me.

Then I felt the 'crump' again. He was starting to hit me. I was too low to try to dive away. I reached down to release my harness to try to bale out. Then I heard the Swede: 'OK, I'll have him off you in a jiffy,' he said.

I looked back. The Jerry's grey fuselage was covered with flashes. He flicked over and dived down. He went into a field on his back, leaving a trail of fire behind him.

Then suddenly — the way it often happens — there weren't any other planes in the sky. Just me and the Swede formating on me and grinning.

There was something wrong with the feel of the plane. I checked the instruments but everything was OK, and the engine was running smoothly. Then I looked out at the wings and saw the hole. It was a foot across, in the middle of the left wing, right where the star was. The metal around the edges was curled up where the slug had exploded. There were other holes behind me, but it was the one in the wing that was holding me back. Even pulling 40° I couldn't clock more than 130 mph straight and level. Even the bombers were well on the way out by now, so I called the Swede and told him to go on home. There was a good chance I wouldn't make it, and there was no reason for him to fritter away his gas, lagging behind with me.

He didn't answer me, and when I repeated, he said: 'Oh, I reckon I'll stick around for a while.'

He stuck around all right. It seemed like we'd never see that coast-line, and by the time we did finally cross out, we could hear the rest of the outfit asking for landing instructions. But the Swede kept on weaving around me. We crept out over the Channel, and it had never seemed so wide. Before we saw the white cliffs, I was sweating the gas out plenty.

We landed at a base on the south coast with the gas gauge kicking the bottom. The Swede landed right behind me, and when he walked over to my plane he was grinning from ear to ear.

'Nice going,' he said.

Like I said, the Swede wasn't rated among the top aces, but he was usually around when you wanted him. If they sprang a dawn mission on us the morning after a party, the Swede was always on the spot. Maybe he had to be poured into the cockpit, and maybe he swooshed around in the air more than somewhat, but he was always there.

He stuck around for quite a while for those days, but when he ended his combat career, he went out in style.

I was already in the bag, a guest of the Third Reich; but the day after it happened, the story was all over the big Prisoner of War camps of Barth on the Baltic and Sagan on the Oder, where the Allied air force officers paced around their barren compounds behind the rows of barbed wire fences, under the constant threat of the guards and their machine-guns in the wooden watch-towers.

The Swede got it strafing an aerodrome, the way all the best ones did. Some say strafing's fun, and it's the fastest and most effective way to knock out an enemy air force, but for those who try it, no amount of skill does you any good. We used to say it was non-habit forming; definitely no future in it!

When the Swede's time came, he slipped and slid his dying Mustang onto the aerodrome they were strafing. They figured they'd heard the last of the Swede, but then they started getting orders on how to direct their attacks. Pierce McKennon was leading the group and yelled: 'Hey, Swede, where the hell are you? What's your altitude?'

'My altitude is nil, Mac, I'm on the ground, but my radio's still working.'

And so he conducted the show until there wasn't much left to strafe. But just as the last squadron had turned for home, the Swede called them back: 'Hey, Mac, there's two 190's coming in to land, come back and get 'em!'

Through the smoke and haze the pilots in the air couldn't see them, but Carlson guided them right onto them. The kills were accredited to Morgan and Brooker, but, as usual, the Swede had played his humble part.

The mass of armed Germans converging on Carlson's plane were furious. Not only did they know he'd been conducting the operations which had destroyed their base, but the last 190 which had crashed in flames had been piloted by Hauptmann Hoffmann, their commanding officer. Maybe one reason he didn't get torn limb from limb is I'm sure, when they got to him, the Swede was grinning from ear to ear.

No, he was no big-time hero, and you probably never heard of him. But there were a lot of guys like him, and when you need someone to loan you a buck, or fly on your wing — or help win a war — they're nice guys to have around — if you know what I mean.

CHAPTER SIX

The Kid

And the Kid! What else could you call him? The Kid! With that round beautiful baby-face, the wide, laughing blue eyes, the long, full, wavy hair falling across his eyes, you couldn't call him anything else. He first picked up the name as an amateur boxer, and in 1940 he won a trophy in the Golden Gloves Tournament. But his trainer always told him he wouldn't make the big time. 'You're too nice a guy!' And he was right. The Kid didn't like the dirty part, so when he was in Detroit to pick up a car to hit the boxing trail to California, he just crossed over to Windsor and joined the Royal Canadian Air Force.

He arrived in England as Sergeant Pilot Ralph K. Hofer. I never met anyone who could explain how the RAF and RCAF decided which pilots should graduate as pilot officers and which as sergeant pilots. If it was on the basis of flying ability and aggressive leadership, the outstanding success of pilots who started out as sergeants should have made it obvious that there was something wrong with the system. But the fact that sergeant pilots like the brilliant Canadian 'Buzz' Buerling were often leading flights with officers under their command, never seems to have caused any re-thinking on the part of the top brass.

Usually, of course, the mistake was corrected, and the sergeant duly got his officer's commission, but he never quite caught up with his colleagues. No matter how brilliant his career, he usually ended it with a lower rank than the less successful officers who had had the luck to be commissioned when they got their wings.

And so it was with Kid Hofer. Not only was he a sergeant pilot in the RAF, but the US Army Air Force continued the farce when he transferred by giving him the grade of Flight Officer, which, in spite of its sound, was still a non-commissioned rank under that of second lieutenant.

Knowing the Kid, I don't imagine he gave a damn about rank,

but he made his point, anyway, on his first combat mission. I
remember meeting Jim Clark, who was leading 334 Squadron,
as I went into the mess after a rather routine show escorting
bombers over France. It was an early mission in our relatively
new P-47 Thunderbolts and we didn't have the range the droppable extra wing tanks gave us later.

'Did you do any good today?' I asked Jim.

Jim shook his head. 'Some kid on his first mission is claiming a
190, but nobody saw him, and I won't believe it before I see his
combat film.'

'Yeah. That one I want to see too,' I said. I suppose there have
been pilots who have shot down enemy planes on their first 'do',
but it would be close to a miracle. Usually the only victory they
could hope for was to get back in one piece. All too often they
never saw the one that shot them down.

I remember taking Swede Carlson on his first mission as my
wingman, and telling him to stick to me like glue. It was an
exciting sweep taking Boston bombers to hit the hornets' nest of
Abbeville, home of the yellow-nosed Me109's of Galland's Jagdgeschwader 26. They gave us all the action we wanted, but when
the Swede and I straggled back to base and landed I said:

'I'm claiming one destroyed and one probable. Can you confirm them for me?' and the Swede grinned sheepishly and said:
'Goody, all I saw was the tail-wheel of your Spitfire!'

So I went along with Jim Clark to see the combat film of the
young upstart who not only pretended to have seen enemy planes
when no one else had, but even claimed to have shot one down.
As we went into the small room by the photographic section, Jim
asked Grover Hall, the public relations officer, and later historian
of the Fourth: 'Anything on it?'

'I don't want to spoil it for you', said Grover. 'Roll it, Izzy.'

Combat films were flickering, jumpy things at the best of times.
The camera in the wing was activated by the trigger and, even
though there was a slight over-run, the flashes of pictures followed
the spasmodic bursts of the guns firing, and were all over in seconds.

When Hofer's brief film was finished, Grover said: 'It ain't
Gone with the Wind but it ain't bad!'

Jim said: 'I'll be damned!'

Although the film had flickered and jerked and although the 190 was hard to distinguish as it swam and danced across the screen, all of us knew it was a kill, and we looked at the 'frozen' frames, not so much for confirmation as for artistic appreciation. 'Still slightly out of range, but definite hits in the right wing root' . . . 'That burst got the cockpit and probably the engine.'

'Maybe a fluke . . . but it's a kill.'

But the Kid went on to prove it wasn't a fluke. In a couple of months he became an official 'ace' with five neat swastikas on his P-47 just above his insignia. He was proud of his home town, Salem, Missouri, so his emblem was a rampant Missouri Mule in boxing shorts and Golden boxing-gloves, with an incongruous pair of wings on his back; the whole was dominated by a large-lettered inscription: 'Salem Representative.'

I remember Jim Clark ambling over to Hofer's plane after one of the Kid's more erratic performances, and eyeing the flying mule. Jim's handsome face was impassive. Finally he took his pipe out of his mouth and said to the Kid: 'Looks like you can't make up your mind whether to be an ass or a flyer!'

Because, for all his brilliance, Kid Hofer was a pain in the neck to his commanding officer. A CO had above all to keep his unit together as a fighting force so that it could perform its all-important tasks. In the case of a fighter squadron, this was primarily to protect the bombers. But the Kid was a loner and his squadron discipline lasted only up to the moment there were enemy aircraft in the area, and then he was gone. He knew that the standard German fighter pilot's defence from attack from above was a vertical dive, so he peeled off before the rest of the squadron were given the order to attack and was down among the enemy before the others.

His flight leaders and squadron commander gave him hell, but were never able to dampen the Kid's laughing exuberance and happy enthusiasm, and anyway, how do you chew out someone who's just chalked up his fifth victory in a couple of months?

But one day even the easy-going charm of his CO, Jim Clark wore thin. Hofer had had to turn back from a mission because one of his droppable tanks wasn't feeding through. The Kid screamed back to base, landed in a steep turn and sped over to the revetment where his faithful Alsatian dog, Duke, and his capable crew chief were waiting. The mechanics quickly fixed the block in the fuel system, and Hofer immediately took off again. But it was too late to catch the main mission, so he simply flew his own separate show, scouring Belgium and France for German aircraft. Not finding any, he did a little ground strafing on his way out over Holland. He dodged the flak coming out over the coast, but the real flak was waiting for him when he got back to base at Debden. Not only his squadron commander, Jim Clark, but the Commanding Officer of the Group, Don Blakeslee, were waiting for him.

That evening, Don, Jim, 'Gunner' Halsey, 'Deacon' Hively and I were discussing the problem of Ralph Hofer. Someone wanted him busted, someone suggested the toughest punishment would be a transfer to another outfit, and someone said the problem would soon handle itself. If the Kid continued to goof off on his own, one day he wouldn't come back.

When Blakeslee asked my opinion, I thought awhile before answering: 'First, as far as Hofer is concerned, I don't see him as plotting to break out of formation, just to build up his score. His reaction is as spontaneous and uncontrollable as that Alsatian pup of his when he throws a stick for him. But what we're really talking about is the old argument of flight defensive discipline versus individual aggressive attack. The team approach versus the Prima Donna.' The average age of our foursome must have been about twenty-three, but they solemnly nodded when I went on:

'We had flying discipline drilled into us in the early RAF days, and the worst imaginable sin was to go off on your own or attack before ordered to; but we were fighting a defensive war then, and everyone from Air Marshal Dowding on down knew that if we didn't conserve our outnumbered planes and pilots, we'd probably lose the damned war. But the Battle of Britain is over now, and the Battle of Germany is starting. We're now on the offensive and they are on the defensive. We've got the planes with the range and performance to do it, so we better use them. After all, a fighter pilot is either the hunter or the hunted, and, if he's the hunted, he's in trouble. I'd hate to think there was no place in this outfit for guys like Hofer, even if they are wild. The thing is to control

them without killing their spirit. After all, the spirit of the outfit is
the spirit of the people in it, and we need all of that we can get.
You'll always have plenty of good pilots to keep the squadron
going as a fighting force — offensive and defensive, but let's find
a way to keep the wild ones with us.'

The old argument went on until we heard there was a dawn
briefing the next morning, and we decided to call it a day.

The Kid's name wasn't on the board for a few missions, and
Jim Clark told me he had really reamed him out and he was in
disgrace.

But at the end of one mission I drove past 334 Squadron's
dispersal hut to ask them how they had made out. In front of
the hut, pilots and ground crew were grouped around what seemed
to be a wrestling match; and a sort of wrestling match it turned
out to be.

On the ground was a tangle of rolling, laughing, barking bodies
which turned out to be an enormous Alsatian dog and a mop-
haired laughing young giant; Kid Hofer and his faithful dog Duke.
Duke had attached himself to the Kid after his original master,
'Digger' Williams, had been shot down. Deacon Hively, who'd had
his share of trouble trying to discipline the bounding Duke and his
equally irrepressible master, said the dog must have been attracted
to the only guy on the base as dumb as he was.

Jim Clark ambled out and stopped to view the scene. His dis-
approval made itself felt without his having to say a word. The
spectators fell silent, and finally the Kid and the dog unscrambled
themselves.

'What the hell do you think you're doing?' Jim asked.

Hofer tossed his mane of tousled hair out of his eyes, and with
that broad smile of his, which was more like a silent laugh, said:
'Well, sir, I figured if I was in the dog-house I might as well play
the part!'

He snapped a jaunty salute which ended in a happy wave and
ran off with Duke leaping all over him. He flung himself into the
back of the weapons-carrier as it took off for the mess, and Duke
made a flying leap after him.

Jim turned to me, shrugged his shoulders and said: 'What can
you do?'

'Not a damn thing!' I said.

But those were busy days, and though Hofer's name wasn't put up on the board for missions, he wasn't grounded, so he kept his hand in, checking out aircraft after they'd been in for maintenance. This was usually in the evenings after the planes came back from the day's show.

It was at that time too, that I usually took a new pilot up for training. They came over with little training in low-flying and formation, and almost none on instruments. Even after a tough mission, I felt it was worthwhile. It helped me to get to know a pilot's potential, and maybe give him a slightly better chance when he went into combat for the first time.

Besides it helped me unwind. Sometimes it was fun. To show how important instrument flying was, with the amount of cloud flying we had to do, I used to have the new pilot fly into a cloud and stick myself close on his wing. Whilst he was concentrating on his instruments, I would drop back, turn on my back, and pull back into formation upside-down. Almost always, the new boy would take a quick glance at me, do a double-take, and roll over himself. He usually lost all orientation as his artificial horizon toppled, and ended up in a spin, but if he was able to keep his heading and altitude, I would drop back again, roll over and come up right side up. This resulted in our coming out of the cloud with him upside down and me straight and level.

One evening I was breaking in a new boy, Ralph Saunders, and flying on his wing, when I saw another P-47 pulling up on the other side of him. It came in close with the prop spinning a few inches from Saunders' wing tip, and sitting in the cockpit sat a large Alsatian dog — and no sign of anyone else. The plane then dived ahead of us, pulled up into a perfect loop and ended up behind us.

When we landed, we climbed into the jeep, and without a word, drove off to 334 Squadron dispersal. The Kid and his dog came over and clambered into the back.

'Duke's getting real good at flying!' said Hofer.

'Any damn fool can do a loop', I said, 'but how is he on instruments?'

'Great!' said the Kid.

'Sounds like a show-off,' I said.

After we dropped them off, Saunders could not restrain his curiosity any longer. 'Sir, did he have that dog on his lap?'

'Yeah,' I said sourly.

'That's fantastic.' Then, sensing my mood, he added quickly, 'But I guess you disapprove.'

'To get enough room, he leaves his parachute off,' I said.

During those evenings when I drilled my new protegés, I glimpsed a lone plane cavorting among the clouds, diving down the white valleys between them, pulling up vertically until it stalled and fell off into a spin, pulling out at the last second and zooming back up in a glorious Immelmann or loop and rolling off the top. And after landing I would drive around the perimeter track to pick up the laughing Kid and his happy dog.

But the group couldn't afford to keep a pilot like Hofer out of action in those early days of 1944 when we were flying mission after mission, and casualties were mounting. Nearly always it was the inexperienced pilots, fresh from the inadequate training in the States, whom we just didn't have time to whip into shape before they went out and got shot down.

Kid Hofer was the amazing exception. If asked, the Kid, who had the superstitions common to most fighter pilots, would have attributed his luck to his beloved big snake ring on the third finger of his throttle hand, and his faithful blue football sweater with the lurid orange '78' on the front, which he always wore on missions.

Yet those of us who watched his performance realised that this was one of those rare natural pilots, whose enthusiastic, aggressive, brilliant flying ability, and a certain unique flair, combined to make them stand out from the rest of us, who, over a long combat career, flew their missions or led our squadrons as best we could, and in the process, if we survived, inevitably built up our scores. But they were the loners who blazed their brief trail through the skies like a shooting-star. Since World War I there have been many of them in all air forces, but probably the most dramatic was Hans-Joachim Marseille of the German Luftwaffe. In less than two years' flying in North Africa, he shot down 158 RAF planes, 57 of them in the one month of September

1942, and 17 of them on the single day of 1st September. By the end of September he was dead. He was twenty-four. Like most of those rare birds, he was considered a Bohemian, with a tendency to wear his hair long, ignore discipline, operate on his own, and able to charm every man and, particularly, woman, he met with his extraordinary good looks and happy personality.

He also started his combat career as a sergeant pilot, but ended it as a captain with Germany's highest decoration: Knight's Cross with Oak Leaves, Swords and Diamonds and Italy's 'Gold Medal for Bravery'.

Finally, Hofer also became a second lieutenant, and his victories continued to pile up. If anyone got a kill on a mission, it was usually the Kid. Our new P-51 Mustangs allowed us to range further afield and add to our scores.

On the morning of 18th March, we took off for Munich. We climbed through some 20,000 feet of cloud, and even there, the visibility was bad. Don Blakeslee was leading the Group with 336 Squadron and I had a flight on his right. We were really in the soup and I was on instruments, but constantly glancing around to avoid collisions. 334 was the low squadron. They must have had a little more visibility down there, at least occasionally, because we heard Gerry Montgomery, who was leading one of their flights say, 'Blue Section, let's go down on those 109's.' Hofer was number 4 in that section and they confirmed that he got one of the 109's, but that was the last they saw of him.

Up at 27,000 feet, the weather got worse. Blakeslee realised the chances of a rendezvous with the bombers was practically nil and called for us to turn back for home.

That evening in the Mess Jim Clark, 'Bee' Beeson, 'Red-Dog' Norley, and some of the others were sitting together. Things were quiet and the conversation lagged. Ashcraft, 334's Intelligence Officer, had reported that Hofer was officially NYR (Not Yet Returned). Jim kept looking at his watch, but we all knew that he had to be down somewhere.

Pierce MacKennon had been playing the piano, but the usual boogie bounce wasn't there, and he finally gave up. Suddenly everyone looked up as Ashcraft came straight to Jim Clark, and said, 'Kid Hofer's landed at a base on the South Coast.'

Nobody said anything, but you could feel the tension ease like an unheard sigh of relief. Jim put one hand over his eyes and rubbed them, then lurched out of his chair. 'That god-damn stupid bastard!' he said, and abruptly left us. Ashcraft looked surprised rather than shocked. I had never heard Jim use that kind of language before.

'It was a term of endearment,' I said.

'I know,' he replied.

The next day, Hofer flew in to face the inquisition from his squadron and flight commanders. Apparently his radio had gone dead on the climb out, and although this was normally a good reason to abort, he had decided to keep going. He hadn't heard Montgomery's order to go down on the two 109's, but he followed them down, picked out his target and shot him down. In the process, however, he ended up below the clouds, saw an airport which he circled, but found no joy, so started climbing back to join the Group. On the way up, he found and attacked a second 109. The pilot bailed out. The Kid found a third 109 which escaped him by flying into some of the cloud which constantly blanketed most of the sky and towered from about five thousand feet up to thirty thousand.

After chasing around and through the clouds, the Kid set course for Munich at full bore, but couldn't see a single plane. The Group by this time was on its way home, but Hofer continued on course. He spotted two 109's above him, and immediately zoomed up to attack them. Before he could get in range, however, he ran into technical problems. He described it as 'the prop running away'. The RPM's went up and the engine boost was strong, but there was no thrust and the plane started losing speed and altitude. The problem, I believe, is caused by the pitch control malfunctioning so that the angle of the propeller blades changes to high pitch, taking smaller 'bites' of air. This is fine for take-off but serious at altitude. The Kid's Mustang lost altitude fast and dropped under the clouds where the weather was clear. He knew he had to bail out, but glancing south and west, he could see snowy mountains, which he knew should be the Alps. Checking his map, he figured he was close to that corner of Europe where Germany, Austria and Switzerland meet. This was confirmed when he saw Lake Constance, and he realised he had a chance to cross into neutral Switzerland and bail out into a friendlier reception than he could expect in Germany.

The Kid gave a breathless account of trying to nurse his struggling plane over the forbidding snow-covered peaks of the Alps. But somehow he made it, prepared to bail out over Switzerland, and jettisoned his canopy. He pulled the plane up to reduce the wind pressure and had actually crawled out of the cockpit in order to slide off the wing when he felt the prop suddenly begin to operate normally. He climbed back into the plane. The prop continued to pull normally, and he considered the possibility of heading for home, but a glance at his fuel gauge told him he could hardly make it. Maybe he should play it safe and drop into Switzerland. What decided him was the thought of the precious film in his wing camera, which, since he'd been alone, carried the only proof of his two 109's destroyed. So he carefully nursed his plane back over those miles of enemy territory and English Channel, landing on a small South Coast airfield with an empty tank.

After this recitation, Don Blakeslee and the squadron commanders stayed behind. Each had some caustic comments to make. Finally Don asked me: 'Goody, what do you think of The Perils of Pauline?'

'Well', I said, 'I imagine his precious film will confirm his kills, and I suppose when he pulled the plane up to bail out the additional strain on the prop in the climb plus the lower speed could have snapped the prop back into normal pitch, so I'm willing to give him the benefit of the doubt for most of the story, but, in that case, he was a long way south of where he says he was.'

'How do you figure?' the Colonel asked.

'There are no mountains between Munich and Switzerland, unless you go way south and cross Austria.'

On my way round the airfield to 336 dispersal area, I saw the 'Salem Representative' outside the big hangar waiting for a new cockpit canopy. I got out of my jeep and climbed into the cockpit.

As I climbed out, I met the Kid heading for his plane. 'Hi, Major,' he said. 'You want to trade planes? You know it's bad luck. Five guys who borrowed my kite went down with it.'

'No, no, I was just relaxing.' I got into my jeep. 'And listening to the radio.'

His face was suddenly serious; then he gave me a sheepish grin.

The Kid continued his happy-go-lucky meteoric career. Whenever there was a spontaneous breach of radio silence, it nearly always came from the Kid, as on the first long mission to Munich when, just as we got over the target, and could see the mountains down to the south, the tense silence was broken by a gleeful voice: 'Gee, ain't the Alps pretty?' Don Blakeslee didn't need to ask who it was.

'God damn it, Hofer, shut up!'

But also, the Kid was usually among those who reported victories. When asked how he did it, he would laugh and show his snake ring. 'I'm one of the lucky ones,' he would say.

I tried to draw him into discussions on tactics, strategy, methods of attack, deflection shooting, and all the tricks of the trade that I was constantly discussing with the others, and particularly with those great technical and strategic perfectionists 'Millie' Millikan and 'Bee' Beeson. The Kid would just laugh and say: 'Hell, if I worried myself about all that theoretical stuff, I'd never shoot anything down. I just go get 'im. I don't aim my guns at them, I aim *myself* at them.' And I think he meant it sincerely.

What came to most of us after years of training, study, trial and error, came to pilots like Hofer perfectly naturally and intuitively. I believe most of those virtuosos were the same. General Galland rated Marseille the best shot in the Luftwaffe, scoring kills with fewer shots expended and from more impossible angles than anyone else. Indeed it was Galland who gave Marseille the name which stuck with him: 'The unrivalled Virtuoso of the Fighter Pilots', but he admits that Marseille never spent much time studying tactics and theory. It all came to him suddenly and naturally, as if his mind was a computer operating subconsciously. Most of us made it the hard way, like Millikan who flew fifty-two missions before scoring his first victory. Hofer shot down his first enemy plane on his first mission, and kept right on going.

The flair didn't only apply to attack. Anyone else operating as much on his own as Hofer did wouldn't have lasted more than one mission, but the Kid survived what would normally be fatal situations time and time again, and I don't believe it could be entirely attributed to luck, or even to the fact that he was always attacking.

For instance, when D-Day finally came, the Fourth Group flew three missions, mainly concerned with preventing German reinforcements from coming up to attack the landings. Most of us were strafing the roads up to the beach-heads, and finally virtually nothing could move during the daylight hours.

The Luftwaffe didn't come up in strength. During the three missions, I saw no enemy planes at all. Nevertheless there were some concentrations. Kid Hofer was leading a flight of four. Although he was only a first lieutenant, he had Captain 'Big Bernard' McGrattan under him as number three. Handsome Mac was due for rotation to the States after a long and brilliant tour of duty. His bags were packed, but he insisted on being in on the big show for which we'd all been waiting so long, so he joined Hofer's flight, with Lieutenant Hal Ross as his wingman flying in number four position.

The flight was jumped by fifteen German fighters. They broke into the first attack, but there were always more coming, in waves. Mac probably shot one or more off Ross' tail, but then got it himself. Ross went down next as they came in one after the other. In the same way the Kid lost his wingman. Somehow, out of the mêlée, Hofer, alone, got home. It was the only time he ever came back from a sortie without his happy smile.

But he was on the next mission making his presence felt — and heard — as usual.

For five days, we flew sortie after sortie, strafing every road south, east and west of the beaches. When nothing more was moving on the roads, we sprayed alongside the roads where we knew the Germans were hiding under cover waiting for dark when they could start to make their night-time move. A few days before, at Debden, Eisenhower had asked me if I thought we could keep the German reinforcements from moving up in force. I said, 'During daylight hours, yes.' And that promise was kept. Even the powerful Panzer Lehr Tank Force, which was deployed around the Le Mans area ready to rush to any landing site, didn't get up in time. All the Germans could do in the daytime was drag their damaged and burnt-out vehicles and material to the sides of the road, where it lay rusting like an almost continuous wall, for many long months: impressive evidence of the awesome weight of air power.

On D-Day plus six, the Fourth were strafing in front of the American forces advancing down the Cherbourg peninsula. Kid Hofer was with 334 Squadron and was gaily pouncing on anything that moved. Suddenly, he reported to Deacon Hively, who was leading the squadron, that he'd been hit, was losing oil pressure, and would have to go down. While strafing, a shot, possibly from an infantryman's rifle, had punctured an oil line. This was not as improbable as it may seem. As soon as Allied fighters appeared overhead the Germans would leave their vehicles and dive for safety in any protection they could find at the sides of the road. From their cover, they would shoot at the low strafing planes with rifles, light machine-guns, and heavier machine-guns which they could mount on tripod stands in seconds flat. As a result, we were often flying into a cloud of small-arms fire.

Hofer headed for the beach-head where one lone Allied airbase had just been established. Later, those who didn't know the Kid as well as some of us, marvelled at his luck in finding himself right over this lone airfield when he broke out of cloud on his way down. I remembered seeing a Mustang low over the beach-head when coming out from the last mission the day before.

Anyway, the Kid was greeted by the ground troops like a hero. They had seen the effectiveness of their air umbrella, and wanted to show their appreciation. Major-General Ralph Royce of the Ninth Air Force was on the base and from him Hofer obtained a jeep ride to tour the battle area, while the mechanics repaired his oil leak.

That evening, he was back at Debden proudly displaying a German helmet and a copy of *Mein Kampf*, as souvenirs of his escapade.

As Deacon Hively and I walked into the mess, Hofer put on the German helmet and saluted. There was an incongruous contrast between that grim-looking head-piece with the eagle of the German

(*Above*) Six leading aces: (clockwise) Lieutenant-Colonel Duane Beeson, Captain 'Cowboy' Megura, Major John Godfrey, Major James Goodson, Major Don Gentile.

(*Right*) Captain Nicholas Megura (The Cowboy), Ansonia, Connecticut.

(Top left) Lieutenant-Colonel James Clark, Long Island, N.Y. *(Top right)* Lieutenant Aubrey Stanhope, a Frenchman. *(Bottom left)* Jim Clark. *(Bottom right)* Lieutenant Steve Pissanos (The Greek), Plainfield, N.J.

◀ *(Opposite, top)* A flight of 335 Squadron P-51's. *(Bottom)* Blakeslee briefing: front row left to right: Clark, Magrattan, Goodson.

General Auton decorates Fred Glover.

(Left) Lieutenant-Colonel Duane W. Beeson, from Boise, Idaho.
(Right) Louis 'Red Dog' Norley.

(Top left) Captain Allen Bunte from Eustis, Florida. *(Top right)* Major Hank Mills from Leonia, N.J. *(Bottom left)* Lieutenant Ray Clotfelter. *(Bottom right)* Major Leon Blanding from Sumter, South Carolina.

Preparations for D-Day. Lieutenant-Colonel Oscar Coen (left, facing camera), Major-General Kepner, Lieutenant-Colonel Jim Clark, Mr Banks (standing), General Eisenhower, Colonel Blakeslee, General Spaatz, Major Gentile, Brigadier-General Auton, Captain Joe Lang, Colonel Fallows (left, nearest camera), Brigadier-General Curtis, Major Goodson, Lieutenant-General Doolittle, Captain Bob Johnson, Commander Harry Butcher, Captain Alfred Markel, Lieutenant Rowles.

Major Hank Mills.

(Left) Lieutenant-Colonel Claiborne Kinnard from Franklin, Tennessee, who succeeded Blakeslee as CO of the Fourth. *(Right)* Pierce McKennon and George Green after 'Mac' was picked up from a field in Germany.

Major Pierce W. McKennon (Mac) from Arkansas.

(Left) Major James A. Goodson, 'King of Strafers'. (Top right) Major 'Bud' Care from Angola, Indiana. (Centre right) Fred Glover, from Asheville, North Carolina, who succeeded Goodson as CO of 336 Squadron.

VF-B, the P-51D in which Goodson was shot down.

Mike Sobanski
(The Pole).

Goodson with
The Pole.

Colonel Blakeslee
and
General Kepner.

Gentile and P-51 with original Eagle Squadron ensignia designed by Walt Disney.

Wing Commander Bob Stanford Tuck, DSO, DFC and two bars, one of the outstanding fighter leaders of the RAF. He was typical of the experienced RAF commanders who helped form the Eagle squadrons.

General Eisenhower pins DSCs on Gentile and Blakeslee. He commented: 'I feel a sense of humility being among a group of fighting men like this.'

Colonel Chesley Peterson (left), CO of the Fourth, and at twenty-three the youngest full colonel in the US Army, with Lieutenant-Colonel Oscar Coen, Carbondale, Illinois, a schoolteacher who became one of the first airmen to be shot down and escape from France.

(Left) The legendary ace of World War I, Eddie Rickenbacker, visits the Fourth Fighter group at Debden. General 'Monk' Hunter is on the left. (Right) 'Deacon' Hively.

(Left) Blakeslee's P-47 after being escorted back to England by Goodson. It had been hit by a total of 68 cannon shells. (Right) The starboard side of the P-47 after the oil had been cleaned off, showing shell holes in cockpit canopy, fuselage and wing.

(Left) 336 Squadron scoreboard with (left to right): Tussey, Patteeuw, Benjamin (intelligence officer), Emerson, Goodson, Hobart, (standing) Blakeslee and MacCarteney.

(Below) General Eisenhower, General Carl (Tooey) Spaatz, commander of USAAFE, General James Doolittle, commander Eighth Air Force, Major General William Kepner, commander VIII Fighter Command and Colonel Don Blakeslee at Debden.

(Top left) Vic France, The Playboy. *(Top right)* Captain Kendall E. Carlson, The Swede.

Vic France and Don Blakeslee.

Ralph Hofer (The Kid) and 'Duke'.

Captain Benjamin (intelligence officer) debriefing Millikan.

(Left) Ruby, 'Millie' and Patsy. (Right) Captain Phillip (Pappy) Dunn, from Portland, Oregon.

Left to right:
Godfrey, Gentile,
Lehman, Goodson
and Millikan.

Godfrey, Gentile
and Goodson.

Major Willard
Millikan just landed
after a mission. Left
to right: Millikan, K.
Peterson, Goodson
(back to camera),
Benjamin, L. Norley,
MacCarteney.

336 Squadron dispersal hut with Goodson in the background, and Gentile leaning on the table.

(Left) Johnny Godfrey and 'Lucky'. (Right) Captain Kenneth Peterson (Black Snake) from Arizona.

Reich on the side, and the laughing, boyish face underneath it. The Kid handed the helmet to the Deacon who passed it on to me. From the inside came the strong acrid sickly-sweet smell of stale sweat. To me, it brought home in a flash the dirty side of war, which we never really felt in the clean, clear air. The war on the ground was something unreal and far away. Even when we saw the flashes of bombs bursting and the towering palls of black smoke; even when we strafed and saw vehicles and bodies smashed by our guns, it was like looking at something through the wrong end of a telescope, or perhaps in a film. But that stinking helmet was real. It was the trenches, the Poor Bloody Infantry, Verdun, Flanders' fields, and a million crosses. I thought of the neatly made bed in my room which hadn't been slept in since D-Day, when Mike Sobanski, who was so much more than just a room-mate, had been shot down. I thought of all the happy warriors who weren't around any more — and I passed the helmet back to the Kid.

'It smells of piss!' he said.

I shook my head. 'It smells of Death!' I said.

Hofer's position by now was unique. In the 'scores' charts, he was jockeying for pride of place with Godfrey, Gentile, Beeson and myself, all of us having close to thirty victories. The difference was that the rest of us had years of experience as squadron leaders or deputies and carried the rank of major. The Kid was still a lieutenant.

His lack of experience showed up in his navigation, which might not have been so serious if he had always stuck with the rest of the outfit, but his tendency to 'goof off' on his own meant that he had to rely on his own dubious talents of navigation.

On 21st June the Fourth Group was given the task of escorting bombers on the great Shuttle raid: England to Russia, Russia to Italy, Italy back over Europe to England. In his briefing, Don Blakeslee had stressed discipline and said 'No landing errors. The Russians shoot people who make mistakes.' Moreover the available maps of Russia were almost bare of any details, and it was obvious that beyond the Russian frontier only dead reckoning could be relied on. There would be no landmarks to go by. During the battles over Germany, Hofer got separated, and finally landed

in Kiev, while the rest of the Group were at Poltava. It took a
telex from Kiev to Debden to check his identity.

This prevented the Kid from joining the rest of the Group
before they left Poltava for Foggia in Italy. Nothing daunted,
he took off, but this time he not only missed the air base he was
headed for; he didn't even hit the right country! He landed in
Malta, but still got to Foggia in time to join the Fourth's next
mission.

This was the famous mission to Budapest in which the Fourth
tangled with JG52. The Kid was probably in on the main battle,
in which the Fourth scored seven for a loss of one and may
well have scored himself; but, true to form, he must have followed the scattered German planes as they turned back north-
wards.

His course was converging with that of another 'Kid', but when
his friends called him 'Kid', they used the German *Bubi*. He, too,
at first was a happy youngster, not very amenable to discipline
or spit and polish. His officer's hat was as crushed down as Hofer's,
and his ways were free and easy, and his buddies loved him.

But his grey 109 carried the black crosses and swastikas of the
Third Reich. Under the cockpit was his insignia of a bleeding
heart pierced with an arrow, and the word Ursel, for his wife
Ursula. Fortunately their devotion was mutual. At the end of
the war, he burned what was left of his planes and led JG52's
remaining personnel on foot to surrender to the Allies. In the
worst sell-out of the war, the Allies turned the heroes of Germany over to the Russians to be treated as criminals, only to be
released after ten years of hell. But when he came back, Ursel
was still waiting, and so was an elite of devoted and admiring
friends from both sides. For this was Erich 'Bubi' Hartmann,
the greatest of the fighter pilots.

So, if the Kid had to be shot down, I'm glad it was by the
best, and I know the Kid would agree. They were about the same
age, but Hartmann's enormous experience and cool technical
proficiency had to tell.

Back at Debden, they knew before anyone else. And they
knew the exact time. Duke, the big Alsatian, leaped up and
let out a series of doleful howls and then went and lay down in

the empty revetment where the 'Salem Representative' would never be parked again.

They identified his body from his dog-tags — and the lucky snake ring. They buried him in Hungary, between Budapest and the Czech border.

He was the happiest of all those happy warriors. He was twenty-one.

CHAPTER SEVEN

Millie

But there were the others. Some had natural flair; some had to make it the hard way. That was Millie's way. It started way back in Malvern, Iowa, where his father's heavy drinking and Irish temper kept the family desperately poor. College was out of the question. Millie had to work to support the family. What free time he had he spent developing his talents for baseball, which he studied with the same intensity he later brought to flying; because flying was what he was determined to do. Probably no one ever aspired to become a pilot with more strikes against him than Willard W. Millikan. All he had was iron determination. He gradually overcame every obstacle through enormous personal sacrifice. One of the last hurdles to be overcome before he could qualify as an aviation cadet was the expense of dental work to repair the damage done during fist fights with his father, and in the ball games of those rough days. He had to borrow $350 to get his teeth fixed, but the worry of paying back the money, and Millie's own intensity, made him another victim of Lindbergh Field's elimination process. Like Peterson before him, Millie was washed out for 'lack of inherent flying ability'. He headed straight for Canada and the RCAF. Again through sheer determination, he got his wings, but his instructor recommended that he become a ferry pilot, since he would certainly kill himself as a fighter pilot.

At first it looked as if Lindbergh Field and the RCAF instructor had been right. Millie flew fifty-two missions before he made his first kill; but during those missions, he was probably the most effective and reliable wingman in the squadron. Only one or two of Millie's fifteen victories were scored while we were flying P-47's, but he was always around. I remember an early mission to Kiel, which brought home to me again the dependability of the P-47. It also showed something of the dependability of Millikan.

The bombers were hitting the German U-boat and naval base.

As usual, we were giving them close escort over the target area. Suddenly the heavy flak opened up, and almost immediately there were black woolly clouds with bright flashes in them floating by. One hit my engine, rocking the plane and filling the cockpit with the acrid smell of cordite. I heard the crump. Black oil hit the windscreen and I started losing power. Fortunately I was at 25,000 feet and already heading for home. I followed the Kiel Canal to the coast of Schleswig-Holstein and had to face the miles of North Sea. I was still at 20,000 feet, but I saw the cylinder-head temperature gauge had gone up to the red danger point. I remembered how Blakeslee's plane had made it back to Manston covered with oil. I also remembered that a rich fuel mixture made an engine run cool. On the instrument panel was a primer level which we used to pump a squirt of straight fuel into the cylinder for starting. I pushed it in and out, and, after a number of shots, I saw that I was able to get the temperature down a bit, but the moment I stopped the needle started up again, and I had to start pumping again. Soon my arm was aching, and my hand was in agony. I always wore gloves; I knew what fire could do to bare hands; but under the leather, the skin of my fingers, and then of my palm was being rubbed raw. I kept the speed just above a stall to maintain as much altitude as possible. The squadron were weaving over me, but when I figured they would need their remaining fuel to get home, I told them to leave me.

There was some argument. I heard Millikan's voice: 'Millie here. I'm staying with you.' — He was probably my closest friend, and not easy to argue with. He had married an English girl, Ruby, and had just had a daughter, Patsy.

'Go home to Ruby and Patsy. I'll be OK. I'll call Air-Sea Rescue if I have to get out and walk,' I said.

'You think you can walk on water?'

'Why not? It's been done before!'

I looked down at the expanse of sea. It looked flat, but I could see the white flecks of the wave caps and knew that down on the surface there were towering waves making rescue almost impossible.

Millie was now close on my wing. He slid underneath me and came up on the other side. 'How's it look?' I asked. There was no answer. I flicked over to the emergency 'May Day' channel. As I suspected, he was talking to them. He was giving my altitude and heading, and added, 'He'll never make it. He'll have to bale out soon.'

'Can he give us a long transmission so we can get a fix on him?' said an unemotional English voice.

'No problem!' I said, but it wasn't easy. The RT button was on the throttle on the left. My left hand was busy on the primer so I had to take my right hand off the stick and reach over. I sang the words of a popular song: 'Don't worry about me, I'll get along!'

'Damn fool!' said Millie.

'Jesus Christ!' said the Air-Sea Rescue.

'No,' I said, 'I've been on to Him. He doesn't want to cramp your style.'

'You're a long way out and the weather conditions are bad, but we'll do our best!' Then somewhat despairingly, 'Good luck!'

When I figured I was halfway across, I was down to 9,000 feet. My left hand was in agony, and I could feel the sticky blood around my fingers.

I was heading for Martlesham Heath airfield by Ipswich on the East Coast. When I calculated I should be sighting land, I was down to 2,000 feet and nothing but sea. I opened the canopy, undid the harness and started to struggle up ready to bale. I got my feet on the seat, crouching behind the windscreen. I pulled my goggles down and started to straighten up. As my head came above the oil-smeared windscreen, I found I could see better.

There it was: the low line of Orfordness, the sandy marshland on the other side of which was the airfield. I clambered back into the cockpit. I tried to stretch the glide but she was going down fast. Suddenly she shuddered on the point of a stall. I eased the stick forward and dropped five degrees of flap. By now I was under 500 feet still over marsh and streams. I was preparing to belly in, wheels up, when I saw the edge of the airfield ahead. I dropped the undercarriage and prayed it would get down in time. I eased the stick back and plopped her down on the grass just inside the field. The wheels must have locked down during the stall just before touching down. I switched off and rolled to a stop. A P-47 roared over me and landed. It was Millie.

I climbed out onto the wing and looked at the smoking, shattered engine, covered in oil. The top of the front cowling was torn to bits and two cylinders were completely blown apart!

Like most of the Group, Millie really got going when we got our Mustangs, but he was one of those guys that always got things the hard way. The Group's first Berlin mission was a case in point. I rated Millie, along with Beeson, as the most capable and dedicated tactician and deflection shot in the Group. They weren't natural pilots like Gentile and Hofer, who simply had the flair to be able to aim their planes — or themselves — rather than their guns. Millie had to develop his talents by constant practice in attack and shooting. By 3rd March 1944, Millie's determined dedication was beginning to pay off, and his score was beginning to build up. So naturally I put Millie's name up, as number three in Gentile's section.

But, although our red-nosed Mustangs were the first Allied fighters over Berlin, it didn't happen until 4th March: 3rd March was a bust; and very nearly eliminated Millie, and eight other top pilots of the Fourth Group, including two of its leading aces, Godfrey and Gentile.

The weather was foul when we took off, and got steadily worse. As the cloud got thicker, I called the squadron in closer to me. I knew that the newer pilots didn't have much experience of instrument flying, and in those storm clouds, the violent turbulence was making it ten times tougher. I figured it would be better if the two planes next to me flew formation on me, and the others formated on them, and so on. Then only I would have to keep staring at the instruments, as I tried to keep the plane right side up.

To make matters worse, the weather people had told us to expect icing, particularly in cloud, and we heard the short transmissions from pilots aborting because their engines were running so rough they couldn't stay in the formation.

I think almost everyone expected Blakeslee, leading the Group, to call it off, but I knew he would never let the bombers down; so we stuck it out, cursing and fighting the controls, expecting at any moment that the turbulence would hit so hard that the artificial horizon would topple and we'd spin out, or collide with the other planes.

Then we heard it. 'Cobweb Green section to Horseback. Bandits all around. Sixty plus. Are you receiving me, Horseback?' It was Millie.

Blakeslee didn't reply. Neither did I. There was nothing we could do. We were due to rendezvous with the bombers in a few minutes. In any case, there was little chance of finding the others among the cloud banks in time to help them.

Apparently the two sections being on the far right of the Group had lost contact, and been forced to fly blind on their own course which had taken them into a comparatively open space where the massed German fighters were waiting. The nine Mustangs were immediately bounced by about thirty Germans. They turned into the attack. The Germans took their usual evasive tactics by diving away, and the Mustangs followed. This was the signal for the rest of the German fighters to peel off and follow them down. Glenn Herter from Detroit, a relatively new pilot who had been separated from his section and had attached himself to the others as tail-end Charlie was hit by three 109's and blown out of the sky. The others broke into the new attack, and a general mêlée ensued.

Gentile and Millikan found themselves free of the battle and could have got away, but they didn't hesitate and turned back to help the others. Almost immediately Gentile was being attacked by ten 190's, but Millie was there. He turned into the 190's and most of them broke off, but some of them continued to chase Gentile. He broke into them so violently that two of them flashed by him almost colliding with him.

I heard him yell: 'Are you with me, Millie?' and Millie's breathless reply: 'I've got ten 190's chasing me.'

Finally the weather got too much even for the bombers. The stable four-engined planes with two pilots could cope much better with blind flying than the single-engined fighters, but by now, the thick clouds and general confusion precluded any effective hit on the target. The order was given to turn back, and we were free to go to the help of our friends — if we could find them.

Blakeslee for once didn't bother with call signs: 'OK, Millie, Don here. Calling all Mustangs, let's give Millie some help.'

But Millie wasn't the only one in trouble; all eight of them were mixing it with an armada of everything the Germans could put up, even including twin-engined Ju88's, Me110's and Dornier 217's. Normally these would have been easy meat for the Mustangs, but every time they lined up on one, they were attacked by 109's and 190's and had to break into the attack.

Gentile saw two 190's closing on 'Gunner' Halsey. He started to attack them and yelled for Gunner to break. The break was so violent, the plane went into three snap rolls, which probably saved Gunner's life; but before Gentile could fire on the 190's, he had to break off to meet eight 190's which were bouncing him.

Millie told me afterwards that he had given up any hope of getting out of the mess, and was just trying to sell his life as dearly as possible. If the others had had time to reflect on it, I think they would have felt the same. Millie, Johnny Godfrey, Swede Carlson and Vernon Garrison attacked a gaggle of Me110's, which immediately went into their only possible defensive manoeuvre when attacked by single-engine fighters. They formed a circle so that each one covered the other's tail, and their rear gunners prevented an enemy plane from breaking into the circle. The Swede, followed by Garrison and Millie attacked them head-on, going around in the opposite direction. He shot one down, and he and Garrison were lining up on a second one when another Mustang cut in front of them and blew the 110 apart. It was Millie.

Suddenly the three found themselves alone. Both Millie's and Carlson's engines were running rough and cutting out, and they were out of ammunition. Garrison's super-charger had been out since the beginning, which was a good reason for aborting, but he had kept going at the risk of not making it back because of the additional fuel needed. I had never known this quiet, modest ex-school teacher from Kentucky lose his cool. He was as steady as the rock of Gibraltar, and one of the best shots in the Group. As soon as they had started to tangle with the German fighters he had shot one down, but most of his guns had jammed. Nevertheless, with what he had left he knocked down a 109 with a 90 degree deflection shot as it flashed past in front of him. That brought his total score to ten. From then on, like the others, he had been turning and twisting, sweating and cursing, as he fought for his life.

I heard Millie say: 'OK, we'll head back ' and a little later: 'Millie here. I don't think I can make it back.'

I said, 'It's probably ice. Drop down below the soup.'

This apparently cleared the engines, but left the three of them racing across Germany at tree-top height. They pulled up over a hill and suddenly found themselves zooming across a city. Judging from the amount of both heavy and light flak that came up, they were over the Ruhr.

Garrison said: 'We'd better get out of here.' Then almost immediately, but strangely quietly, 'That's me, boys.'

He had just enough speed to pull up and bale out.

Millikan, Gentile, Godfrey, Halsey and Carlson got back to England completely exhausted.

Pappy Dunn wasn't quite so lucky. In the bad weather, he got separated from Gentile and Halsey. His radio could transmit but not receive, so he probably flew a wrong course home. When he was finally able to pinpoint himself he had missed England altogether and found himself low on fuel over Brittany in western France. He could have turned north to try to make it across the Channel to the West of England, but with no radio, and almost no gas, he decided not to chance it over the water. Instead he headed for Spain, and might even have made it, if he hadn't spotted a Heinkel 111. It was too good a chance to miss.

Pappy had done everything in civilian life from flunking out of medical school to running a funeral parlour in Alaska. In the squadron he was loved by everyone, but more as a comedian than as a fighter ace. On that day he had a 48-hour pass, but when he saw we were going to Berlin, he saw his chance for glory, and begged me to put him on the board.

As Pappy floated down into the arms of the waiting German soldiers, I'm sure he felt it was a reasonable price to pay for his victory. Usually when we asked him if he'd scored a victory, he would reply: 'Hell, yes! I got back in one piece, didn't I?'

This time he was not getting back, but he was going out in style.

If he had one regret, it turned up shortly after the rest of us landed back at Debden. An irate British lady naval officer had been asking for Lieutenant Philip Dunn, and was now demanding to see his CO.

'Lieutenant Dunn was to meet me at the station. Where is he?' she asked primly.

'He hasn't got back from a mission to Berlin,' I said.

'Berlin! What was he doing over Berlin when he was supposed to be meeting me?'

'What time was he supposed to pick you up?' I asked.

'Five o'clock!'

'Oh, he'd have had time to do that. We landed about four,' I said.

'You mean he was going to Berlin and back, pick me up, take me out for the evening, and — and — everything —?'

'Well, that's par for the course around here,' I said.

Her indignation was giving place to amazement. 'Well, where is he now?'

'Like I said, he didn't come back.' Slowly it was beginning to dawn on her. 'You don't mean — he's not coming back?'

'That's sometimes par for the course around here too,' I said. 'I'm sorry! Can I offer you a drink?'

She stared at me in a state of shock. Her face was white and her eyes were glazed.

'My God!' she said, and turned and left to return to the calmer and more dignified environment of the Royal Navy.

The mission had been a failure, but it proved something. On most of our Mustang missions we had met equal or inferior numbers of enemy planes. In this case, over sixty Germans had attacked and fought nine Mustangs over Berlin. They had shot down one for the loss of six of their own. The success of the Fourth was proof of the remarkable performance of the Mustang, but it also showed that experienced pilots constantly attacking aggressively, and helping one another were more than a match for the Luftwaffe.

Pappy's navigational problems made me wonder why the leaders didn't have the same sort of problems, considering the distances we had to travel, often in bad weather, and after mixing it up from 30,000 feet down to the deck.

Less experienced pilots who got separated from their squadron often got lost, but they had been given a compass heading which would at least get them back to within radio range of England where they could be pinpointed and given a new heading; but we leaders seemed to develop a sort of sixth sense, perhaps like migrating birds. On this mission, after collecting the squadron together, setting an estimated course for home, letting down through the solid cloud undercast, I broke out right over our base at Debden. Map-reading didn't play much of a part, although we did, of course know all the landmarks near our base, from Orford-ness over Ipswich, Braintree etc to Debden. Even on the way to Berlin we could recognise the Hook of Holland, The Zuider Zee, the Ruhr, the round Dummer Lake north of Osnabrück, Hannover, Magdeburg and Braunschweig. But they were only of help in good weather, and that was the exception rather than the rule.

The map with the lines drawn on it indicating our course to and from the target, and the compass headings was most important, and we could do some calculating on our knee-pad; but, above all, some of us developed a sense of direction, which once acquired, stays with one, even on the ground.

Millie was involved in more of the action than some of the more celebrated aces, but his emphasis was as much on protecting the bombers, and other members of his flight, as building up a score.

Most pilots new to combat were terribly vulnerable, many were shot down before we even got to know them. No matter how tired Millie was after a mission, he always had time to take the new boys up for training; and he kept a protecting eye on them during the missions.

I remember Pete Lehman casually remarking: 'Once over Emden, Millie saved my life by shooting a Hun off my tail that I never even saw.'

Pete survived to become a valuable and reliable member of the squadron. He was one of the few who had left a wife and two child-ren and a career in the famous family investment banking business. His brother followed him by serving in the tank corps; and his father renounced another term as Governor of New York to become director of the United Nations Rehabilitation Relief Administration, at an age when most men have long since retired.

Pete's goal was to win the coveted Distinguished Flying Cross for his father's seventieth birthday on 28th March 1944. He just made it. His citation was dated 28th March; he was killed on 31st March.

After the fiasco of 3rd March, the next day Berlin was on again; but this time we made it. This was the day when Göring said he knew the war was lost: the Mustangs of the Fourth were protecting their big bomber friends over the capital of the Reich. Millie wasn't with us. I told him he better give his plane a thorough testing to make sure his engine troubles were only icing. He could have taken another plane, but we were all superstitious about that. No one liked lending their planes and no one liked borrowing one. But, of course, it wasn't the plane I was thinking of. Like most of us, Millie had been flying all of the missions without a break, but the difference with Millie was the terrible intensity he put into it, and the training he put in after the gruelling missions. And Ruby had let slip that he was dog-fighting and dodging flak in his sleep during most of the night. I'd noticed the night before that the big, raw-boned Iowa farm boy was finally beginning to feel the strain, so Millie was to have a day of rest. As it happened, in his quiet way, he made himself at least as useful as the rest of us. There wasn't as much German fighter reaction as we had expected. They were probably waiting for the escorting fighters to turn for home before attacking the bombers, but this time, they didn't leave.

The most frustrated was Blakeslee. Just after we'd taken over from the escorting P-47's who were at the limit of their range, we saw the green flares coming from the bombers to ask for help. Fifteen 109's were lining up for a head-on attack on the leading wing. Blakeslee gave the order to attack, flipped over and split-essed into a vertical dive to cut them off. The speed of the dive enabled him to get behind a 109 which saw him, but couldn't shake him. Soon Blakeslee was right in his slip-stream. He pressed the firing button — and nothing happened. Red Dog Norley who was flying on his wing couldn't contain himself and yelled, 'Let him have it, Colonel!' but not one of Don's guns would fire. His speed took him right up alongside the 109. The Luftwaffe pilot stared at the Mustang, unable to understand. Blakeslee gave him a friendly, if frustrated wave, he waggled his wings in grateful reply, flipped over on his back and dived for the deck. Red Dog wasn't close enough to follow so they climbed back up to resume the escort, with the only consolation that the attack on the bombers had been broken up.

Meanwhile, a number of planes had had to turn back with engine trouble. It may have been the continuation of the icing problems of the day before, or maybe the long distance missions day after day were taking their toll.

One of those forced to turn back was Charlie Anderson. Not only was he nursing a rough-running engine, but his air speed indicator wasn't working.

As he limped into the circuit at Debden, he faced the daunting problem of trying to land without an airspeed indicator; but, as he radioed the control tower, and the ambulances and fire trucks raced out to the runway, he heard another voice: 'OK, Andy, Millie here, I'll get you down.'

Millie had been testing his plane over the base, and was soon on Andy's wing, nursing him down. On the first approach, Millie, the perfectionist wasn't satisfied, and took Andy around again. With infinite patience, he led him in on his wing, at the same time calling out the airspeed, and talking him down.

The day came when Millie, the slow starter who didn't score till his fifty-second mission, had fifteen victories in the air, four of them on one mission, and two destroyed on the ground. He had over 400 combat hours, about eighty missions, without a rest, and was showing the fatigue. A few of us had more, but the difference was that Millie put so much of himself into it. Also having to say goodbye to his wife Ruby and little Patsy every day had to mean more strain, although he would never admit it. I noticed, too, that most of Millie's victories were scored after violent, drawn-out dog-fights, and almost all were the result of his going to the rescue of someone in trouble.

On his last mission, he led his section into an attack on about thirty 109's to rescue Deacon Hively. He chased them right back over their own air base. Suddenly the flak came up, and Sam Young, flying on Millie's wing, was hit. His windscreen was shattered and his plane knocked sideways, right into Millikan's plane. When he recovered from the shock, Millie found he had no controls; stick and rudders flopped around uselessly. Sam's prop had sliced Millie's plane in two just behind the cockpit. The front half, with the engine still roaring away, was spinning wildly. Somehow, Millie managed to jettison the hood, undo the safety harness and bail out.

Millie survived POW camp and the war, and went on to become an outstanding aviation personality and Brigadier-General of the Washington Air National Guard.

But I only learned all this much later. I also learned that, on that May day in 1944, when Millie found himself sitting in a field near Braunschweig surrounded by German soldiers, all the tension and fatigue of the last few months rolled away, and he found tears rolling down his cheeks.

And strangely enough, back at Debden that evening, as I was eating dinner, I became aware of something dripping on my plate. I looked up, and discovered that tears were streaming down my face. Funny what can happen when you get a little tired.

CHAPTER EIGHT

The Battle of Germany

In many ways, Don Gentile was the opposite of Millie. Millikan's rawboned, angular frame was typically Nordic: both Gentile's name, Dominic Salvatore Gentile, and his dark good looks were typical of the first generation Italian American. His surname was pronounced Gentilly, but some of the pilots called him 'Gentle', almost as a nickname.

In character, there was even more difference. It was brought out on one of our P-47 missions to Paris — a mission which also showed Gentile's natural flying ability, and his amazing ability to get out of impossible situations alive.

It was in late '43, when a raid on Paris still got a strong German fighter reaction. 336 Squadron first spotted the FW190's heading for the bombers, swooped down on them, and were soon in a swirling dog-fight. Gentile got on the tail of two 190's flying abreast, the basic formation which the Luftwaffe called a *Rotte*. They dived for the deck in their usual defensive manoeuvre. Gentile, knowing the seven-ton P-47 could catch them in the dive, once its speed built up, took after them. He got the first one and continued after the second. When the massive Thunderbolt got to within 300 yards of the 190, Gentile gave a long burst and the German pilot never pulled out of his dive. The 190 exploded as it hit the ground and Gentile just had time to pull the P-47 out of its screaming dive to climb back up to the squadron. His wingman hadn't been able to stay with him in the dive, but he saw him pull up, and we soon heard his urgent cry: 'Break, Gentle, break!'

The *Rotte* Gentile had attacked was part of a gaggle of four flying in the loose, spread-out formations the Luftwaffe used so effectively. Now the second *Rotte* was on Gentile's tail.

Don racked the heavy plane into a tight turn, but at 500 feet the FW190 was in its element, whereas the P-47 only came into its own above 20,000 feet. The leading German plane started to gain on the heavy Thunderbolt in the turn. Gentile pulled his plane into a tighter circle, until it started to shudder and buck on the point of a stall. He had to ease off to avoid spinning into the trees only feet below. Right away the 190 gained in the turn, and started firing, but he didn't have enough deflection. We heard Gentile calling the rest of his section, led by Millikan: 'Help! Help! I'm being clobbered!'

Millie's calm, controlled reply was in sharp contrast to Gentile's screams. 'If you can give us your approximate position, we'll try to help.'

'I'm down by a railroad track with this 190!'

There was no way Millie, or anyone else, could find Gentile down on the deck, or get to him in time to help. Don was on his own and he knew it! When the rest of the Group heard Gentile's breathless transmission: 'If I don't get back, tell them I got two', they thought it was his last.

The second 190 had been lost in the gruelling dogfight, but the remaining one was a real pro and determined to get this P-47 which had shot down two of his squadron, and must by now be almost out of ammunition, and short of gas.

Only Gentile's flying ability was keeping him alive, but the 190 was out-performing the Thunderbolt at that low altitude. Each time he started to gain in the turn, Gentile, fighting for his life, pulled his heavy plane right to the point of stall, and then fought it off. The German probably knew what Gentile didn't know: the FW190 was far more vicious than the P-47. If he took it too close to the stall, the 190 would flip into the ground long before the stall could be corrected.

Gentile finally found himself in a tight turn, hanging on the stall. Looking over his shoulder, he saw the nose of the German plane inexorably gaining on him until the leading edge of the wing lit up as the guns fired. In one last desperate effort, he racked the plane up until it hung shuddering on its prop in a stall turn. The German plane slid by underneath. Gentile nursed his plane off the stall by stomping rudder and diving for the deck. He had reversed his heading. By the time the 190 had come around, his prey had been lost.

When Don landed, he was exhausted and shaken to the core; but in a day or so he was back in character, eager to be included on every mission, and, once on the mission, the first to peel off to attack. Don Gentile's obsession was to become America's leading ace, anything else was secondary. His first question on returning from a mission was to check on his nearest rivals: 'How many did Beeson get? How many did Goody get?'

I once passed the hut that housed the Catholic chapel, on my way to a briefing, and met Gentile coming out.

'What were you doing in there, Don?'

'Praying. I go there before every mission.'

'What do you pray for?'

'To shoot down more planes, of course! This time I prayed for three!'

Although most of the Fourth's pilots were keen to build up their score, I think there were only two others as completely obsessed as Gentile. One was Beeson, who flew with 334 Squadron. The other was Johnnie Godfrey.

Back home in Woonsocket, Rhode Island, Johnnie had been a problem for his parents; refusing to go to university, seemingly without ambition, and finally running away to join the Royal Canadian Air Force. For the first time in his life, he was doing something he liked, and took seriously; but, before he got his wings, another event occurred which hardened his character and gave him the drive which had been lacking. His brother, Reggie, an aircraft mechanic, was torpedoed and drowned en route to England.

He told me the story when I was welcoming him to 336 Squadron in late 1943 and he was supervising the painting of his insignia on his newly assigned P-47. Instead of some lurid caricature, the carefully spelt out letters simply read: 'Reggie's Reply'.

Johnnie was 6'2", dark and good-looking, with jet-black, piercing eyes, which became the best in the Group at picking out enemy fighters. He was not easy to get to know, but was very close to Bob Richards. The two, accompanied by Johnnie's mongrel dog, 'Lucky', were inseparable, and when Richards was shot down and killed in March 1944, Johnnie became even more of a loner — and even more of an aggressive attacker. He and

Gentile were soon engaged in a fierce competition to become the leading ace.

It was a close contest. Everyone has his own score-card, but the official War Department figures show that, after those wild days of spring 1944, Godfrey, Gentile and myself were credited with 30 each. Hofer had 27, Beeson 25 and Glover 24. In other groups, Henry Brown, Bob Johnson, Gaby Gabreski and Dave Schilling were also approaching 30.

The intensity of the competition posed a problem for the group and squadron commanders. Although they wanted to encourage aggressive tactics, the first priority had to be protection of the bombers. This was more difficult to guarantee if pilots attacked and followed their prey far from the bomber stream.

Blakeslee, thanks to his RAF training, was a strict disciplinarian and was particularly rough on the mavericks. Kid Hofer in 335 Squadron was the outstanding example, but every squadron commander had the problem. Most of us worked out a compromise. In 336 I usually had Gentile leading one of the four flights with Godfrey flying as his wingman in number two position, and a strong, reliable, solid pro, like Millikan, or Glover, with a good wingman to give cover. It worked beautifully, and even when Johnnie had caught up with Gentile's score, and finally had the same rank of captain, he never minded flying on Gentile's wing. They became one of those brilliant teams of two.

The Battle of Germany reached its crescendo during March 1944. It actually started on 20th February when General Toohey Spaatz gave orders for the launching of Operation 'Argument', a concentrated attack with all forces available, including the Fifteenth US Air Force from Italy, and the RAF operating at night. Its purpose was to destroy the production centres of the German fighter planes on the ground, and the fighters themselves in the air — and on the ground, as an essential prerequisite of the invasion of the Continent. It could only be contemplated because the Mustangs of the Fourth, with their two droppable wing tanks could now escort the bombers all the way to the target.

We fought the Luftwaffe over the aircraft and components factories at Brauschweig, Leipzig, Aschersleben, Gotha, Augsburg, Stuttgart, Fürth, over the ball-bearing factories at Schweinfurt and over the Messerschmitt works at Regensburg.

Sometimes bad weather made form-up and rendezvous difficult for both fighters and bombers, and whenever the bombers went without fighter escort, the Luftwaffe pounced. On 23rd February, bad weather, particularly over England, resulted in the bomber stream being late and strung out. The Luftwaffe, forewarned, seized their opportunity. Instead of waiting to attack over the target area, where our Mustangs would be escorting, they hit as soon as the bombers crossed in over the coast. The Thunderbolt escort, including the 56th Group protected the strung-out stream as best they could and scored many victories, but, as we came in to take up our escort duty over the target, we followed a trail of crippled bombers. In all, 41 bombers were lost, and only 99 out of the original 430 got through to the target.

It was now the turn of Berlin. We set out for the German capital on 3rd March, but the bombers had to turn back. We were over Berlin on the 4th, over Bordeaux in Southern France on the 5th, over Berlin again on the 6th, and on the 8th, and on the 9th, and so on.

I think the 6th must have been a decisive day. On the 8th we encountered fewer German fighters, and on the 9th, none at all!

But on the mission of 6th March, we didn't know this. The first Berlin show had shown us that the German fighters would come up for the defence of the capital, and our relatively defensive attitude for the first Berlin show was now dropped for an aggressive desire to take advantage of the opportunity to add to the score.

Once again, the Fourth Fighter Group with their Mustangs were to cover the bombers over the target, taking on the escort work when the shorter range P-47's had to turn for home. Obviously it was out here on the far end of the loop that the German fighter defence would concentrate their attacks. They would know that the bombers would be concentrating on their bomb run, and that the fighter escort would be thinner, and that even the P-51's would be operating at the limit of their range.

I had just identified Magdeburg on my left, when I saw the bomber fleets ahead. Although we had seen their con-trails for some time, now we saw the flashes as the sun glinted on their canopies, and then the small black forms of the different 'boxes' gliding majestically through a few flak puffs toward their target.

We caught up with them on schedule and started to weave over them; but almost immediately we saw that the forward elements were under attack, and the RT reports were coming in: 'Bandits at 12 o'clock!' 'Millions of 'em at 1 o'clock!'

Blakeslee led the Group into the attack. He was heading for a gaggle of attackers ahead of us which seemed to include Ju88's firing rockets. As the speed built up in the dive, the slight curve of the attack brought my squadron lower and closer to the bombers. Glancing towards the nearest group, I saw they were about to be jumped by some ten 109's. We were in a good position and had the speed. A quick look behind indicated that we could get in a quick attack and break back up to join the rest of the Group before the top German cover could hit us.

I told Blakeslee I was taking my squadron down, and increased the angle of the dive almost to vertical to pick up the speed necessary to close faster with the 109's before they could reach the bombers. I still had time to check behind to see that the squadron was following and that there was nothing on our tails. Then I saw about thirty 109's starting down after us. I figured with our speed we could still make a good attack and a quick get-away. I told the squadron to make a hard break right after hitting. Then I pulled out of the dive to come up under the gaggle of 109's. We were closing very fast, but I forced myself to keep looking behind. I picked out my 109, and bored in until I could see the black crosses. I had found this to be the best way to judge my range if the target was not yet alerted and if I wanted to be sure of a kill. The 109's were close to the bombers and concentrating on their attack.

I got hits on mine as soon as I opened fire and more hits and flashes with each burst. When I broke hard right to avoid ramming him, I saw him spiralling down smoking and with flames along the side of the fuselage. I often see that scene in my mind's eye. Somehow there is something terribly stark about that cold combination: grey fuselage, black cross, black smoke, yellow and red flame. It is brought back to me every time I see the black, yellow and red of the German flag.

By now we were in the thick of it with planes everywhere. My plan had been to pull around in a hard break to come in behind the last section of the squadron to protect their tails, and I guess that's more or less what happened. I checked and found my three wingmen with me, and then almost immediately saw a 109 on the tail of a P-51. I dived, pulled in behind and below and soon had the German fighter in my sights. I was lucky that he was concentrating on his attack. Again my first burst hit him, but almost immediately a piece flew off his plane and loomed up in front of me. I threw the stick into the corner, but not soon enough to avoid the piece of fuselage from the German plane. I felt a jerk and heard a 'chunk' as it hit my propeller.

I was amazed to find that my engine continued to operate, but we had lost our quarry. He had broken off his attack and dived for the ground. At least we had got him off the Mustang's tail.

Suddenly all was quiet and I led my flight back up. We had dropped behind and below the main bomber stream and as we caught up we saw a B-17 straggler. They were always easy meat for German fighters, so I eased over to come up behind him. Then I saw two FW190's closing on him. By this time we were above the Fortress, so were able to pull in behind and dive in to come up behind the two Germans. I selected one, but before I could close, he flipped into a tight break. I immediately followed — but maybe not quite fast or tight enough. It had been a long time since a German fighter had stayed around for a dog-fight, and we believed the P-51 could out-turn the 190 anyway. That day I learned the hard way. I suddenly realised the 190 was gaining on me in the turn. And yet I was fighting it around as tight as I could. The gravity was pulling my oxygen mask down from my nose. My breath was coming in gasps and gulps and still that spinner of the sinister 190 crept up. I thought he must have enough deflection to hit me and I pulled tighter and felt my plane judder and buck on the edge of a stall. He was firing now, and would soon be hitting. In my moment of need, I dropped my right hand to the flap lever beside me and dropped just a few degrees of flap. Miraculously the plane stopped its bucking and I pulled out of the line of fire. Immediately the 190 dived for the deck in the usual Luftwaffe evasive action and I was after him.

But now something strange happened. Normally a P-51 could at least stay with a 190 in a dive, and maybe catch him — at least when he pulled out. But here was my 190 pulling away from me as if I was standing still. Then it came to me: 'Idiot' — the flaps were still on. As I took them off, the plane picked up speed. We were hurtling down in a vertical dive. But, although it had only been a few seconds, my 190 was gone. Then I spotted him again, in a shallower dive, but now three Mustangs were behind him. They were firing, and maybe hitting, but they weren't closing. I had the advantage from my vertical dive and was able to cut across and close slowly. I didn't get to within range until we were almost on the deck. I checked the fuel gauge and knew I should have turned for home ten minutes before. What was more the 190 was streaking eastwards. I closed until I was at about 300 to 250 yards — beyond my preferred range, especially when he was jerking and evading. I fired one burst and then another. Little puffs of smoke floated back from the 190. I gave another burst, but it was only for a second. I was out of ammunition! I broke away and headed for home with my three flight members. They too had shot their ammunition and were as low on gas as I.

I nursed my plane back on the deck, just pulling up in time to identify Orfordness on the East Coast and land with empty tanks and a damaged propeller at Martlesham Heath.

I realised I was lucky to be back but it seemed a long way to go for a victory. So when the RAF officer in the mess asked what we'd been doing that day I just said, 'Nothing much.'

So I was surprised some time later to receive a communication which read, in part:

For extraordinary heroism in action with the enemy. On 6th March 1944, Major Goodson while leading a squadron of fighter airplanes furnishing protection to bombers, attacked a force of more than eight enemy fighters despite the fact that they had the protection of 20 to 30 fighters acting as top cover. In this encounter, Major Goodson destroyed one enemy plane. In spite of his unfavourable combat position he engaged and damaged another enemy fighter. Although his own airplane was damaged by flying pieces of this enemy plane, he attacked and fought another enemy plane until his ammunition was exhausted. Again on 23rd March . . . .

It was the citation for the Distinguished Service Cross.

Still later, I was intrigued to read in General Adolf Galland's book under the caption *'Von Mustangs Nach Hause Gejagdt'* ('Chased home by Mustangs') an account of an attack on a B-17 straggler by himself and Trautloft near Magdeburg. While Galland attacked the B-17, Trautloft reported a Mustang attack and stated that his guns were jammed forcing him to break off combat. Galland then describes the end of his combat as follows:

I simply fled. Diving with open throttle, I tried to escape the pursuing Mustangs, which were firing wildly. Direction East towards Berlin. The tracer bullets came closer and closer.

As my FW190 threatened to disintegrate and as I had only a small choice of those possibilities which the rules of the game allow in such harassing situations, I did something which had already saved my life twice during the Battle of Britain. I fired simply everything I had into the blue in front of me. It had the desired effect on my pursuers, who suddenly saw the smoke which the shells had left behind coming towards them. They probably thought that they had met the first fighter to fire backwards or that a second attacking German fighter was behind them. My trick succeeded, for they did a right-hand climbing turn and disappeared.*

It was on the 8th March Berlin raid that the Gentile-Godfrey team gave a supreme example of how they could work together. We took up our escort of the bombers as usual as they reached the outskirts of Berlin. As we drew ahead of them, we saw the green flares asking for help from us, and twenty to thirty 109's preparing for a head-on attack. 336 was the nearest squadron so we attacked immediately. As usual, during those Berlin days, there were about fifty 109's flying top cover. Their job was to deal with

---

*   *The First and The Last*, Methuen, 1955. Translated by Mervyn Savill.

the fighters while their buddies were hitting the bombers. I called for cover from the other two squadrons as I was diving into the attack.

We were soon in a swirling dog-fight. Gentile and Godfrey both got on the tail of two 109's. Gentile said, 'OK, I'll cover you!' and then: 'Give him more!'

Godfrey's 109 rolled over and the pilot baled out.

Then Gentile continued after the other 109 while Godfrey gave him cover. Gentile closed to 75 yards dead astern, and shot the German out of the sky.

'Johnnie, give me cover. There's another at two o'clock.'

'I'm with you!' from Godfrey.

Don got this one in a tight turn, and the German baled out.

'OK Johnnie, there are two more at 1 o'clock. See them?'

'Yep.'

'You take the one on the right. I'll take the one on the left.'

'Right!'

They were able to sneak up on these two from behind and below, and blast them from short range. Both 109's went down burning. As they climbed back up to the bombers, Johnnie's sharp eyes caught sight of a 109 coming in on Gentile.

'Break! Break starboard!' he yelled.

They both broke into him and he whizzed past them head-on. As they came out of their turn they saw that the 190 had turned back into them and was again coming at them head-on.

'Johnnie, you break right, I'll break left.'

That way one of them would probably end up on the Jerry's tail. After the break, the German had had enough, and dived for the deck; but Godfrey was after him with Gentile not far behind.

Johnnie caught up with him as he pulled out of his dive at 500 feet. He gave him a telling burst, but then had to call on Gentile: 'You take him, Don, I'm out of ammo.'

Gentile finished the job. They had shot down six between them, and Johnnie had got the five he needed to become an official ace with one to spare. He had planned to be an ace by his twenty-first birthday, and he just made it.

During March the Group destroyed 156 enemy aircraft and damaged 60. It was a record for any group. What was more important, the bombers who recorded their most successful missions, also had a much lower percentage of losses. On the way home, if we spotted a lone bomber straggler, we always dropped down to nurse him home, while the crew waved, blew us kisses and went down on their knees in a salaam in thanks. Sometimes they went out of their way to get their grateful message back to us.

'Black Snake' Peterson got his nickname from his dark lean features, wiry frame and his pride in his Indian blood. He'd been around since the RAF days, not building up a big score, but always there when needed, doing a steady, reliable job; but to Staff Sergeant Ed Johnson of the 306th Bombardment Group, he's one of the war's greatest heroes. After over a year in prison camp, he insisted on writing this official combat report:

On 29th March 1944 I was flying as left waist gunner on a 1st Division B-17 raid to Brunswick. Between Brunswick and Hanover, our formation was attacked by about 60 Focke-Wulf 190's and Me109's. All members of the crew up forward were killed. We went into a dive and dropped out of formation.

Twelve 190's were continuing their attacks as I baled out. I opened my chute too soon, at 20,000 feet, and saw the ensuing action. The 190's were still firing at our plane when I saw a red-nosed P-51 (Peterson) dive over the tail of the Fort, close to point blank range on a 190 and cause it to blow up immediately. The plane caught fire and the left wing came off. The 190 pilot did not get out. At this time there were still several members of my crew trying to bale out. They owe their lives to the fierceness of Captain Peterson's attack.

Immediately after Captain Peterson shot down his second 190, I saw a third 190 fire at him at a range of 100 yards. This lucky shot must have put out the controls, for I saw the P-51 shudder and wallow badly ... Captain Peterson baled out ... That night I was put in jail in Hildesheim along with Captain Peterson ...

Captain Peterson's action saved the three men besides myself who baled out successfully ... He attacked 12 enemy aircraft alone, with full knowledge that his chance of survival was very small.

Yes, Pete probably knew his chances were slim. Two fighter planes together had a fighting chance against overwhelming odds; but one on his own needed more than just skill, he needed a hell of a lot of luck.

One who had it was 'Cowboy' Megura. On three Berlin missions, the Cowboy had found himself alone, and come back every time with two destroyed in the air, and more on the ground, with a few trains thrown in for good measure. The third Berlin do on 8th March was typical for Megura. Clark took 334 Squadron to help a bomber group under attack. Right away they were in the thick of it. Jim Clark shot down one 109 and the Cowboy got another, but he had to chase him from 33,000 feet down to 8,000. He shook another 109 off his tail in a tight skidding turn.

He then shot down one of a gaggle of 190's attacking a lone Fort straggler. The pilot baled out right over Berlin. Megura then spotted a group of 190's preparing to land on an airfield on the outskirts of Berlin. He simply joined them in the circuit and lined up on one of the unsuspecting Germans coming in to land. Before he could fire, he was bounced by two 190's who had recognised the Mustang. The Cowboy broke into them and came on around to hit the 109 again just as it was landing. But the two 190's came around again, and he had to break off to confront them. They chased him eastwards but he finally gave them the slip by twisting and turning among the buildings of Berlin. He turned back and headed west, taking out a train as he left the outskirts of the sprawling city. On the way home, he was jumped by six Germans, and again got away by dodging among the hills and forests. He attacked a Ju88, but ran out of ammo before it went down. He zoomed past the bomber, saw that one engine had been shot out, thumbed his nose at the pilot, dodged and jinked his way through the murderous flak, and somehow got home. Jim Clark, like most squadron leaders, discouraged maverick loners, but it was typical of him that he put the Cowboy in for the Distinguished Service Cross.

Megura's luck still held, particularly on one of his last missions. At 30,000 feet north-east of Berlin he was attacked and badly hit by an American P-38 Lightning which mistook the Mustang for a 109. The Cowboy tried to bale out, but couldn't release his cockpit canopy. Even this turned out to be lucky. His engine was shot out, but he had enough altitude to glide to neutral Sweden. A few months later he was back at Debden, giving his crew-chief hell for the jammed canopy, and clamouring to be put on the next mission.

I remember 21st March 1944. On that day the Group destroyed twenty-one enemy aircraft, and Jim Clark was awarded a well-deserved Silver Star. It was also my 23rd birthday.

Jim Clark and I were convinced, that although strafing planes on the ground was far more dangerous than attacking them in the air, it was far more effective, and was indeed essential if we were to knock out the Luftwaffe before the invasion. In particular, they had to be driven from their bases in France.

Jim was a quiet, handsome giant from New York. At that time, he was not only commanding officer of 334 Squadron, he was also Deputy Group Commander under Blakeslee. It was therefore natural that he should plan and lead the first, destructive, long range, low level mass attack.

The Group flew into France skimming the roof-tops, spread out to cover an area at least 100 miles wide. We swept down from the Channel coast all the way to the Pyrenees and the Spanish border, turning to streak across Southern and Central France, coming out by way of Paris and Northern France. In addition to the twenty-one planes destroyed, countless other planes, trains and airfields were damaged.

Seven of our planes were shot down. Godfrey's plane was hit, Jim Dye was severely wounded, and 'Georgia' Wynn, whose first three kills had been with the RAF in Malta, had the belly of his plane ripped open by scraping it on a flag-pole, but they made it back.

Jim's citation read:

... For gallantry in action over enemy occupied Europe on 21st March 1944. Knowing of a concentration of enemy aircraft deep in occupied France, Col. Clark asked for and received permission to lead a fighter group against this heavily defended military installation. He personally planned the entire mission and selected the routes and targets on the longest sweep into enemy territory yet made by American fighter aircraft from bases in England. . . .

The importance of the raid was that it was the first of many strafing missions, including one in which we destroyed over 100 planes on the ground; and the result was seen on the morning of 6th June when the Luftwaffe could only put two planes up to attack the invasion landings: 'Pips' Priller, CO of JG26 and his wingman.

Jim Clark was a worthy deputy to Blakeslee, although in many ways they were complete opposites. Blakeslee was rough and tough, often lost his temper, drank heavily and swore frequently. Jim was every inch the gentleman, so quiet I never saw him lose his cool; so modest he protested that he was unworthy of the Distinguished Service Cross. But they had one thing in common: they had the respect and even devotion, of every man in their command, all of whom were not only willing, but eager, to follow them to hell and back.

This was true of the other squadron commanders as well. They inspired their men by their experience, professionalism and sense of duty. They led them, not by preaching or directives, but by example. They never pulled rank: they didn't need to. In fact, only the new pilots ever addressed us as 'Major' or 'Colonel'. The rest of us had been through too much together. When someone's screaming for you to get a swarm of 109's off his tail, you don't say, 'Call me Sir!'

Freddy Glover had been a problem to his superiors as a ferry pilot in the RCAF. To get rid of him they acceded to his persistent request to be transferred to the Fourth Group. When he met Blakeslee in the bar, the Colonel raised his eyebrows when he heard that Glover had no experience on single-engined fighters.

'I think I can fly a plane as good as anyone I can see around here!'

It was blasphemy! This unblooded lieutenant was surrounded by most of the leading aces of the US Air Force.

There was an electric silence.

Blakeslee and Glover glared at one another.

'Have a drink!' said Blakeslee.

'I've had a drink!' said Glover.

In any other group, with any other CO, Glover's flying career would have been over. In the Fourth, Glover survived to become Blakeslee's closest friend, an aggressive fighter pilot with twenty-four victories, and eventually my successor as commanding officer of 336 Squadron.

Glover's other close friend was 'Red Dog' Norley. Although he had a shock of red hair, his nickname came from his addiction to that form of poker. He started off as the Group jester with an inexhaustible sense of humour, but in the air he became more and more serious. Eventually he became CO of 334 Squadron with sixteen victories.

Douane 'Bee' Beeson was the opposite. To look at this slight boyish-looking youngster, you'd think he was one of those naive innocents who would never survive the first few missions, and indeed, when he first joined 71 Eagle Squadron in the summer of 1942, they dismissed him as an eager beaver and a pest.

In fact, he had a steely determination to destroy more Huns than anyone else, and, like Millikan and Garrison, schooled himself night and day in tactics and deflection shooting. He was one of the few who had a vicious hatred of the Germans, and soon had a score of twenty-five destroyed, rivalling Gentile.

If he hadn't been shot down by flak while strafing an airfield on 5th April 1944, he would probably have achieved his goal of becoming America's leading ace — but then, I suppose you could have said that a dozen of us who would probably never have been shot down by a German fighter, but lost the gamble with flak.

That 5th April was a sweet and sour day for the Group. Once again we showed that we had gained air supremacy over Germany; once again we proved the terrible effectiveness of ground strafing by fighter aircraft; but once again, we saw the price we had to pay. The Group destroyed fifty planes on the ground and seriously damaged thirty-eight more. That was a substantial part of the Luftwaffe's strength in the West at that time.

The price was the loss of Beeson and four others. One was Allen Bunte from Eustis, Florida, who always reminded me of the actor Ray Bolger when he played the scarecrow in *The Wizard of Oz*. Bunte narrowly escaped being blown apart by flak, burned to death in his plane, killed by crashing into a lake, and finally drowning, all in the space of a few seconds. While strafing an airfield, his plane was hit by heavy flak, and burst into flames. He was too low to bail out, but just as the heat was getting unbearable, he spotted a lake and made a dive for it. The crash on the water knocked him out, but the shock of the cold water as the plane sank revived him. The oxygen mask may have helped him to avoid drowning while he struggled out of the cockpit. He managed to inflate his life-jacket before collapsing.

Bob Hobert wasn't so lucky. I had led the squadron down on an airfield near Berlin, and continued to zig-zag between the smoke of the burning planes until I was sure we had destroyed them all. Before leaving, I counted twenty-five burning wrecks, of which Gentile had got five and I six; but Hobert reported being hit by flak. I looked over his plane but couldn't see much damage. Indeed he kept up pretty well with us on the way home. At the Dutch coast I asked him if he wanted to risk the long hop over the North Sea. He didn't hesitate.

'Temperature's going up a bit, and I can't get full power, but I think I can make it.'

'OK,' I said. 'I'll stay with you.'

About half-way across, things took a sudden turn for the worse, and finally the temperature went over the top, and his engine seized. He bailed out. I made sure the Air-Sea Rescue people had a good fix on him, and headed for home. Even if it took a while for him to be picked up, it was April, and not all that cold. I figured he'd be OK, but as soon as I landed, I cut my way through the excitement of the ground personnel's urgent questioning, and the pilot's flustered, disjointed replies, and made for the telephone. The Air-Sea Rescue launch hadn't picked him up yet, and a sea was running. I knew that meant they'd have trouble finding Hobert in his little inflatable dinghy. As I ran through the dispersal hut the Intelligence Officers, Benjamin and MacCarteney wanted my combat report.

'I'm going to look for Bob Hobert!' Some of the pilots were so exhausted, their ground crews had had to lift them out of the cockpit, stretch them out on the grass, and massage them before they could trust themselves to walk. Dick Braley, who was prone to back trouble struggled to his feet and tried to crawl back into his plane. Benjie Benjamin climbed onto the wing of my plane as I was strapping myself in.

'You'll kill yourself!' He looked at me so earnestly, I had to laugh.

'Probably', I said, 'but not right now. I've got something to do — and before it gets dark.'

The blast from my propeller blew Benjie sliding down the wing.

I think if all the planes had already been refuelled, the whole squadron would have followed me. As it was, I had a section of four. I had noted my compass heading when I had left Hobert, and I knew exactly where I had crossed in over the English coast, so it was easy for me to fly back.

After spiralling down to about 2,000 feet, I spotted the yellow speck surrounded by the colouring which could be released to help an aerial search. We circled until the Air-Sea Rescue launch picked him up.

It was a little after midnight when I walked into the bar. There were still some diehards rehashing the events of the day. Grover Hall, the Public Relations Officer, and some of the Intelligence Officers, including Benjie were hanging on hoping to pick up more information.

'Benjie,' I said, 'I'm sorry I left you a little abruptly this evening.'

'No, it was my fault; I shouldn't have interfered, I was just worried about you.'

'I seem to be able to take care of myself,' I said. 'It's the others I can't take care of.'

They loyally protested. 'You're the most conscientious CO there is. You're always putting your pilots first. Look at what you did for Hobert today!'

'That's what I am looking at. I've just been on the phone. He was suffering badly from exposure when they picked him up. He never regained consciousness. He died half an hour ago.'

Finally, after all the rumours and false alarms, it began to look as if the invasion was really going to happen. We had a meeting at

Debden with Eisenhower, Doolittle, Spaatz, Kepner and all the brass to discuss our role on D-Day. It was an eye-opener to me. I realised why Ike had been chosen to be supreme commander over more senior generals. It was a lesson in leadership and motivation. He went around the table and asked for everyone's input. No officer was too junior, no comments were too inappropriate not to be listened to. Only once did Eisenhower cut anyone off. When someone said: 'Ike, I've got a great idea,' he replied, 'It's too late for great ideas. We now have to make sure that the plans we have work.'

After the meeting, Ike asked me to accompany them back to HQ, I found myself sharing the back seat of a command car with the great man himself. Having led the squadron on a number of successful strafing missions, and having destroyed fifteen enemy aircraft on the ground myself, I was considered to be somewhat of an expert on the effectiveness of fighters attacking specific ground targets deep in enemy territory by strafing or low-level pinpoint bombing. It was the theory of the Stuka, but without its lack of speed and vulnerability. He was intrigued by the possibilities. He also asked who it was that had developed the close cooperation between land forces and air forces that had given Germany its early victories. I reminded him that it was Ernst Udet, the World War I ace, but that he had learned most of it when he visited the United States in the thirties, and had even been allowed to purchase a Curtiss dive bomber which went to Germany to become the inspiration for the Ju87 'Stuka'.

My main interest was to take advantage of this unique opportunity to find out from the one man who had all the plans and strategy in his head, just when the war would be over. A lull came in the conversation, but I hesitated. It would be stupid and naive simply to blurt out, 'General, when is the war going to be over.'

But he beat me to it. He rubbed his bald head wearily and said: 'Major, you've been close to things here for some time, when do you think this damned war will be over?'

Mac allowed the boogie-woogie to die out, finished his beer and closed the piano. As a youngster, Pierce McKennon couldn't make up his mind whether to follow in his father's footsteps and become a doctor, or follow his mother's advice and become a classical concert pianist. He won a music scholarship to the University of Arkansas.

But there must have been another side to Mac's character. He dropped Mendelssohn and Bach to enlist in the US Air Force, and, when they turned him down as unfit, went to Canada to join the RCAF. When he arrived at Debden, he endeared himself to one and all by playing the fool to Deacon Hively's brilliantly solemn, and howlingly funny 'sermons'. He was always ready to play the piano into the small hours of the morning; but here too there had been a change: Beethoven and Mozart had been dethroned by Cab Calloway and the current leaders of jazz and swing. Mac could transpose any melody into a rolling, rumbling Boogie-woogie. He could always transform gloom, fear and grief into relaxation, happiness and hope. Our warmest memories of Debden were those precious evenings, each one of which could have been our last, with Mac, a cigarette dangling from his lower lip, pounding away till the beer in his mug perched on the piano was slopping over the top.

The serious side of Mac's character gradually made itself felt. After many narrow escapes, including being shot down over occupied France, and getting back to England, Mac took over as CO of 335 Squadron. He had nineteen destroyed, and more experience than anyone still left in the squadron, with the exception of Red Dog Norley. He also had a problem pilot in his outfit. George Green had been grounded time and again for misdemeanours both on the ground and in the air. His final crime was committed while flying number two to Red Dog Norley. They bounced two 109's. Norley ordered Green to stick with him and give cover while they took one after the other, but when Red Dog had shot his down, he found himself alone. Then he spotted Green way down on the clouds, having goofed off after Jerry number 2, and lost him. The 109 was positioning himself for an attack on Green, and it took all Norley's experience and skill to chase him off, and join up with Green.

Red Dog wanted Green transferred out of the squadron, and Mac was inclined to agree. It was the classic dilemma for a squadron commander: how to deal with a keen, aggressive and capable pilot who was not amenable to squadron discipline.

Mac, perhaps thinking of Kid Hofer, or Don Gentile in his early days, decided to give him one more chance. He put him on his own wing on 18th March 1945, on a mission which ended up strafing Prenzlau airfield near Berlin. This time the flak got McKennon. He was able to pull up to 4,000 feet and managed to bale out, fighting his way out of the stricken plane. He parachuted down into the same field in which his plane had crashed.

Green had stuck close to his leader, and now saw him on the ground disentangling himself from his parachute. Green now made a typical decision. He would land in the rough field and pick Mac up. He knew it had been tried before, but only once successfully, and that by a P-47 with its roomy cockpit, and from a smooth field. He also knew that, as a result, it was automatically a court-martial offence. There could be only three possible results of his action: court-martial and disgrace, captivity in a German POW camp, or death. Green didn't hesitate.

He judged the wind direction from the smoke coming up from the burning plane. As he started in with wheels and flaps down he saw German soldiers and dogs heading for Mac.

'Take those Germans out,' he yelled.

One of the circling Mustangs came in, guns flashing. The surviving Germans scrambled back to cover.

Green came around again, dragging the plane in with full flap, and dropped it over the fence into the bumpy field. Mac ran to meet him, and clambered onto the wing. Green put on the parking brake, clambered out onto the other wing to get rid of his flying gear and parachute. It was the only way they could both squeeze into the tiny cockpit. Mac squeezed his 6 feet 2 inches frame into the seat. Green climbed in and sat on his lap. To get the canopy closed, Green's face was pressed against the gun-sight. Mac's face was pressed against Green's back.

Green had to do the flying. He took the plane back to the far edge of the field, stood on the brakes, opened up the engine to maximum power, and released the brakes.

The plane sprang forward and bounced and lurched over the rough field. He dragged it off after only about 300 yards. It fell back down, bounced hard, staggered back into the air, and wobbled over the trees at the end of the field. They had made it!

They still had plenty of problems. Mac was in agony from the weight of Green's body which pressed his legs against the sides and bottom of the cockpit.

They ran into fog, and, since neither of them could see the instrument panel, Green had to take it up to 15,000 feet. He was able to plug in his own oxygen tube, but Mac didn't have one. Finally Green felt Mac's body go limp. Squeezing his head around, he saw that he'd passed out. Taking off his mask, he placed it over Mac's nose and mouth. When he came to, Green took the mask back to keep himself from passing out.

They somehow made it back to Debden and landed. Now Mac was confronted by a worse problem: he had to have Green court-martialled.

I was never able to check with Mac as to what happened. When I got out of prison camp, he'd made the final flight when his luck had run out. I do know that there was no court-martial. I asked a high-ranking friend of mine in Headquarters, how come.

He said: 'Yeah! I heard that story, but everyone knows it's impossible for two pilots to get into a P-51 cockpit.'

'Sure it's possible,' I said. 'It happened.'

'Whose side are you on?' he asked.

We had good generals.

When they asked Green why he had done it, he shrugged his shoulders and said, 'I figured I owed the guy a favour.'

Meanwhile Gentile and Godfrey's free-wheeling heroes' tour of the United States was running out of steam, and they were posted to training assignments. Don Gentile seemed to enjoy the publicity and adulation, but Johnnie Godfrey became more and more frustrated. He requested to be transferred back to the Group to continue his combat career, and pestered everyone until it was granted.

Johnnie was delighted to get away from the States and back to Debden. Just before leaving he gave an interview in which he expressed his feelings about Stateside training restrictions.

The story read in part:

Capt John T. Godfrey, Rhode Island's leading fighter ace, is 'burned up' by what he calls America's present policy of 'spoon-feeding' its thousands of future pilots.

'I stood six days of their constant silly restrictions ... then I said to hell with it and went back home,' he told a United Press reporter.

'They won't let the kids fly when it's cloudy ... I can remember taking off in England when you jumped straight into overcast and stayed that way up to 30,000 feet or more,' Godfrey added.

He expressed the opinion that a kid-glove policy by 'brass hats' in this country is endangering the lives of all youngsters now in training camps ...'

If he had still been in the States when this hit the fan, he would probably have been court-martialled. As it was, he kept one jump ahead of them; or perhaps the 'European brass' protected him from the 'US brass'. In any case, Johnnie flew every mission, and announced his intention to take his score to fifty.

He started off on 5th August 1944 in style by blowing up a 109 when he was so close that the explosion damaged the prop and blackened the paintwork on his plane as he flew through the blast. He then destroyed three more planes on the ground, damaged another three and attacked eight locomotives — all in one mission.

But by this time, the Battle of Germany had been won, and Johnnie had to find his victims on the ground. Freddie Glover was CO of 336 by now. As they searched for German aircraft in the Berlin area, they spotted 109's on an airfield. Freddie took them down, and destroyed a taxiing 109. Godfrey took out another. As they zoomed low over the airfield, they flew through a curtain of flak. Johnnie's windscreen was shattered and a glass sliver cut through his helmet into his forehead. Worse still, the glycol cooling system was hit.

He pulled up to 2,000 feet, and saw his cylinder head temperature starting to climb. Glover heard him say, 'Afraid I'll have to bail out!'

Freddie saw that Johnnie had been hit in the coolant system, but he remembered something else; he'd been on that mission when I had nursed my plane back to England by pumping the primer to flood the engine and keep the temperature down.

'Don't jump, Johnnie, don't jump! Grab your primer handle and pump like hell!'

The temperature stopped climbing. They started for home along the old trail: Hannover, Bielefeld, The Ruhr, dodging flak over each city; but Johnnie suffered the same agonies as I had. The constant priming wore through the leather gloves, and by the time he reached Amsterdam, his hand was a bleeding mess.

'I'm not going to be able to make it across the drink. I'd better bail here.'

'Don't give up, Johnnie, we'll stick with you. Give it a try.'

But finally Godfrey could continue no longer. He figured that even if the engine didn't seize up through over-heating, he would run out of gas before reaching the English coast. He went over to the emergency channel and called for Air-Sea Rescue: 'Mayday, Mayday, I'll have to jump!'

'Just keep sending so we can get a fix on you,' they replied.

'Sorry, I have to get out before I get lower.' He had lost too many friends who had left it too late, and died in the fall into the sea before their chute could open.

His canopy had already been blown off by the flak. He disconnected his oxygen tube and his earphones, undid his sea harness, and stood up in the cockpit. Just before he dived out he took one last look ahead — and there it was: the low-lying East Coast of Essex!

Even Johnnie's luck couldn't hold indefinitely. By August 1944, the long-range fighters of the Eighth Air Force, were encountering fewer Luftwaffe planes in the air. That month, for instance, the Fourth shot down only 28 against 207 in April. They therefore stepped up the destruction of the German Air Force on the ground.

On 24th August 336 Squadron spotted a number of Ju52 transport planes on an airfield deep in Germany. Godfrey destroyed four on his first pass, bringing his score to thirty-six, at that time the highest in the US Air Force. But he had made too long a run. As he pulled up at the end of it, he heard the deadly 'crump', felt his plane knocked sideways, and smelt the cordite of the explosion. He knew that the plane had had it. He continued to attack, trailing a plume of black smoke from his dying engine. Finally the plane stalled out and crashed in a field. Johnnie was knocked out, but not badly hurt. He joined the thousands of us already in prison camp.

In ancient Greek tragedies, the hero's own pride or 'Hubris' leads inevitably to his own destruction. When we returned from the last mission Gentile flew before going back to the States, there was an incident that should have been a warning.

Before the mission he asked me: 'Goody, you've learned the knack of real low flying. That's how you get away with your strafing missions. What's your secret?'

I should have told him it was nothing but experience. Foolishly, I tried to be funny. I said: 'Well, Don, I guess you go as low as you dare, and then take her one foot lower.'

Humour was lost on Gentile. He must have taken me literally. When we came back from the mission. I saw the reason for his questions. The press corps and their cameramen were lined up on the far edge of the field. Don decided to give them their money's worth. He came zooming in low straight at the photographers. The field at Debden was slightly higher in the centre. Don came in low over the perimeter track, but didn't pull up enough to clear the knoll. There was a horrified gasp from the onlookers as the propeller of his plane gouged into the ground and the plane crashed in the middle of the field.

Don climbed out unscathed, until he was summoned by Blakeslee. The CO's dressing down cowed even Gentile. He called him a spoiled show-off, and much more which hasn't been preserved for posterity.

Gentile was being built up as America's greatest ace, so he got away with it. He and Godfrey went off to the States and were fêted as they deserved; but as the PR campaign ran out of steam, more and more often they ran foul of the flying restrictions and military discipline back home.

Thinking it over much later, I guessed it might have been the way he would have wanted it. Above all else, he had to be the star, and like a shooting star he had a brief meteoric career. While taking off on a training flight, he crashed and was killed.

His old buddies were genuinely sad. We may have laughed at the euphoric press releases, but we admired him as a great natural pilot.

And we loved him for himself. You couldn't help it.

CHAPTER NINE

Borrowed Time

The scene was changing.

There were very few of the old gang left, and in July 1944 most of the faces in the officers' mess were strange to me. Don Blakeslee was still there, but I found myself leading the Group more and more often, as there were fewer and fewer of the experienced old-timers.

Even the war was changing. The Air Force and the Russians were no longer fighting alone. The Allied armies were breaking out of the Normandy beach-head and making steady progress in the Mediterranean theatre.

And the air war was changing. The air armadas were enormous. Sometimes the streams of bombers and escorting fighters seemed to stretch from the bases in East Anglia all the way to the target, which, now that the invasion beach-head had been secured, was often Berlin.

The depleted Luftwaffe fighter force, stretched between the Russian front, the southern front and the Western or Home front fought as gamely as before, but their relatively small numbers couldn't stop the growing overwhelming mass of aircraft. So, there were now missions where even we in the Fourth Group, almost always at the target end of the fighter escort relay, didn't encounter any enemy fighters; but when we did see them, we still had to admire them. They had to run the gauntlet of risks, first from the umbrella of escorting fighters above, below and all around the bomber stream. Then from the criss-cross fire from the gunners in the bombers who sprayed out their stream of tracer bullets like firemen using hoses. Because of the formation of the bombers in their boxes, an attacking fighter could find himself in the firing range of twenty or more machine-guns. And, as the German fighter broke off his attack, added to the danger from the hail of bullets was the ever-present risk of collision as he cut in and out of the bomber stream.

All these dangers were magnified when the fighters made a head-on attack. I once led the squadron down to break up a frontal attack by German fighters and found myself following a 109 through a bomber formation. The stately procession of bombers which usually seemed almost motionless, suddenly became a maelstrom of hurtling juggernauts. As soon as I slipped past one, another was rushing down on me, followed by another and another. When I thought I saw a gap, I simply jammed right rudder, and shoved the stick into the front right corner and prayed. When I opened my eyes, I was alone. I looked up and back and saw far above me, looking like little minnows in a stream, the last boxes of the bomber formations. I had been lucky.

In his outstanding book *Fighter Aces of the Luftwaffe* Colonel Ray Toliver quotes from the report of Helmut Lipfert of JG52 on one of his missions against some 120 bombers with fighter escort. He led nine Me109's in three head-on attacks on the bombers. After the first attack, he had five of his nine left; after the second, three left, and after the third, the only survivors were his wingman, Tamen, and himself. They returned to base only because they were out of ammunition. They each claimed one B-17 destroyed. I think this was no unusual episode, but typical of the Luftwaffe's performance.

When we first saw German fighters crashing into bombers as the result of a head-on attack, I thought they had been less lucky than I. There was even a B-17 that got back to England with its tail almost slashed off by a 109. It wasn't until after the war that I met Colonel Hajo Herrmann. After piloting bombers against England in the Battle of Britain and elsewhere he organised and led the Wild Boar night fighters who flew through their own flak and used day fighter tactics to inflict terrible losses on the RAF night bombers, including fifty-six downed in one Berlin raid. He then organized JG300 'Rammkommando Elbe', an élite corps of specially armoured FW190's dedicated to stopping the four-engined US bombers even if it meant ramming them. This was no Kamikaze group. The pilots were trained to aim their planes at the bombers, and bail out at the last minute. This involved staying with the plane till the last split second, crouched on the seat, ready to be catapulted out when the plane plunged into its victim at a closing speed of close to 1,000 mph.

However there were two much greater dangers to the Allied Air Forces during this crucial time in mid-1944. The first was the twin-jet Me262. At the briefing at which top brass and the intelligence officers told us about this revolutionary fighter, it was obvious that they were seriously worried. The jet era had started and we had no entry. The 262 was faster than any Allied fighter. It could outclimb them and outdive them. It could carry more armament and more protective armour plating; and its two jet engines were less vulnerable than the single glycol-cooled engine of the Me109, or Mustang.

Hitler had another secret weapon even more potentially dangerous than the Me262. The Me163 was rocket-powered and therefore probably faster than the 262. It would be in and out of the bomber formation so fast, no fighter could touch it, and even the gunners in the bombers wouldn't have time to concentrate their fire on it. Not only its speed, but also its diminutive size made it an impossible target. It was rocket-propelled up to the normal flying height of the bombers, between 25,000 and 30,000 feet; it would shoot down one or two and then, its rocket fuel expended, dive back down to land at its base. It was smaller than any other fighter, with short, stubby wings, so, in addition to being incredibly fast and hard to hit, it could be mass-produced much more easily, using less material, than the Me262. We estimated that, if the Germans switched their production lines from current production, they could produce 500 Me262's and 500 Me163's a month.

Since each new fighter would be capable of shooting down at least one US plane per mission, we were looking at losses in excess of 1,000 planes per mission, and therefore the end of Allied air supremacy on which victory depended. We couldn't know that Hitler was more concerned with revenge on the enemy than protection of the German cities and therefore gave priority to V-1's and V-2's, and the bomber version of the Me262. To us it seemed that Germany had an enormous technological advance over us, and was about to take full advantage of it long before we could catch up with them.

By the beginning of July the Normandy beach-heads were firmly established and we had established air supremacy over France. The short-range Spitfires and Typhoons of the RAF, and the fighters and bombers of the US Tactical Air Force were giving air cover and ground support to the armies, and the roads of Northern France were lined with the wreckage of German transport and armour. So we of the strategic Eighth Air Force went back to the long-range bombing of targets deep within Germany.

It was on a Berlin raid that we first saw an Me262. I had taken the squadron down on a gaggle of 109's about to make a head-on attack on the leading box of bombers. We broke them up and dived after them. I was able to catch the last one and 'clobbered' him from about 200 yards dead astern. Like most fighter planes shot down on both sides, he never knew what hit him. We would have gone on down after the other 109's, but that would have taken us away from our main task of protecting the bombers. I broke hard right and up, calling on the others to follow.

We were just coming up to the level of the bombers and were swinging around to sweep past them and clear the way ahead over the target area when we saw it. It came from above and behind and sliced down and through the fighter escort and the bomber formations as if they were standing still. Without slackening speed, it lined up behind a B-17 which immediately fell out of formation, trailing smoke, as the Me262 raced by to disappear far ahead of us. It was all over in seconds. All any of us could do was gape. For all we knew, it knocked off another B-17 before it zoomed away, leaving us all far behind.

Then came the day when the bombers were to hit Stettin, north-east of Berlin almost on the Baltic coast. It sounded like a routine mission and one I could sit out. I had flown every mission for the last month or so and maybe I did need a rest.

The trouble with that Stettin mission was that the really experienced pilots had either been rotated to the States or shot down. Emerson was the most senior and yet it seemed only yesterday that he had joined the squadron. Still, I'd always advocated training on the job, and here was a good chance to put it into practice.

I went and sat through the briefing. The mission was routine, escorting the bombers over the target area. Only one thing was a little out of the ordinary. The line showing our return route passed over Peenemünde which we knew to be the centre of Germany's rocket research.

Back at dispersal, Bob Gilbert, my crew chief looked surprised and hurt, as he leaned against our Mustang VFB. It was his as much as mine, and he was proud of its polished silver finish, its diving eagle ensign which he had painted on, along with the neat rows of thirty-two swastikas.

'She's all ready to go,' he said.

I shook my head. I watched as one propeller after another started to turn and each engine spluttered into life.

Then suddenly Emerson cut his engine and the others followed suit. I ran over to his plane and clambered up on the wing. He pulled back his perspex hood and took off his helmet.

'Five minutes delay!' he said.

'How do you feel?'

'What worries me is how the others feel. If I don't feel good myself I might let them down.'

It was then I realised that every pilot in the squadron was watching.

'Okay', I said. 'Yellow section is one short. You take it! I'll take the squadron.'

I ran back to my plane, jumped in, started up and taxied out to lead the squadron.

As I had expected, it was a run-of-the-mill mission. As usual, we formed up over Saffron Walden, set course almost due east over Essex and the towns I knew so well from the air but not from the ground: Sudbury, Braintree, Ipswich and Orfordness with the sandbanks on the coast. By the time we were over the North Sea we were at our cruising altitude of about 30,000 feet and with our speed at that height it wasn't long before we were crossing the Dutch coast north of Haarlem and south of the Hook of Holland. Then in only a few minutes we crossed the Zuider Zee and on over the flat East Holland and North German territory, pinpointing ourselves as usual by the distinctive perfectly-round Dümmer Lake, north of Osnabrück and south of Bremen. Vis-

ibility was so good we could vaguely see Hannover and Braunschweig down to our right. Then, still to the right, we saw the
bombers feinting towards Berlin. Soon we saw our bomber fleet
swinging north and east. I led the squadron above and across
them to protect their flank and then swept around in front of
them as they started their bombing run.

Apparently what German fighters there were, had been protecting Berlin. There seemed to be no activity around the bombers, and soon I saw the relieving fighter escort coming in from
the west. I figured our only chance of finding German fighters
would be to drop down in the hope of spotting some diving
home from attacking the other bomber groups. I was also thinking of continuing on down to strafe those special air bases we
had not yet hit. We went down in front of the bombers which
were now heading homewards and were well protected by the
new escorting fighters. At about 20,000 feet I could just make
out the thin shape of fighters heading north well below us. I
rolled and went into a steep dive to catch them. I kept my eyes
on them with an occasional glimpse behind to make sure that
the planes behind were ours.

Because I had rolled into a steeper dive sooner than they
had, I was well ahead of them, and I was closing on the last of
the German fighters. I could see it was a 109. I could also see an
airfield ahead and knew it must be Neu Brandenburg.

Suddenly I was catching up fast and I realised he was throttling
back, entering the circuit to land. It also meant he didn't know I
was lining up on him. I waited until I estimated I was less than
200 yards behind him and closing fast. The first burst scored
hits all over him. I immediately pressed the trigger again. I was
still hitting him when I had to stomp rudder and throw the stick
forward and right to avoid ramming him. I looked back and saw
him dive straight down to explode on the deck.

I was down to about two thousand feet now. Ahead of me I
saw the airfield. Then I saw the other 109's. Two had already
landed but one was coming in to land, from the other direction,
almost head to me, but dropping fast.

I pushed the stick forward, I had to dive almost vertically to
get down to his level. He was almost on the ground, but still

slightly in front when I had to pull out of my dive or hit the ground. As I pulled back on the stick, I pressed the trigger and sprayed him as he flashed underneath me. I saw the hits rake the length of the 109, just before I pulled around into a climbing turn.

I saw him go into a ground loop and start burning. But out of the corner of my eye I glimpsed something else. It was almost an unconscious recognition; a short stubby profile, a caricature of a plane hidden in a revetment on the perimeter of the airfield.

I pulled up higher. As I turned I saw it clearly. It was an Me163.

I stayed in the turn. A number of thoughts flashed through my mind. I could call down the rest of the squadron. They would be coming in above by now. But I was already down here and I knew where the plane was. I had only used a few bursts so far and knew I had enough ammo to take it out. Most important, this must be one of their few prototypes. It was a fantastic chance.

I tightened my turn to line up on it, but by now I had to cross the airfield. Much worse I couldn't hug the ground as usual; I had to be high enough to aim over the protective walls of the revetment which were covered with sandbags and camouflage.

So far there had been no flak but the moment I started across the airfield it started. The bright balls of fire came sailing up, seeming to move slowly until close and then whizzing by. There were the little black clouds of heavier flak, with exploding flashes inside them. They were mostly above me. Automatically I was taking evasive action, weaving and jinking, stomping one rudder and then the other, skidding and side-slipping, so that the fire balls passed underneath or behind. But I always kept my eye on the target and soon my shots were slamming into the prototype as I steadied the plane. At the same moment I felt the plane shudder. I heard the crump and smelt the explosive. I felt a numbness in my right knee, and knew I was hit. But it was the plane I felt for. She was like a stricken war-horse. She tried to respond but the life-blood was ebbing. I tried to hold her up, but as I sensed her start to stall, I gently eased the stick forward. And so, tenderly and sadly I nursed her down, feeling her, caressing her, until as softly as I could, I let her settle on the rough ground. As we hit the ground I cut the switch. We bumped and skidded to a halt. Suddenly everything was quiet.

I slid back the hood, undid the seat harness and the chute and started to climb out. My right leg didn't seem to be working. I looked down. There was a lot of blood and the brown cloth of my pant leg was torn and shredded. I saw too that there was a gaping hole in the floor of the cockpit.

I hauled myself out and stood for a moment on the wing. I looked at my name and the thirty-two swastikas representing the official victories. I patted the side of the plane.

'Two more now, old friend, not bad! We went out on a high note.'

There was an incendiary device to stick in the fuel tank to blow up the plane when it went down; but by now I heard and saw the rest of the squadron coming in above me. I waved to them to shoot up old VF-B and limped off into the nearby woods. I heard the whine of the planes diving and the firing of the guns as they gave her the *coup de grâce*. Then suddenly everything was quiet.

In the few minutes after I'd been hit, I'd been able to coax the wounded plane a few miles from the airfield. That part of northern Germany was heavily wooded; but as I stumbled deeper into the trees, I saw that these woods were not like the civilised oak and beech woods of England. They were more like the northern bush of the States and Canada. The trees were fir and birch and the soil was sandy. As I crashed through the under-brush, I suddenly saw four deer bounding away; I had dropped into a completely different world.

I kept going as long as I could, and then slumped down. I looked in a bemused way at the blood seeping through the khaki fabric of my pant legs. The fur-lined flak boot had protected my leg below the knees and the bucket seat and the parachute had partly shielded my body, but the insides and backs of my legs, from above the top of the boots to the back of the thighs, were peppered with little pieces of shrapnel. That wasn't serious, but there was a numb feeling around the right knee, and a lot of blood. As I probed with my finger, I saw that a piece of flak had gone right through the fleshy underpart and come out on the other side.

I was still wearing my Mae West inflatable life jacket. I took it off and found the escape kit in the pocket. Inside was a first-aid kit and I used it as best I could.

Then I took off my oak-leaf rank ensign and my dog-tags, remembering being told by our intelligence officer once that, if I ever went down in Germany, I had a good chance of escaping because I spoke French and some German.

'Tell them you're a French worker,' he said. 'They're allowed quite a bit of freedom.'

I looked at my waterproof synthetic flight jacket and my khaki shirt and slacks, and doubted that they were what the well-dressed French worker in Germany wore. Still maybe through the International Red Cross or something, US khaki clothing got through to them. It was worth a try.

My flak boots were made so that the tops could be torn off to leave the rest looking like a pair of shoes. I decided against this. My slacks covered the tops in any case, and in this rough under-brush it would be better to roll up the pant-legs and use the protection of the boots, at least for now. Anyway, like all fighter pilots, I loved my boots, and thought they were lucky. After all, they'd protected me that day, and many times before. In any case in my state I realised I would have to keep out of sight and travel rough.

Stuck in the top of one of my boots was an air map of Germany. I pulled it out, and pinpointed Neu Brandenburg. It con-firmed what I knew. I was only some eighty miles from the Baltic Sea; and only some seventy miles across that sea was neutral Sweden. Obviously the thing to do was to head north-west to Rostock. It had to be a main port for Swedish ships and even if I couldn't smuggle myself on to one of them, I could find a small boat and get across to Sweden or Denmark on my own. Looking back on it, the chances of a wounded pilot avoiding capture while limping miles through hostile territory penetrating the closely guarded coastal area, and somehow getting across the heavily patrolled Baltic Sea, were dismally small; but it was about the only chance, so the decision was easy.

I got up and carefully tried putting my weight on the wounded right leg. I felt no pain, but when I started to walk, it crumpled and I fell. I tried again, slower this time. I learned how to limp along without the leg collapsing and as I struggled deeper into the forest, the knee seemed to lose some of its stiffness.

In the escape kit there was a minute but accurate compass. I think pilots learn to know directions and keep them in their minds almost automatically, and I had a good idea of which way was north. The compass proved I was right, so I stumbled along in that direction.

My leg didn't hurt much. It was more of an ache and a numbness. But one effect of the wound was to make me weak. The going got harder and harder, but I forced myself on. The Baltic Sea seemed further and further away.

Finally I saw more light through the trees and came to the edge of a wheat field. Across the field, in the distance, I thought I could see a road. I realised a field of grain was a good daytime cover. I could even make my way slowly crawling through the wheat as far as the road. There I would wait for darkness, then follow the road until dawn, and then back into the protection of the wheat fields or the woods.

I ducked down and started my painful crawl through the wheat though it was more of a side stroke than a crawl. My right leg was hard to bend, and I couldn't put any weight on my knee. I had to keep the leg straight as I trailed it behind. But I had plenty of time. It was July and I knew it wouldn't be dark until about nine in the evening.

When I reached the edge of the field, I gave one quick look at the road and then ducked down again and retreated a few yards into the covering wheat. The last planes had long since disappeared from the sky, and the evening was quiet and still. I saw a wheat stalk sway. At the top was a small field mouse nibbling the unripe ear of wheat. It ran down the stalk and scuttled away. I reached up and picked an ear of the wheat and started nibbling it.

There seemed to be no traffic on the road, but then I heard a distant regular squeaking. I raised myself up just enough to peer out through the grain. Down the road a man was approaching on a bicycle. I quickly ducked down again. Then I heard another sound over the squeaking; a man's voice singing. As it came closer I recognised the words and the tune. It was 'God Save

The King!' Then came 'Hello there! Where are you? I help you,' with a German accent.

My first reaction was that it was obviously a trick. Someone on a bicycle would have had time to get there from the airfield, — or the local police had been alerted. The police in England rode bicycles, why not in Germany? But there was a doubt in my mind which I couldn't pinpoint. Then suddenly I knew. In my brief glance at the cyclist, I couldn't see whether he was wearing a uniform, but I had the definite impression that he was not wearing any kind of helmet or cap. He was bareheaded. I felt sure that no German policeman or soldier would take off his helmet, even when riding a bike.

I stood up. The cyclist was a few hunderd yards past me. Should I call out? No! I was a lone enemy in a hostile country, and I might as well face up to it. I sank down into the wheat!

Years later I learned that there were secret anti-Nazi movements in Germany, particularly towards the end of the war. I have often wondered about the mysterious singing cyclist.

As it got dusk I heard voices and what sounded like the clop of horses' hooves. I peered through the tops of the wheat and saw a strange sight. Two horses were trotting down the road pulling an old-fashioned open carriage. There were three rows of high seats filled with men in uniform. The whole scene was hard to believe. Then I realized that there would probably be many horses in the agricultural north of Germany, and, with a shortage of fuel even more acute than in England, it would be natural to use the old carriage for transport especially for an evening out.

It was then that I got the feeling, the strange feeling I always had about wartime Germany. I think it started when I saw for the first time the black crosses on an Me109 reminiscent of the First World War. It was underlined by the horses and carriage, and by the close-fitting green uniforms of the German officers. It wasn't just a different world I had been dropped into, it was a different and older time. I had stepped back into the past. Perhaps that was one of the main reasons for this war; for the Nazi philosophy. They were still fighting the 1914—18 War. Perhaps German political development had always been behind that of other European nations. It was reflected in the old Gothic charac-

ters which were still used and encouraged in German print. It was
behind their fantastic loyalty to *Führer* and *Vaterland*.

After the coach-load of laughing army officers had disappeared
in the distance, I felt it was dark enough to venture out of my
cover onto the road. My knee was very stiff now, but I hoped
it would ease up as I used it. I also hoped the pain would stop.
In the beginning there had been numbness, but now it was hurting
badly.

There was another problem. I hadn't eaten since an early
breakfast. It wasn't that I was very hungry, but it made me weak.
Down the road I could see a collection of farm buildings. I was
sure I would find some sort of food on a farm in mid-summer,
perhaps even some warm milk straight from a cow.

Like most country areas, people apparently retired early in
this sparsely populated part of Germany, and I was able to hobble
down the road to the farm without having to avoid any traffic.
The farm buildings stood back from the road. I turned in and
headed for the barns and stables praying there would be no dog.
The house was well separated from the other buildings. I headed
for a large barn which seemed to have a stable under it. There
was a large wooden door. I raised the wooden latch and pushed
and pulled. The door was firmly locked. I went around the building. There was another door at the back, but it was as solidly
barred as the first. I went quickly to the other barn buildings. All
were bolted and barred. I realised that the methodical German
farmers kept everything locked away. Whether this was due to the
many foreign workers on the land; the German troops based in the
area, or passing through; or just the general shortage and rationing
of food; or a combination of all these factors, I didn't know; but
it was obvious I wasn't going to find any food in the farm buildings, even though I could hear the scuffling of the animals behind
the barred doors.

I was just leaving the farm when I saw a brick building apart
from the others. I hobbled over to it. There was a strong rotten
smell coming from it, but at least I was able to force the door
open. Feeling around in the darkness, my hands picked out two
or three rounded objects which I guessed were potatoes. Most of
them seemed to be rotting, and I guessed they were being kept to

feed pigs. I found four which seemed more solid than the rest and put them in my pocket. In the farmyard was a pump and trough. I washed my face and hands and drank the cold water.

As I walked, I cleaned one of the potatoes as best I could and bit into it. It was so unpalatable it took my hunger away, but I continued to chew it, hoping it would help keep up my strength. Strange how delicious a potato can be when it's cooked and how unappealing when raw.

Occasionally a military vehicle came along, but the headlights were blacked out and it was easy for me to dive into the side of the road and wait for it to pass. It was the third time that I got a shock. The car was coming from behind me. I limped off the road and lay face down in the long grass and weeds. I waited. The car didn't come. I raised myself on my elbows and looked over my shoulder, I saw the car not far away. Almost at the same time the bright blinding beam of a searchlight came from the side. It started sweeping the fields at the side of the road; stopping, searching, then sweeping again. At the same time, another searchlight stabbed out from the other side of the car.

It was too close for me to get up, and move into the field. All I could do was to roll over twice to get further from the road and flatten myself against the earth. I turned my face away from the road and pressed my cheek into the grass. I could see the light coming and going as the beam swept and probed. Soon I could hear the car, getting close to me. I could see the field light up almost opposite me. I waited to be blinded by the beam catching me in its glare.

Then I could hear the car almost on top of me. Still I stayed in the shadow. Then the beam swept down the field towards me. I could see how it lit up every stalk of grain, as if it was in bright sunlight. I waited as the light came nearer. It was lighting the tips of the grain a few yards from me. Then it stopped. It started to lift and sweep back up the field. I couldn't believe it. The car moved on. Soon I could risk looking up. I saw the rear of the vehicle moving slowly down the road.

I watched fascinated, still unbelieving. Then it occurred to me how I had escaped being seen. As the beam swept down towards the road, it always stopped just before it lit up the immediate road-side. I realised that the searchlight could not be depressed below a certain angle. It was probably calculated that, in the unlikely case that their quarry would be that close to the car, either the dimly diffused headlights or the glow from the powerful searchlight's glare would give enough coverage to spot it. But there was a narrow strip between the two patches of light, and of course eyes used to looking into light can't see into the darkness just beside it. It was in that dark gap that I had been lying.

So I continued to hobble along through the dark summer night. Before long, I came to a neat metal sign, black German Gothic letters on a yellow background. I later learned that these same plates marked every village and town throughout Germany, and as far as I know, still do. They not only give the name of the village but also the name of the *Kreis*, or district, which takes its name from the main town or city. In this case, I was relieved to see that the *Kreis* was given as Demmin, and my map had told me that Demmin was the first big town I should head for. I was on course!

By now my most immediate problem was food; not so much because I was hungry, but because I still felt weak. The trees around me were small pine; probably the only tree that could be grown in the sandy soil. I knew pine offered no food, but I was hoping to find some berries. So I kept going; even if there was nothing to eat in the woods, I could get out of them into farmland again. It was mixed farming country, so there must be cows somewhere.

So I stumbled on through the woods. It was flat land until I came to a slight decline. I went down into the small valley. At the bottom, as I had hoped there was a stream. I drank and bathed my face. As I rubbed my chin, I realised that I badly needed a shave. I imagined that beards were pretty much out of fashion with the Aryan master race, and my unkempt stubble would be a dead give-away if I should be seen, which was always a possibility. This was a problem which had been foreseen by the geniuses who had designed the amazing escape kit. It contained a miniature razor and a sliver of soap.

An hour later I was stretched out, naked and clean-shaven, in a small, sunny clearing surrounded by my newly washed clothes spread out on the grass, drying in the sun. My knee was clean and doused with iodine. I was on top of the world. I was lord of all I surveyed.

The only slight problem was food. I had been chewing wheat ears, raw potatoes and grass, but this had made matters worse by upsetting my stomach. So I was soon struggling along through the woods. When they petered out, I found myself on the edge of a wheat-field. I crawled in and started to make may way through the grain, hoping I was going parallel to the road. Suddenly I saw a field mouse scurrying away in front of me. I lunged at it. It wasn't hard to catch. I soon had it firmly in both hands. It bit my finger, but I still held it. I suppose I had some idea of sucking its blood to give me some strength. I looked at it as it wrinkled its pinkish nose. I felt its trembling heart-beat under its soft body. I opened my hands to let him scurry off. But he seemed mesmerized. He sat in front of me, his little heart beating. 'You'd better get going, buddy,' I said. 'You're up against the scourge of the Luftwaffe!'

I watched him disappear into the forest of wheat stalks and felt better.

As night fell, I was back on the road, but my knee was really hurting now but above all, I was weak. The moon was out, and, looking out to the side of the road, I saw pasture land. I kept looking, and stopping and listening, praying for some sign of cows.

And finally there they were; a large herd, black and white in the moonlight. I climbed the fence and slowly, painfully, moved towards the nearest one. It didn't panic. In fact it kept on grazing. It was only when I was within a few feet of her that she casually moved away. Once again, slow step by slow step, I approached. This time she moved away faster. I decided to try another one. The whole minuet repeated itself. Once I even put a tentative hand on her rump. She started and moved away. I tried a new strategy. I lay down on the grass and painfully inched towards her. As she grazed, she would step forward, but I slowly gained on her. I wasn't trying to hide my presence; just hoping she'd gradually get used to me. I finally got so close I could reach her udder. My hand slowly closed around a teat. At the same moment she walked on.

Slowly I crawled after her. Each time she moved on at the last moment.

I realised I was up against two problems. First these cows were not used to being milked in the fields; and, second, they had probably been milked in the evening, and felt no desire to be milked again. I decided sadly that I was wasting too much time.

It seemed food was not to be found in the open. I would have to continue my trek, and try one farm after another.

The first farm, set back as usual from the road, had a dog. It started barking almost as soon as I turned into the lane leading off the main road. I turned back, and kept going. I didn't come to another farm until I reached the outskirts of a village. I thought at first this would be more dangerous, or at least more difficult. But then I wondered if being close to a village might not make the farmer less nervous about intruders. Besides it was a small farm; maybe not so well organised; The barn was at the back of the house. I went back to the road, climbed a fence into a field, and approached the farm from the rear. I saw by my watch it was 4 a.m.

The barn was small, not more than a shed, and, more important, it had only a wooden latch. When I gently lifted it, the door swung open. An odour of chickens, manure and hay hit me. But there was also a pungent smell which I recognised as soon as I heard the staccato bleat. Somewhere in the darkness was a goat. A goat meant milk and a goat in a shed meant I could catch her.

I closed the door behind me to keep the clucking of the hens and the noise of the goat from being heard in the house. I stood still to let them calm down and to get my eyes used to the darkness. I thanked God for the goat but I prayed it was tethered. Slowly I moved towards the sounds and smell of the goat. I heard it moving to avoid me, and then I could just see it. I kept on moving towards it and, from its movements, I saw that it seemed to be tied. I went to the wall and moved along until I came to the rope. With one hand I held the rope; with the other I reached out and stroked her head.

I worked my way down her neck, caressing the coarse hair on her body; but as I dropped to my knee, and groped for her udder, she shied away from me. I tried again. And again. Then I realised my only chance was to tether her so short she couldn't move. I remembered the blacksmith when I was a kid. He had me twist a horse's nose with a small loop of rope and a wooden handle.

'It doesn't hurt him, it just holds his attention, and keeps his head up,' he said. So I took the rope, pulled the goat's head up to the iron ring, and tied the rope as close as I could. She wore a loose sort of halter so there was no danger of choking her, but it didn't stop her bleating. It didn't stop her kicking either, but I was still able to reach one of her teats, and squirt a stream of warm milk into my mouth as I knelt on the floor.

It was the answer to all my prayers. I felt strength, well-being and joy flood into me with each grateful swallow.

But I was only just getting the hang of squirting the milk into my mouth when the shed was suddenly lit up. I turned to the source of the light. In the doorway, holding a lantern, was, an elderly farmer.

They say it's the essential characteristic of a good fighter pilot to react quickly and decisively. At least in this case that's what I did. I scrambled to my feet and lunged towards the light. The old man staggered backwards. His face still showed amazement at the sight of me. I brushed passed him. He crumpled and fell backwards to the ground in his frantic effort to get out of my way.

I dodged around the shed and headed back into the field the way I'd come in. It was beginning to get light in that northern latitude, and the locals would be quick to respond to the old man's alarm.

The field was pastureland, but behind it I could see woods. That's where I headed, loping along as best I could. The trees were pines or spruce, and as I plunged in, I saw that they were regularly spaced; obviously planted like most of the woods in Germany. They were tall and closely enough planted to prevent any protective underbrush from growing. The tree-trunks were mostly bare, as if the lower branches had been trimmed. The ground was sandy and partly covered with dead pine-needles. I felt very exposed, as I kept stumbling on.

When I could keep going no longer, I flopped down to rest.

Then I took out my map. I was making my way around the large town of Demmin. I had covered about half the distance from Neu Brandenburg to the Baltic, and I was determined to make it. I knew my knee was getting worse, and I was getting weaker. I knew they were looking for me, and would have alerted police and military all along my route, and especially in the densely patrolled coastal area. But, just as these thoughts were going through my mind, I froze. There was no doubt about the sound I heard; it was the barking of dogs: not happy barks, but the excited yelping of hounds on a scent.

I realised there was no sense in just running. There was no stream to cross to throw off the trail. I looked around desperately for cover. There was none. Then I looked up. I saw the thick, dark umbrella of evergreen above me.

I remember reading somewhere that searchers seldom looked up. I picked out a group of trees that seemed to be closer together. One of them had vestiges of branches left where they had been trimmed. It wasn't easy. It took all my strength and several attempts to shimmy up the smooth trunk to where the branches started. Then it got thick. I had to fight my way up into the pine branches at the top. I went up as far as I dared. It swayed alarmingly, but settled down when I clung to the trunk and kept still.

Now there were men's voices mixed with the barking of the dogs, and they were getting closer. Soon they were underneath. The noises of men and beasts indicated they were confused. I could only see the ground immediately under the tree just around the trunk. My cheek was against the rough bark as I strained to see. I was dreading the sight of a dog following the scent to the foot of the tree, and then barking up at me.

For almost five minutes they milled around below me. Then to my amazement they moved away. I still don't know why the dogs didn't surround the tree. Maybe they weren't good tracking dogs, Maybe a trail over pine needles isn't that easy to follow.

I clung to my perch after the sounds of the men and dogs had died away. I kept expecting them to come back, but after about fifteen minutes I had to move my stiff limbs. Slowly I climbed down, dropping the last twenty feet to the ground. I lay still and listened. Only the sounds of the forest! I couldn't believe my luck; but I also knew it would get tougher from now on. The whole area would be alerted. It would need more than determination to get to the coast now; and then there was the problem of crossing the Baltic! Still I wasn't downhearted. At least, even if I eventually got caught, every day of freedom was one day less in the prisoner-of-war camp. I set course for the North, and limped off.

I crossed the main road from Demmin to Jarmen and Swinemünde, which meant I was due east of Demmin. My next landmark would be the river. When I crossed that I could turn west to pick up the main road running north from Demmin to Stralsund on the Baltic.

When I reached the river it was wider than I had expected. What's more there were houses along the opposite bank. I followed the river bank westward, looking for a clear crossing. As I picked my way along the river bank, I saw a bridge. I knew a bridge could be a serious trap.

A small road led up to the bridge. I dare not cross it close to the bridge, near which there were buildings. I followed the edge of the road away from the bridge before crossing; then I followed the road back towards the bridge again, then veered off into the field, hitting the river again about a hundred yards upstream from the bridge. I slithered down to the water's edge; then into the river, boots and all. There was no problem until I had to start swimming; then the current started floating me downstream towards the bridge. I tried not to splash, but they must have heard. Suddenly there were searchlights. Almost immediately there was gun fire. I dived under water and let the river carry me down under the bridge, helping the current by trying to swim underwater. When I could stand it no longer, I surfaced for a gulp of air, then dived under again.

When I finally had to surface, all was quiet and dark. I made for the far bank and by the time my feet touched bottom I was well past the bridge. Slowly I crawled to the bank and lay half in, half out of the water catching my breath.

After about ten minutes I started to crawl up the bank. I knew there were houses there, but I figured I was coming up behind them through their back gardens. They might give me some cover to reconnoitre before venturing out to cross the road, which I expected to find on the other side of the houses.

There was a clear space between me and the buildings. I decided to make a rush across it. Half crouched, I hobbled across as fast as I could. Then I saw my mistake. Right in front of me was the road. I wasn't behind the houses. I was in front of them. Suddenly everything happened at once. I heard the sound of running. Orders were barked out in German. Beams of light caught me in their glare. There were men and vehicles behind the lights in front of me.

I turned to run back to the river. They were behind me too, cutting me off. There was no alternative so I kept going. I had some hope of diving back into the river, and being carried downstream out of range. I didn't make it. The last thing I saw was two uniformed, helmeted soldiers. Both had their guns pressed into my stomach. Both looked determined, desperate and frightened. It was time to change tactics. In my best German, and with as charming a smile as I could muster, I said:

'Gentlemen; good evening! Where have you been? I've been looking for you everywhere!'

It didn't raise a smile, but they didn't shoot.

They took me to a modest village police station. I sat surrounded by what seemed to be the entire complement. Five men were seated on wooden chairs. All had guns pointed at me, except for the man seated behind a desk who seemed to be the boss. Two men were wearing what I took to be police uniforms. Two seemed to be wearing SS uniforms. The other two, including the man behind the desk, were in civilian clothes.

The man behind the desk was strangely friendly and cheerful. He seemed more like a farmer than a Gestapo boss. Of course he was probably happy to be responsible for my capture, but I had the feeling that he was a nice guy; probably the local police chief. He was smiling as he said in German: 'Let's try it again, shall we! Who are you and what are you doing here?'

'I'm a French worker. I got separated from my work party which was on its way from Stettin to Rostock.'

'And where are your identity papers?'

'Lost during the bombing of Stettin. We were completely bombed out.'

'You are supposed to keep your identity papers on you all the time.'

'I was knocked out and wounded in the leg during the bombing. Maybe they were stolen.'

'*Komische Geschichte*, but it's nothing to do with me. You'll have to tell it to the others.'

'What others?'

'You'll see.'

I was still puzzled by the fact that he was in civilian clothes. Maybe he was a Nazi Party boss, a *Gauleiter*, or even the mayor. I hazarded a direct question.

'Are you Gestapo, sir?'

'Mixed,' he said. 'But we are all Nazi dogs.'

I showed my surprise at the use of the word '*Hünde*.'

'You understand? Dogs!' he repeated, and started to bark like a dog.

Then he laughed. To this day I don't know why he used those words. Was he showing that he knew that foreigners and non-Nazis referred to them as 'dogs'? Was he using the word to indicate their solidarity and loyalty to one another like a pack of dogs? Or was he by any chance expressing some underlying disillusion with the Nazi force?

A truck pulled up outside. Doors banged; orders were barked out; heavy boots stomped and the door to our room was thrown open. The smiles and friendly atmosphere vanished. The men leaped to their feet, stamped to attention, and gave the Nazi salute almost in unison. A man in civilian clothes, wearing a rather wide-brimmed hat came in, followed by a uniformed sergeant and a soldier armed with the small sub-machine gun, which I soon learnt was called a '*Maschinen-Pistole*' by the Germans.

The civilian obviously inspired respect, if not fear, in the others. He beckoned to the chief, and they left the room. Some ten minutes later they were back. The civilian sat down behind the desk and with a wave of the hand, dismissed everyone but his own military escort. The chief was dismissed with the others.

The man then opened a thin leather brief-case, took out a sheaf of papers and a fountain pen, and prepared to write. Then the questioning again. If I was a French worker, where were my identity papers? Where had I been working? Why was I over a hundred kilometres from Stettin? The interrogator seemed very cool, even bored. He was endlessly patient, simply repeating questions and copying the answers. I had expected threats, badgering, third degree, even torture. I was confused, perhaps even a little disappointed, and also a little apprehensive at the 'ho-hum' attitude of my interrogator.

Suddenly to my surprise, the interview was over. The questioner stood up and his henchmen leapt to their feet. I was jerked to my feet, had my arms pulled behind my back, and an old-fashioned pair of hand-cuffs clapped on my wrists. I was pushed out the door and was soon blinking in the morning light. A military truck drove up, and I was bundled into the back, followed by the two guards. A few minutes later, the civilian interrogator came out, got into the front of the truck, which drove off.

We bumped over the cobbled roads for over an hour. I reckoned we were travelling north-west.

Finally we turned off the road and drove up to a forbidding steel door in a brick wall. The heavy door swung open and we drove through into a cobbled courtyard. Things were getting serious. This was a jail!

I was thrown from the back of the truck and fell face forward on the cobblestones. Almost immediately I was kicked, and prodded with a gun-butt. It was difficult to get up again because of the handcuffs. My two guards jerked me to my feet and prodded me towards the door of the prison. The guards were rough, but, during all my captivity, I never had the impression that there was any malice or deliberate cruelty. It was just the way things were done in political captivity, and if the guards acted less aggressively, their NCO's and officers would soon show them how to act. I've always thought that one reason for the efficiency of the German war machine was the fact that the soldiers were more afraid of their officers than of the enemy.

I was marched down concrete corridors past helmeted armed

guards who snapped to attention with loud stamping of boots which echoed through the barren building. Finally I was thrown into a small cell. It was completely empty except for a folded blanket in one corner and a battered old metal bucket in another. There was no bed but that was probably because no bed could have been fitted in.

They unlocked the handcuffs, stamped out and slammed the door. I heard the iron bolts being shot across and a key turned in the lock. The heavy footsteps died away. There was no sound. I explored the cell. It didn't take long. Three concrete walls, one steel door, concrete ceiling, concrete floor; no windows, not even a barred slit for ventilation. The only break in the monotonous surface was in the grey steel door, which itself formed one wall of the cell. At eye-level there was a small closed panel with bars in front of it. At floor level, there was another panel. I tried both. There was no give; no play. I was sealed in.

This was a new situation for me. Even when I was captured I immediately thought of escape when the right opportunity came along, but I had never considered this sort of maximum security prison.

I began to realise the French worker story was hopelessly weak. It might have held water if I'd been better briefed on the status of forced labourers in wartime Germany. Although technically they may have had civilian status, they really had little more freedom than prisoners of war. They too were kept in camps and barracks at night, and closely watched at all times. They too were checked and double-checked. Like everyone in the Third Reich their every movement was controlled, and their very existence depended on their identity papers.

Gradually I was becoming aware of Nazi Germany's overwhelming phobia. As the tide of war began to turn against them, the German leaders' greatest fear was not the menace of the mass of the Russian army; it was not the vast fleets of Allied aircraft which were systematically and inexorably destroying German cities; it was not even the threat posed by the massive might of the Allied armies building up in preparation for the invasion of Continental Europe. No, there was another enemy army, even larger than those outside their frontiers, and more imminently dangerous because this force was already right inside the country, and growing daily. This menacing army was made up of the millions of prisoners of war, political internees, and foreign labourers within the borders of the Third Reich. Many of them were highly-trained military experts, all of them shared a burning hatred of the Nazi regime. And there were millions of them. Estimates of their numbers vary wildly, but one thing is certain, they outnumbered the security forces within Germany who were responsible for controlling them, and indeed preventing them from taking over the country. They probably even outnumbered the total number of able-bodied German males left in Germany. Armed forces could be brought back from the front to put down any insurrection, but then the delicate balance of the battle fronts would be upset, with the probability of complete collapse.

The most amazing aspect of this extraordinary situation was that, although the Nazis recognised it as their greatest danger, the Allies ignored it completely, and never thought of exploiting it. The German leaders and the Gestapo could not believe that the Allies would overlook this heaven-sent opportunity, and their fears influenced their treatment of all foreigners within their borders; political internees, foreign workers, and even prisoners of war, such as the fifty Air Force officers who escaped from Stalag Luft III, were recaptured and shot by the Gestapo. The Nazis from Hitler on down were convinced that the only element missing to set off the explosion was leadership and organisation. Therefore, the Allies would do everything possible to supply that catalyst by sending specialists into Germany either as shot-down aircrew, as foreign workers, or simply by parachute. From the German point of view those potential homefront organisers had to be eliminated as quickly and quietly as possible, and, if some innocent foreigners and bona fide prisoners of war got caught in the net, that was nothing compared to the risk if a real nucleus of officers were able to organise even a part of the vast potential army.

As I slumped down on the rough folded blanket in my cell nursing my injured leg, I only sensed a part of all this, but the pervading atmosphere of fear and evil in that place made me aware of the fact that I had fallen into a sinister sort of underworld.

As the hours crept by, I began to understand why people break down in solitary confinement. The feeling grows on one that one is completely deserted, forgotten, almost ceasing to exist and no one knows, or cares, or will do anything about one's existence. It came as an enormous relief when I heard footsteps outside the door. The small trap door at the base of the main steel entrance opened. A small piece of rough brown bread was pushed through, followed by a tin container with water. Almost immediately, the small grille was slammed shut and I heard a bolt shot home. I was hungry enough to eat the bread, which was obviously very wholesome. This was my first taste of the *Kommis-Brot*, which was the standard fare of the German Army and all prisoners of war.

It was about an hour later that the top grille was slid back and a voice said, '*Kanne*.' I understood this to mean that he wanted the tin drinking pan back, because at the same time the lower grille was opened. Instead of immediately passing the tin back, I put my face to the upper slit and peered through. Since my cell was dark, and the corridor outside was lit, I found myself gazing into the pale blue eyes of a young, blond guard in an SS uniform. I smiled and said, 'Good evening. I didn't quite understand what it was you wanted.'

'*Kanne*!' he barked again.

'Ah,' I said, 'I think I understand.'

I pushed the tin drinking cup through the lower grille. He took it, and the grille slammed shut. He was about to slam the upper grille shut when I asked him as politely as possible if it would be possible for me to use the toilet facilities. He replied, 'It's in the corner there.'

'Yes,' I said, 'but I think you understand my feelings. I give my word to cause you no embarassment if you could just escort me to the toilet and back.'

The slit was slammed shut and that was the last I heard for about three hours.

Then I saw a shaft of light as the upper slit was opened. When I looked out, I again saw the blue eyes of the guard. Again I tried to charm him. 'May I ask your name?'

For a few seconds the blue eyes stared at me and then he replied, 'Hansen.'

'Ah!' I said. 'That's a northern name!'

'Schleswig-Holstein,' he said with obvious pride. 'Who are you, then?' he said.

I decided then that the French worker story was a loser and that I had nothing to lose, and possibly something to gain by telling this youngster the truth. Immediately, his face came alive and he asked me about flying and America until he realised that he was going too far. The grille suddenly slammed shut.

About an hour later, the shaft of light came again. This time, his voice was an urgent whisper.

'*Schnell!*' he said. To my amazement, the bolts were shot back and the heavy lock opened and the big main door swung open. He hustled me down the corridor and pushed me into a primitive toilet and slammed the door.

'*Schnell!*' he said 'I've stolen the keys and I've got to get them back!' When I got back to my cell, the door was slammed, the lock was turned and the bolt shot home, but by now I had a fellow conspirator. He had shared with me what, to him, must have been a terrible breach of discipline.

We now had something in common. He explained to me that he was the night guard and that I would be making a dangerous mistake if I were to speak with the daytime guards. He need not have worried — I knew when he was off duty. There was no conversation possible with any of the others.

Gradually, our conspiracy was compounded. Not only did he let me out to go to the toilet, but he even pushed through to me the bowl of soup which was served to him in the middle of the night, explaining that the minute he opened the grille, I was to push it back to him, because it meant someone was coming.

It was five in the morning when I was awakened by a staccato noise. Shortly afterwards, the upper slit in the door slid open and Hansen said, 'Until this evening. I'm off now.'

I said, 'Till this evening!' and then added, 'What was that noise just now?' The question obviously embarrassed him.

'You know,' he said.

I said, 'No — I don't know!'

'Well, it's the others,' he said.

'What others?'

'The other prisoners,' he said.

Then it started to dawn on me. 'You mean . . .'

He nodded solemnly.

'And me?' I said.

I could see my questions were hurting him.

'You must tell me,' I said.

'*Morgen oder Übermorgen,*' he said. 'Tomorrow, or the day after.'

'Friend,' I said, 'you know I'm an American flying officer. You must tell the Commandant that I have to see him. I am a prisoner of war and shooting prisoners of war is a crime.'

His eyes opened in bewilderment. 'But I can't talk to an officer! I can only talk to the *Feldwebel*. He can talk to the *Leutnant* and he might talk to the *Hauptmann.*'

'Hansen, my friend,' I said, 'you have to do it for me. Not only for me, but for you and all your officers. If I am shot, it would be a terrible crime and everybody would be held responsible when it came to light.'

He was obviously frightened. 'I'll try,' he said.

All through the day, I worried and waited, and nothing happened.

At 8 pm the stamping of heavy boots and crashing of steel bolts echoed through the corridors again.

"*Raus!*' I was marched off between two guards, with a sergeant in command. We stopped in front of a door. The *Feldwebel* knocked.

"*Rein!*'

The *Feldwebel* stamped in, came to attention in a stiff brace, and gave the straight-armed Nazi salute, reminding me again that I was in the sinister secret world of the SS and Gestapo rather than the true armed forces, which, at that time, still used the traditional military salute.

I had hoped and expected to find myself in front of the *Kommandant* but the *Feldwebel* addressed him as '*Herr Hauptsturmführer*', which was the SS equivalent of captain.

He looked at me with obvious distaste.

'So! You have something to say to me? I'll give you five minutes.'

My German was slow and hesitant, but in those few minutes I was a German-talking fool. I gave my name rank and serial number.

I stressed the fact that I was a leading American fighter pilot. I indicated I was known by reputation to Galland, Göring and even Hitler, all of whom would, of course, be furious if anything happened to me. He could confirm my identity by simply contacting the Luftwaffe, who were undoubtedly looking for me.

He interrupted me in full flight. 'I don't give a damn whether you're a *Terror-flieger*, an escaping foreign worker, a spy, or a saboteur. In any case, you are an enemy of the Reich, and the Führer has entrusted us with the task of eliminating all such enemies. As for your Luftwaffe friends, what have they done for us? Where are they when you and your murderous friends come over and kill our women and children and destroy our cities?'

As I listened to him repeating the words of the Nazi propaganda machine, hope drained out of me and fear came in. I felt it as a sick feeling in my stomach.

It wasn't only propaganda. Underlying it was the days and nights and years of fear and frustration as they watched helplessly as friends and families were killed and maimed, and historic cities and beautiful buildings collapsed in flame and ruin never to be replaced.

If we thought of it, we knew we were spreading death and destruction, but dismissed it, as well-deserved retaliation for what Londoners had suffered in the Blitz. What we didn't know, but should have, was that the reaction of the German population was the same as that of the British: bitter hatred of the enemy and determination to endure and win through so that vengeance could be wrought on their murderers.

The words 'Murderers', 'Gangster flyers', 'Terror flyers' were constantly repeated in the Nazi press, coupled with the story that America had assembled its gangsters and murderers to man its air force. Photographs of the name on the B-17 'Murder Incorporated' were featured. The campaign was successful. They were ready — even anxious — to believe the worst.

I had to give up on the Captain, but I wasn't going to quit. 'I don't accept your decision, Sir!'

That stopped him. 'What do you mean? Why not?'

'I outrank you. I insist on seeing the *Kommandant*. That is my right!'

'The *Kommandant* is in Berlin. He won't be back till tomorrow.'

'Then we must wait!'

He hesitated. The argument about priority of rank obviously impressed him, but then he made up his mind.

'No. I have complete authority in the absence of the *Kommandant*! That's it! Out! *'Raus!'*

That was it.

Back in my cell, I sat back on my blanket. I was surprised that I was so calm. Why wasn't I terrified, or at least frightened? There was no possible escape. The next morning I would be shot. It wasn't like combat where one had a chance. Even if the odds were against you, you had a chance, and most of us believed in our luck. We had to! Death was something that happened to others. But now, in this hermetically sealed cell, there was no chance, no odds, no doubts — so why did I feel no fear?

I began to realise that it was because it was inevitable that I was so calm. Nothing I could do would change anything. The die was cast! Fear is indecision. It's not knowing what to do, when not making the right decision could mean the difference between life and death. The tingling nerves are messages from the brain telling them to stand by for action. The pounding of the heart is to pump the blood for the actions that have to be taken.

I had taken all my actions, made all my moves and come to the end of the line. It was too late to send messages to the nerves and my brain knew it. I think it was Dr Johnson who said that nothing so wonderfully concentrates the mind as the knowledge that one will die tomorrow ... or words to that effect. He was absolutely right. As I sat in my cell, my mind was clearer than it had probably ever been. There was nothing to interrupt my thoughts. The prison was absolutely quiet. Hansen had apparently been relieved of his post, and I could establish no contact with his replacement. So I had the rest of the night — my last night — to think.

At first I thought of the unkind fate that had dumped me in this mess. If I hadn't been shot down, I would have wound up the leading Allied ace, but then lots of others had had that chance too, and they ended up dead. You never know what fate may bring but it's almost never one success after another. Usually today's hero is tomorrow's forgotten man. That's why the ancient Greeks had a saying: 'Call no man happy till he dies'. But I still felt cheated. It wasn't fair for my life to be ended at the age of twenty-three. It wasn't fair to my mother. There was nothing else in her life but me.

But I was Aries. It was my decision to volunteer for the RAF. I thought of my mother then, but she was Aries too. It was just as natural, as inevitable for her as for me. She wouldn't have had it any other way. She would be broken-hearted, but not broken. She would understand.

It was my decision to fly every mission to attack wherever and whenever I could; to risk going down on enemy airfields, to destroy aircraft on the ground, knowing it was more dangerous, but also more effective.

It was I who volunteered to take out the Me163 prototype. It wasn't bad luck that my life was now to be snuffed out just as it was getting rolling. If anything I was lucky that it had lasted this long. It was tempting to say I could have played it safer; only flown the missions I had to; only attacked when everything was in my favour; but I knew in my heart that what happened was the expression of myself. I had simply been true to myself. Like a Greek tragedy, my own character almost inevitably led me to this cell.

And as the hours crept by in that silent prison, I realised that if, by some miracle, I had it all to do again, I'd probably play it the same way. Even more, what regrets I had were that I hadn't savoured life fully. I thought of exciting opportunities which I was too busy or timid to grasp and exploit. I had thought life would last forever; that I had plenty of time to do all the wonderful things I thought were possible. I was convinced that I could have done anything if only I'd put my mind to it. Every day offered the chance of a life-time. Every problem could be converted into an opportunity.

It wasn't just the normal 'success'. I'd had my share of that. I was a leading ace, I'd led the leading fighter squadron. I'd knocked out the rocket plane prototype.

Most of all I had experiences anyone could envy.

But I still had regrets. I thought of friends and people I had known and loved. I knew that I had been too busy, too unfeeling or too afraid to show feelings to let them know how I felt. I would have given anything to have been able to reach out to my mother to tell her of my love and how my main sorrow now was the sorrow I would give her. I wanted to cry out to everyone I had known: and say, 'Sorry!'

I felt I should consider the meaning of life in the short time left to me, but there didn't seem to be much sense to it. Maybe it boiled down to a game. You couldn't know the reason for it any more than a football player can tell you why it was vital to kick an inflated leather ball between two wooden poles as many times as possible. The only thing to do is to play the game to the hilt, to throw yourself into it with all the energy and enthusiasm you possess. When you have that joyful uplift, you're winning. When you get weary and don't care any more, it's time to quit.

Come to think of it, that had been my philosophy; the approach of Aries, the sign of the ram; but I could have done so much more. I felt like Scrooge in Dickens' *A Christmas Carol*, endeavouring to change his life and make up for his series of omissions, if only he be granted the chance.

But Scrooge saw the light in a dream. Looking around my cell, I knew this was no dream from which I would wake with the relief and joy of knowing I had the rest of my life in front of me. It wasn't a dream when the stamping of the marching boots echoed through the prison and stopped outside the door of my cell. The bolts and locks crashed and the heavy door swung open. There was a sergeant and two guards, one of which was Hansen. Before we left, Hansen was ordered to relieve the guards, who had been outside my cell all night. He stepped smartly out of the detail, came to attention directly in front of me and saluted. I saluted back. Our eyes met. I was surprised to see a look of intense sorrow and sympathy. The young blue eyes were so close to tears and were trying to say so much. I felt I had to console him somehow. I smiled at him, winked, put a friendly hand on his shoulders.

'Thanks!' I said in English.

The sergeant had been shocked into immobility. He now sprang into action. '*Achtung*!' he yelled. '*Marsch*!'

We marched off; the sergeant in front and the two soldiers behind with their guns in my back. A strange funeral march, I thought. Not much of a Guard of Honour, and the only mourner a young SS soldier. I tried to live up to the seriousness of the situation. I'd always been good at playing a part when in a tight spot even hamming it up a bit. There's nothing wrong with ham as long as it's good ham: — especially if it's your finale.

There was no dramatic background music, just the echo of my marching feet as we tramped through the empty corridors. Suddenly an officer appeared.

'Halt!' We halted.

The officer called the sergeant to him and held a whispered conference.

The sergeant came back.

'*Marsch*!'

We marched off again following the officer. Soon we entered an area of officers and stopped in front of an imposing door. The officer knocked.

'*Herein*!'

I was pushed into the large room. It was well furnished. There was a large desk. There were well-filled book shelves, carpets on the floor, paintings on the wall, including a portrait of Hitler behind the desk. In one corner was a sofa, chairs and a small table. Behind them was a drinks cabinet. In front of it with his back to me was a short figure in black uniform pouring himself a drink.

The door closed behind me. The officer turned. I had always thought that Hollywood was guilty of caricaturing the real thing; but this *Kommandant* could have stepped right out of a war movie. He was a younger version of Erich von Stroheim or Conrad Veidt. From his close-cropped head to his black polished boots, and in his every gesture, he was playing the part of the typical tough SS officer. The only thing lacking was the monocle. He spoke in a high-pitched bark in an imitation of Adolf Hitler:

'I have just returned from a high-level conference in Berlin. I have decided to give you five minutes.'

I came to attention. 'As a major in the United States Army

Air Force, I demand to be handed over to the Luftwaffe as a prisoner of war.'

'By what right?'

'By the terms of the Geneva Convention!'

Now his voice rose to a shriek.

'You have the nerve to mention the Geneva Convention. The enemies of the Reich have broken every rule of that Convention. As for you, if you are a *Terror-flieger*, you are a murderer of innocent civilians, women and children. What right do you have to be treated as a soldier?'

'The same right as the men of the Luftwaffe who attacked Warsaw, Rotterdam and London.'

His eyes were blazing as he stared at me. I stared back. He strode to the door.

'They only attacked military targets! You have the gall to compare yourself to German heroes! Guards!'

He threw the door open. The guard was still standing outside. I had to play a strong card. It was now or never.

'Do you really think Reichsmarschall Göring will thank you for taking the decision to shoot one of his most important prisoners-of-war? Because you will have to answer that question when the Luftwaffe traces me here.'

It worked. Once again I'd played on the fear German soldiers had of higher authority.

He stopped in the open doorway and hesitated. On the other side of the door was the guard waiting to escort me to a firing squad. On this side of the door was at least a chance of survival.

Slowly the *Kommandant* closed the door.

'I suppose you are going to tell me that Reichsmarschall Göring knows all about you!'

I looked amazed. 'But of course!'

He snorted in disbelief but I knew he wasn't sure. He went back to the settee, sat down, picked up his glass and took a long swig.

'I'll say this. Whoever you are, you've got guts!' He was relaxing now. 'We Germans know how to respect bravery, because we ourselves are the bravest race and the best race. That's why our army is the bravest and the best in the world!'

He paused. He was waiting for agreement or argument.

'You agree?' He seemed to need reassurance.

'I don't think any race has a monopoly on bravery. You can find bravery anywhere, just as you can find cowardice anywhere; but I've studied the history of this war and the last, and I've fought the Luftwaffe myself and I won't argue with you about their bravery. They're brave!'

He was delighted. 'And the best!'

'Again I wouldn't argue with you. I think our army would admit they have to have the Germans outnumbered to be sure of winning a battle.'

'How about the Luftwaffe?' he asked.

'Oh, they're brave and good!'

'And better than the enemy?'

I realised I had to keep him interested — and talking. I also had to use every opportunity of impressing on his mind that I was an air force officer.

'Well, in the air as on the ground, equipment and numbers are important. So it isn't only the pilot that counts. But I'm happy to admit that some of the greatest fighter pilots are in the Luftwaffe. Many of them have thousands of missions behind them, and hundreds of personal victories. I have nothing but the greatest respect for them. Galland, Moelders, Trautloft, Mayer, Nowotny, Hartmann — all great men!'

The *Kommandant* was getting mellow, and the names impressed him.

'Sit down,' he said. I took one of the chairs. 'So you admit we're winning the war.'

'No, *Herr Kommandant*, I didn't say that!'

'But you admitted our German armed forces are the best in the world.'

'I admitted they were brave and efficient.'

'So they will win!'

'No, *Herr Kommandant*!'

'Why not?'

'Because modern wars are not won by bravery or even by good soldiers. They are won by production. This war is being won on the floors of factories in the United States, England and Russia.

Rommel's Afrika Korps was great, but it was annihilated because Montgomery had overwhelming superiority in tanks, guns and aircraft. It's the same in France to-day. Not only is the Wehrmacht outnumbered, but it can't move during the daytime because of our bombers and fighters.'

He rose to the bait. 'France! Let me show you something.'

He went to his desk, pulled open a drawer and spread out a map.

'Look! The American army has gone through North-West France and then turned east again along the Loire, leaving their entire right flank exposed. Our German army will come up from the south and cut them to pieces!'

'No. Patton knows what he is doing. His flank is protected by the Tactical Air Force, and he can call on the Strategic Air Force if he has to.'

'An Air Force can't protect an army!'

'It can if it has air superiority. You saw how the Luftwaffe paralysed the Polish, French and Russian armies during the first offensives. They used only a few hundred aircraft. We have thousands! I've patrolled roads leading to the Normandy beach-head. They are choked with the wrecks of military vehicles. We told Eisenhower we could keep German reinforcements from reaching the invasion beaches, and we did. During the daytime nothing can move and the nights aren't long enough for clearing the debris, repairing the roads and getting the material through.'

He was obviously intrigued. 'I've seen the same thing in Poland. You have learned from us!'

'Of course!'

'But why are the Americans fighting us? Why did they side with the British? Britain had already lost her war.'

'It was Germany who declared war on America at the time of Pearl Harbour!'

'Nonsense! America was already keeping Britain going before that and you know it. They were at war without declaring it. But why? We had no quarrel with them.'

'We are defending democracy against dictatorship.' I was very earnest and sincere.

'Democracy! Nonsense!' He used the German word, *'Quatsch!'*;

it was one of his favourites. 'You're defending the dictator Stalin and his criminal Communist system, which he wants to impose on the entire world, including the United States. Only Germany, and now Japan, are stopping them. Only we are protecting the world from the Communist hordes. We are defending you from the greatest danger, and you are stabbing us in the back! Or do you think perhaps Russia is a democracy?'

I was so amazed at this point of view, I found it hard to answer.

'Russia may not be a democracy but neither is Nazi Germany!'

'What do you mean by democracy?'

'Popular government. People having the government they want.' It sounded a little weak, and he hit it hard.

'You don't really think Stalin is more popular in Russia than the Führer is in Germany? Stalin and his government are hated and feared in Russia by most of the people. In Germany, the Führer is loved and revered by everybody. He was voted to power, and if there was a vote to-day he would get 100% of it. That's more than Roosevelt or Churchill would get!'

It had never occurred to me that there was any excuse for Hitler, but I didn't feel I was winning the argument, so I changed tack.

'Democracy has nothing to do with individual leaders. It's government of the people, by the people, for the people.'

'*Quatsch*!' he shouted. 'No country is really governed by the majority and thank God they're not. Do you know that the majority of people in this world cannot read or write? The *majority* don't eat with a knife and fork; they don't even eat with chopsticks; they eat with their fingers. The *majority* of people in this world are not as far advanced as we were in the Dark Ages; most of them are still in the Stone Age or early Iron Age; and you want to entrust the leadership of the world to them! Ha! The first thing they would do would be to wipe out the intelligent minority and set civilization back two thousand years!'

It was the first time I had heard such views expressed, so I was at a loss as to how to refute them.

'So! You can't answer that!' He was delighted.

'The people who are living and dying in your concentration camps might prefer the Stone Age.'

It was the best I could come up with, but he had an answer.

'But they are not the majority. They're a small minority which wants to destroy the majority. They have to be restrained for the good of the majority. They have to be cut out like an infection in the body. The end justifies the means.'

'Nothing justifies causing such cruelty and death to innocent people!'

'What? Such tenderness from a *Terror-flieger* makes me sick. How much misery and death have you and your friends spread by the indiscriminate bombing of German cities. Were those women and children any less innocent? Are you any less guilty?'

I searched for an answer.

'Why do you do it?' he asked.

Still I had no answer.

'Perhaps because you think the end justifies the means?'

'You are a very clever man, *Herr Kommandant*, but you are wrong! There is no comparison. Victims of war are victims of those who start wars.'

'We are all victims of war. That is why I am going to have you shot!'

'I don't follow your logic, *Herr Kommandant*. How can my death help anything? Isn't there enough death — death which can't be helped? My death would be murder. You are making a conscious decision to kill me. How can that help you? It can only cause you trouble!'

'No, my friend, you are very clever, but it won't work! However I have enjoyed talking to you. Sit down. Would you like a drink? This is French cognac, Rémy-Martin.'

I sat down. 'Thank you.'

It was good cognac and I enjoyed it.

'I see you have a box of Cuban cigars,' I said. 'I always think they go well with cognac, don't you?'

He laughed, handed me the box and took one for himself.

'You're right. I too enjoy a good cigar.'

He struck a match, lit his cigar and threw me the match-box. I drew deeply on the cigar, savouring it, and then blew a thick, round smoke ring. Probably because I only smoked cigars and never inhaled them, I had formed the habit of blowing rings. The air was still in the room. The ring rolled across the table and settled and spread on the surface.

The *Kommandant* was fascinated. 'Do that again.'

I laughed and blew another ring.

'How do you do that?'

It was one way to gain time, so I tried to teach him. He was an apt student. The session forged a bond between us. As he wrestled with the problem, he poured me another brandy.

'Thank you,' I said. 'At least I'm going out in style.'

'Yes,' he said. 'You do have style. *Prosit!*' and he raised his glass to me.

'Is there anything else I can do for you?' he asked.

'Of course, *Herr Kommandant*, you could telephone the Luftwaffe!'

'No! I have no desire to make a fool of myself in front of them. I don't take orders from that lot.'

'On the contrary.' I was playing my last card. 'You would be making fools of them!'

'How?' He was interested.

'You would simply say: 'We are, of course, aware of the fact that a high-ranking American flying officer was recently shot down. It has taken you so long to capture him, I thought you wouldn't mind if I mobilized my command to save further waste of time. If you wish to interrogate him, he is at your disposal. If not, I shall deal with him as I see fit.'

He continued his attempts to blow smoke rings.

'Hold the smoke in your mouth longer before blowing it out,' I said.

It worked. He was delighted.

Then he looked at his watch, got up, went to the telephone on his desk and barked out an order. He hung up, came back, and poured us both another brandy.

The phone rang. He swaggered over and answered it. He repeated my suggested script almost word for word. Then all I heard was a series of '*Ja*', '*Jawohl*', '*Ja*'.

He hung up and came back and sat down with his brandy and cigar.

Neither of us spoke.

Finally he finished off his drink and stood up.

'Well, it's been a long day — and night; so if you will excuse me.'

He went to the door and called for my guard, then came to attention stiffly in front of me. He shook hands with me, stepped back and saluted.

'*Herr Major, Leb'wohl*!'

In the doorway he turned. 'The Luftwaffe will pick you up in about an hour.'

I could not believe it! I dared not believe it! It seemed too miraculous to be true that I was to be allowed to live after all. It was like being born again. Everything seemed new and wonderful, and I saw it all in a new clear light. Through the window, dawn was breaking. As in a dream, I walked over and looked at the trees and fields. They would have been ordinary; now they were fabulous.

The guards came to take me. I pointed through the window.

'*Wunderschön*!' I said. 'It's beautiful.'

Back in the cell, I thought of how, an hour or so ago, I had faced my death. Now I faced life; and I knew that for me it would never be the same. From now on, every minute, every event, every person, every thing; every sight, sound and smell would be precious, because I had so nearly lost them. I would be living on borrowed time; precious time; wonderful time; and I would never forget it!

The Luftwaffe, when it arrived, was disappointing. It consisted of a young lieutenant and a *Gefreiter* or private as a guard. They seemed intent on showing the Gestapo and SS that the Luftwaffe could be just as coldly efficient as them. They saluted smartly as the prison guards turned me over to them. The lieutenant produced a pair of handcuffs, snapped one on my left wrist and the other on the wrist of the guard, and marched me off.

Outside a small military car with a driver was waiting to drive us to the nearest railway station. It seemed strange to be standing on the platform among the ordinary German civilians, but, if they were surprised or embarrassed at the sight of an enemy pilot manacled between his two captors, they showed no sign. In fact, I felt that my guards were more ill at ease than the other passengers.

When the train came into the station, we installed ourselves in a second-class compartment, the other passengers crowded in after us, and we settled down for the journey. I tried to engage the lieutenant in conversation. It wasn't easy, but I learned that his name was Albrecht and he came from Koblenz. I knew that it was on the Rhine where the Mosel winds through the hills covered with the vineyards that produce the light Mosel white wines. He was proud of his homeland and of being a Rheinländer, and I realised that Germany still with its regional loyalties, was behind in the historic march of European countries towards nationhood. Maybe that explained the fanatical desire of the Nazis to weld the country into one *Vaterland*, '*Ein Volk, ein Reich, ein Führer*!' I learned that the guard's name was Schneider and that he was a Bavarian. And all the time I was thinking of a way to escape. But not only was the compartment crowded, the corridor was also jammed with people standing, and even a trip to the lavatory, manacled to the guard, was out of the question.

'Where are we going?' I asked.

'To Frankfurt, but first to Berlin where we have to change trains.'

The mention of Berlin reminded me that, just before being shot down, we had been planning a renewed series of raids on the German capital now that the Normandy beach-head was secure.

I remembered the date. At 12.30 two waves of bombers, escorted by as many long-range fighters, the Fourth covering the target area as usual, would converge on the centre of Berlin with the Friedrichstrasse Bahnhof as the bomb-aiming point.

'What station do we arrive in?' I wanted to know.

'Friedrichstrasse Bahnhof,' was the reply.

'When do we get there?'

'Just after twelve mid-day.'

The sirens were already howling as we pulled into the great railway station. People leapt from the train and joined the rush towards the air-raid shelters. We followed as best we could with me manacled to Schneider and Albrecht holding my other arm, afraid of losing me in the confusion.

The *Luftschutzraum* was well sign-posted. We went in through thick concrete walls, and went down solid concrete stairs into a large concrete cellar. There were wooden benches, but, as they crowded in, it was clear that most would be standing. Like most airmen, I suffer from claustrophobia in crowded, confined spaces, and, as the hum of the approaching air armada became audible, I longed to be up there with my boys at thirty thousand feet in the clear, free air.

There was a hush in the air-raid shelter, as if everyone was holding their breath, waiting for the holocaust they knew was about to explode around them.

I'd been in air raids before, but this was like all of them put together. The noise deafened our ears and numbed our brains. The explosions came over us in waves, threatening to crush the life out of us. The dust in the air suffocated us. Through it all came the terrified screams of women and children, and even men.

I counted the squadrons of bombers and thought of the men I knew up there, the pilots holding their course on the bomb run in spite of flak and fighters; the bombardiers peering down through the nose perspex and toggling out their bombs. To them the inferno we were in was nothing but a series of blinking lights on a map, followed by little mushrooms of smoke. They couldn't imagine the agonized faces that I was looking at in the dim light of the naked light bulbs.

Suddenly it stopped. There was nothing but the staccato bangs of the flak; and the whimpering and crying.

Then, to my surprise the siren sounded a steady wail. There were shouts of 'All clear!' and people started to get up.

'No!' I shouted. 'It's not over yet. More are coming. There's a second wave!'

They stopped and stared at me. The lieutenant looked at me, questioning. I nodded. He turned to the crowd and said. 'He knows!'

Almost immediately the siren howled its warning again. The crowd moved back and steeled themselves for the new onslaught. It came.

If possible it was worse than ever. It seemed impossible that even the thick reinforced concrete of the bunker could resist the terrible blasts.

Finally it was over. All eyes were directed towards me. I tried to read those looks. Some were full of hatred, but most were just dumb and dazed. They had stopped asking why. They had lost their feelings of hate and patriotic fervour. They were old and tired. They were only surviving.

The lieutenant asked, 'Now?'

I nodded.

Slowly we moved out; out of the bunker into Hell on earth. It was a maelstrom of ruins, blazing buildings, crashing walls; — and everywhere bodies; writhing bodies, maimed bodies; dead bodies. At the entrance of the bunker, there was a hideous scene. Many had been running to the bunker, but hadn't made it before the bombs started to fall.

Everywhere the fire and police services were swinging into action. They were organizing military personnel into rescue squads to help them in their unequal task. It was the London Blitz all over again, but a hundred times worse.

A security officer came up to the lieutenant. 'Come on! We need you and your men!'

'I cannot leave my prisoner.'

'There are people dying in that rubble.' He looked at me. 'He can help too — or do you just kill people?'

The lieutenant was undecided. 'Will you parole yourself? Will you give your word as an officer and a gentleman that you will not take advantage of this and try to escape?'

'No,' I said. 'It is the duty of any officer to escape.'

In the pathway in the middle of the street, which wound between the hills of rubble on either side, rescue teams were carrying stretchers, and guiding wounded victims to the ambulances. There were weeping women, dazed old men, whimpering children.

I nodded to Albrecht. 'I'll give you my word. Let's go!'

It was hard to believe that this inferno had been the bustling, beautiful, dignified centre of the magnificent city of Berlin, probably the most impressive capital of Europe. Now the great sweep of Unter den Linden was reduced to a winding path between piles of rubble. Behind the hills of bricks and broken masonry were the skeletons of the buildings. Most of them dated from the late 1800's or early 1900's and they were solidly built. This was particularly true of the outside walls. As a result, the inside of the buildings was often gutted, and the floors collapsed, along with the roof, while the walls stayed relatively intact. Often the tall buildings became chimneys with the flames roaring up inside the floors to the roof, until the roof and one floor after another crashed down to the stronger ground floor, until often it too collapsed under the accumulated weight, and the whole mass crashed into the cellar, and it was in the cellars that the people from the apartments in the whole building took refuge during the air-raids.

That was the scene we found in the first building we went into. I had got rid of my handcuffs and we had joined a rescue team. We fought our way into what had been the ground floor. It was a jungle of fallen masonry, burning rafters, twisted girders, and everywhere smoke and dust.

As we groped our way in, bits and pieces, large and small, kept crashing down. So far the ground floor seemed mainly intact, except that the stairs from the cellar had been carried away, preventing the victims below from emerging from their refuge. The shouts and cries from the cellar indicated that there were casualties down there, and an urgent need for haste.

The team leaders started in, but then had to recoil. The debris hanging down from above started to fall. Then there was a louder crash as the ground floor gave way under the weight.

When we came back into the dust and gloom, we saw a gaping hole in front of us. From the depths below, there were now only moans and whimpers. Above, sections of the upper floors, steel girders, burning wooden beams and skeletons of walls continued to fall. The rescue team didn't hesitate. They were experienced and efficient. Ropes were dropped into the gloom below and secured above. The older, heavier men stayed above to handle the ropes and haul up the slings and stretchers. The younger, more agile light-weights were assigned to the job of sliding down into the cellar to dig out the victims, alive, dead and dying, to bring them to where the stretchers, slings and ropes were waiting to be hauled up to the surface.

Most of the men in the security and rescue service were too old for the armed forces. As one of the younger ones, I was immediately selected to go down. One of the older men stopped me, took off his helmet and put it on my head. The lieutenant and the guard followed me down the swaying ropes. These were old buildings, and the cellars had been deep. It seemed a long way down before my feet touched the piles of rubble in the cellar. We followed the leaders and started to dig into the debris, to release those trapped beneath it.

First, it was simply a question of guiding those who were still able to walk to the shaft where the rescuers were waiting. There were not many of these. They were mostly elderly women, crying loudly, moaning softly or just stumbling along, dazed and silent.

Then came the next phase, releasing those who were trapped under girders or rubble. When we had freed them, they could seldom walk, and had to be carried or dragged to the shaft where a medical team gave them what emergency treatment they could before they were lifted out, and separated the living from the dead. Most of the bodies we brought out seemed more dead than alive, but we handled them all with the same gentle tenderness.

It was gruelling work. Moving the debris was back-breaking, but we had to keep going. The moans and cries for help wouldn't let us stop. The dust and smoke choked us and never settled as the smouldering ruins kept collapsing.

Towards the end we were all close to collapse with fatigue. Finally there was only one pile of rubble left to shift. A protruding leg told us there was at least one more body under it. With aching backs and lacerated hands, we slowly moved enough to make sure there were no more bodies.

Suddenly one of the men at the front let out a yell.

'There's another cellar here!'

We all moved up to look. A few steps led down to a small doorway in the thick wall. There was no door left; just a low opening. As we looked through it, we shook our heads. It was almost blocked with masonry. There was a small opening under a fallen girder. When we peered through it, we saw that the cellar beyond was choked with smouldering debris.

'Nothing alive in there!' and they turned wearily away.

I started to follow. Then I heard it. Almost inaudible, unbelievable, but unmistakable, it was the tentative cry of a baby!

'Wait!'

The others turned round.

'There's a child in there!'

'No!' It was the security officer speaking. 'Nothing could still be alive in there! Besides there's no way we can get in there without some heavy equipment.'

'I can get through!' And indeed I was probably the only one slim enough to squeeze through.

'It'll collapse on you!'

'Listen! Can't you hear it?' It wasn't easy to hear, but I was sure of it.

'Well, at least take the rope.'

He tied a rope around my waist, put his hand on my shoulder, and wished me good luck with the slogan of the German coal miners.

'*Glück auf!*'

I was surprised at his concern. 'I'm not a miner, you know.'

'*Ja!* I know who you are!'

I had to wriggle my way through the tangled mess like a snake. It reminded me of burrowing through the hay in the barn when I was a kid on my uncle's farm. I had to lift every kind of obstacle to worm my way through. The danger was, it seemed to crash down again behind me, blocking the way back.

Occasionally I would stop, partly to rest, partly to listen for the fragile cries. Finally I emerged into an area that was at least a little more clear. It was also a little lighter. Looking up, I could see the sky through some of the holes in the ceiling.

Then I saw the body of the woman. At least I saw the upper part of her body. The rest was covered with rubble, and a girder lay across her back. I saw her blonde hair covered in dust. She was lying face down. I turned her head to look for signs of life. In spite of, or perhaps because of, the dirt and dust, it was a beautiful young face. The eyes were closed, but the body was slightly warm. I gently pulled an arm from under her, and felt for a pulse. It was feeble, but it was there. I tried artificial respiration, but the girder was in the way. I put my mouth to hers, trying desperately to breathe life into her.

The eyes opened. She started to move, but the girder was

pinning her down. I turned to try to free her, but she seemed to be protesting, feebly but urgently. I bent over to hear.

'No. I'm dying. Here! Take her!' She twisted her body as well as she could. I put my arms around her and tried to lift her.

Then the cry came again, still muffled, but close. With a great effort she took from underneath her the child she had been shielding. She was a golden-haired angel about two years old. Two blue eyes peered at me solemnly through their tears.

'Take her!' I could hardly hear her now. 'Take her and promise me. Take care of her — always!' There was a terrible urgency in her whisper. 'Promise! Please!'

'You must have relations. Where are they?'

'All gone! Promise!'

'Where is the father?'

'*Gefallen*!'

I remembered they used the word 'fallen' in the First World War.

'Promise! Before it's too late!' She was hanging on desperately waiting for my answer.

'But I'm not German!'

'What then?'

I pointed upwards. 'American!'

She looked confused and pained. 'I'm dying. Promise me!'

'I promise!'

A look of relief, almost a smile came over her face. '*Danke*!' Her head dropped.

The child turned and put her arms around her mother's neck. Slowly I pulled her away and took her into my arms.

That's the way they found us whey they finally dug their way through. They tried to take her from me, but we clung together. Out in the daylight, I was still dazed, and when the First Aid team came up to take her from me, I fought them off. They shrank back surprised at my vehemence. An official looking woman in a Red Cross uniform came up.

'What's the meaning of this? We'll take over.'

I turned away. 'I promised.'

My guard was beside me. He had the handcuffs in his hand. The lieutenant was behind him. I looked at him. He nodded.

The Red Cross woman came to take the baby. I still held on.
The lieutenant put his hand on my shoulder.

'I promised!'

Slowly he took my arms from around the child. He did it gently.
I knew it had to be. The Red Cross woman took her.

'Where will she go? How can I find her? I promised!'

The woman looked at me with hatred. '*Gangster! Terror-
flieger!*'

The guard snapped one bracelet of the handcuffs on my wrist,
and the other on his own.

The train to Frankfurt was to leave from the Charlottenburg
railway station. By some miracle the S-bahn elevated railway
had been kept running. Once more I found myself handcuffed
to my uniformed guard surrounded by a hostile crowd. But
even here in Berlin after days and nights of bombing, there was
not the hatred I expected. The mass of people on the S-bahn
seemed more dazed than bitter. They obviously were not in-
flamed by the vicious Goebbels press campaign against the gangster *Terror-flieger*. There was even a trace of the famous Berlin
good-natured humour. In fact they were not much different
from the crowd in a London tube. The train was terribly crowded.
A little old lady got squeezed between me and my guard.

'Give me a little more room, will you!'

She was being pressed against the arm which was handcuffed
to the guard. I raised my arm and showed the manacles. 'Sorry!'

'*Himmel!* You'd have been better off staying in jail!'

Everyone laughed.

The train came to a halt. A young woman was about to get off
when she remembered the bunch of flowers she had left in the
luggage rack and from which she was now separated.

'*Meine Blumen!* My flowers!'

I was taller than most of the crowd in the train. With my free
arm, I reached up to the rack, took the bunch of flowers and
passed it over the heads to the young lady.

'*Danke schön!*' she said cheerily.

'*Bitte schön!*' I replied.

On the train to Frankfurt, we settled down again in a public
second class compartment. The lieutenant, aware of the reaction

of the other passengers when they saw the handcuffs, made a suggestion.

'If you give your parole again not to escape, we can take off the handcuffs. I trust you.

'No! Thank you!'

I was constantly searching for an opportunity for escape, even if the chances looked slim whilst I sat pressed close to Lieutenant Albrecht on my right and handcuffed to the guard on my left.

Albrecht was obviously upset at my refusal to give my word.

'Does that mean you are going to try to escape?'

'It means I'm not going to parole myself. It's my duty as an officer to try to escape.'

'Why? Who says so?'

'That's what I believe.'

'Then I'll have to prevent it!'

He took his Mauser pistol from its leather holster, flicked off the safety catch, and slipped it back leaving the leather flap open.

'I'm sorry!' he said.

The train was soon out of the city and rattling through the countryside.

I tried my first plan.

'May I go to the toilet?'

'Of course!' The lieutenant nodded to the guard. He stood up. I held up my manacled wrist for the lieutenant to unlock it. He shook his head.

'Only if you parole yourself.'

So I remained manacled to the guard through the whole procedure.

Even when I washed my hands, the two of us struggled to get to the diminutive wash basin, handle the taps, fill the basin, rinse our hands and dry them, while the train rocked and swayed. We struggled out of the narrow door and found the lieutenant waiting outside with his pistol drawn. The three of us stumbled back to our seats.

'OK?' asked the lieutenant.

'Great!' I said. 'That's the first time I've ever done that with an Honor Guard!'

'Well, I'm sorry, but I wanted you to parole yourself. You did it in Berlin, and you were wonderful. Why not now? There's no possibility of escape. Even if you got away from Schneider, I'd have to shoot you! I'm sorry!'

'I understand.'

'Do you?' He looked at me seriously. 'You see, if you escaped, I should be shot.'

'No!'

'Oh yes! Believe me!'

I believed him.

But I still racked my brain to find a way to escape. I considered even the wildest schemes. The main problem was that I was handcuffed to the guard Schneider, but it was Albrecht who kept the key. I even thought of going to the toilet again with Schneider. He was smaller than me, so the plan was to grab him just as we got close to the outside door of the train, throw the door open, and leap out with Schneider in my arms. I would hope that Lieutenant Albrecht would not accompany us the second time or, if he did, that the suddenness of the action wouldn't give him enough time to shoot me. The real problem, of course, would be freeing myself from the handcuffs that bound me to Schneider.

Another plan was to make a grab for Albrecht's pistol, which was now in an open holster, with its safety catch off, hold it to his head, and force him to unlock the handcuffs. Here, the problem was that, knowing Albrecht, he would call my bluff. Also, Schneider, being manacled to me, could throw all his weight away from me and pull me away from Albrecht. He would then have all the others in the compartment to help him overpower me. I looked at Albrecht. He smiled at me, a warm friendly smile. He wouldn't believe I could pull the trigger on him.

So I had to revise the plan. I decided that the first priority had to be getting out of the handcuffs. Using the key seemed to be out of the question, but Albrecht himself had given me an idea when he clicked off the safety catch and left his holster unbuttoned. He wore his pistol on his left side and that was the side of my free right hand. Of course, his right hand was resting on the holster, ready to draw, but I hoped that during the long journey to Frankfurt he would relax, and the moment would come when I could whip the pistol out of its holster, put the point of the muzzle on the large lock on the bracelet on my left wrist, pull the trigger and blow the lock.

Because of the heat, the window in the compartment was lowered. This meant that there was an opening about three feet wide and almost two feet high. I reckoned I could dive straight through it before anyone could stop me.

Things seemed to be going my way. Albrecht, Schneider and I had been going since at least four in the morning, and had worked flat out after the air-raid in Berlin.

Schneider was much older than Albrecht or I, and he was the first to succumb. His head was soon resting on my shoulder, and he was fast asleep. Not long after, Albrecht was asleep too. His hand had fallen away from his pistol. Swiftly, but smoothly I slipped the gun out of the holster, bringing my other arm around at the same time. I put the muzzle to the lock of the bracelet and pulled the trigger.

There was a loud click! And nothing else!

Schneider was looking at his hand in disbelief. I turned to the lieutenant. He was eyeing me perfectly relaxed.

'It wasn't loaded,' he said casually.

It took a little while to sink in. Then I started to laugh. Albrecht smiled, and then began laughing with me. The others in the compartment looked at us as if we were mad.

As we stepped out of the train in the Frankfurt Hauptbahnhof, I was surprised that it was not more seriously damaged. The glass roofing was gone, but the main walls were still standing. Like most of the public buildings built in the golden days of the Kaiser's Germany and the Austro-Hungarian Empire before World War I, the main railway stations were massive edifices constructed of thick heavy stone. Like the great cathedrals, built almost like the pyramids, these monumental landmarks were remarkably resistant, not only to incendiaries, but even to high explosives.

But when we came through the great central portal into the Bahnhof Platz, it was as if we were standing in a bowl, the sides of which were a rubble of bricks and stones cascading down from the skeletons of the few walls left standing. In front of us was what had been the Kaiserstrasse. Between two hills of rubble, like a small stream meandering through a valley, ran a small winding path. It was so narrow that, being handcuffed to Schneider, I had difficulty passing the pedestrians coming in the opposite direction. Twice Schneider fell against the piles of rubble, and I helped him up.

At the bottom of the Kaiserstrasse is a park, the Taunus Anlage, and it was here that we were to start the last stage of our journey. Albrecht consulted the timetable posted on what looked to me like a street-car stop, and checked his watch.

'We have twenty minutes to wait. Would you like to see something of Frankfurt?'

'Of course'

'*Komm!*'

We went first to the end of the Taunus Anlage closest to the River Main. Here we saw the partially bombed-out Frankfurt theatre, the Schauspielhaus. It was half destroyed, but I could see it had been a beautiful building; not large or pretentious, but in beautiful taste.

'Eighteenth century,' said Albrecht.

Then we walked to the other end of the Taunus Anlage: the Opernplatz. Here we saw the burned out shell of the Opera house. It was a magnificent example of German nineteenth-century architecture; far more imposing than the Schauspielhaus, overwhelmingly impressive; even more so because it was a burned out ruin. Like the Schauspielhaus, it was a noble, tragic monument of accusation and reproach.

The three of us stood and looked for a few minutes. Then we turned and walked back through the park.

A few miles north-west of Frankfurt, at the foot of the Taunus hills is the town of Oberursel, and it was here that the Luftwaffe had established their Interrogation Centre. We arrived there in the little electric tram which still winds its way from the Taunus Anlage to the lovely towns of the Taunus.

At the entrance to the centre, Albrecht unlocked the handcuffs. He and Schneider first saluted me, and then warmly shook my hand.

'Thanks!' I said.

'It was a pleasure!' he said.

The Interrogation Centre went by the German name: 'Auswerte-stelle West'. I expected the worst, but nothing about the place was as expected. In the first place, Oberursel was a charming, sleepy town, behind which rose the gentle slopes of the Taunus hills, covered with beautiful trees, with here and there an old castle, perched above its village. There was no industry there in those days, and it was far enough away from Frankfurt, to have escaped bombing. The houses were either solid granite monu-ments of the Kaiser's Reich, or quaint, half-timbered gems of older days, some having remained unchanged and as neat and clean as in the sixteenth century.

The centre itself was a collection of drab wooden barracks, which contrasted with the neater, older buildings of the town, but there was none of the sinister atmosphere one would expect around a German interrogation centre.

Even inside the atmosphere was somehow surprisingly relaxed. I was taken to a sort of small reception area. The facilities were obviously overloaded. Not only were there large numbers of US fighter pilots; there were also American and RAF bomber crews coming through. Sitting on a wooden bench were two American officers. The Captain greeted me:

'Hi, Major, join the club.'

Behind a sort of window, like a bank teller was a German private busily writing. Another German soldier was standing beside the wooden bench.

'Hi,' I said. 'What's the drill here?'

'This guy seems to be the receptionist. He checks you in.'

I looked at the other soldier.

'I guess he's just a visiting fireman,' said the Captain.

When it was my turn, I gave my name, rank and serial number. We were then moved to what I later learned was referred to by both POW's and Germans as 'The Cooler'. This was simply a row of small, clean, simple cells leading off a long corridor. Before I had time to get bored in my cell, a guard came in and asked me to follow him.

We stopped in front of an office door. The guard knocked, a cheerful voice said, *'Herein'*, and I stepped into a small cluttered office and the door closed behind me. A good-looking young man in the uniform of a Luftwaffe private looked up at me. I didn't know it then, but I was in the presence of Hanns Scharff, the Luftwaffe's Master Interrogator.

I stood at attention, steeling myself to give only name, rank and serial number, regardless of threats or even torture.

He got up from his desk and came towards me, hands outstretched and a charming, broad smile on his handsome face.

'Well, Goody! We've been waiting for you for a long time! I'm delighted to see you!'

Goody was a nickname used by only some of my closest friends, and, occasionally, as a call sign on missions.

'Look!' he went on. His English had only the slightest trace of an accent. 'You're in my Hall of Fame. These are the top VIP's (that's Very Important Prisoners) I've been waiting for.'

I found myself looking at a photograph of myself pinned to the wall. There were also pictures of Zemke, Gabreski, Blakeslee, Godfrey, Gentile, and a few others.

Scharff was happily chatting on. 'You'll soon be seeing a lot of your friends from Debden. Some of them you probably thought had been killed. We've got Peterson, Bunte, Clotfelder, Van Epps, Mills, Oh! And your close friend Millikan. I'll try to arrange for you to go to Stalag Luft III. That's where Millie is.'

He was right. I had thought many of the list he recited were dead. What's more, he went on to give me the latest news of the Group. Glover had taken over my job as squadron commander. Bob Mirsch's wife had had a baby boy.

'But it's too bad you missed last night,' he said. 'The Fourth Group were celebrating their one thousandth victory. One thousand destroyed. It was a great party. They invited Bubbles and the rest of the gang from The Rose and Crown in Saffron Walden, and many a toast was drunk to you — and other absent friends!'

He talked of my friends as if they were his friends, as if he was part of it, and understood it, and was a member. It was a brilliant performance, and I could see that it could have a tremendous effect on a depressed and lonely POW, expecting brutality, even torture, from a vicious enemy. He would suddenly find a friend; a friend who knew his friends and his squadron — almost one of the gang.

I prided myself that I recognised his tour de force for what it was. I was amazed at his intimate knowledge of personal details of the Group and its pilots, and couldn't imagine how he had amassed so much information; but there was a hint of the flourish of the magician pulling rabbits out of the hat that strengthened my determination to show no flicker of surprise, nor volunteer any comment. In fact, I resented this impertinent young German outsider intruding on the privacy of *my* Group.

But Scharff seemed blissfully unaware of my cold silence.

'Sit down, and relax,' he said, waving me to one of the two armchairs, while he slipped behind his desk. 'We have something very urgent to do. We must send a telegram to your mother to tell her you're OK. Unfortunately she was informed that you were missing, presumed dead. God knows why. Just the usual Pentagon confusion I suppose! Now, let's see; what's her address?'

I remained silent.

'Well, it will be in your file,' he continued. 'I have it here on my desk. Let's see: "James Alexander Goodson, born New York City, 21st March 1921" — Ah, you're Aries, I might have known it — "University of Toronto ...".' He mumbled through a complete and accurate curriculum vitae, including such details of the fact that I had been on the *Athenia*, and that I spoke French and German. Finally he came to my mother's address.

'Ah! We had to bring this up to date just the other day. You probably haven't heard yet. Your mother has moved down to Nassau in the Bahamas.'

He wrote out the address. 'Now, what would you like to say?'

'You're on your own.' I didn't know why he was going through this farce. Surely he didn't think I would believe that I could simply send a telegram from a POW camp in Germany to my mother in Nassau, Bahamas.

Scharff ignored my lack of cooperation. 'How about: Alive and well as Prisoner of War, Love Jim.'

'James!'

'What?'

'James! She calls me James.'

'Good! James! Now we'll send this through the Swedish Red

Cross. She should have it in about three or four days.'

It was some time before I learned about it, but he was absolutely right.

The next day, I was back in Scharff's office. 'It's a beautiful day. Feel like a walk?'

'Do I have a choice?'

'Of course!' He looked shocked. 'I just thought you'd like a walk up into the Taunus. It's very beautiful. Also, you've still got some shrapnel in you. We have a nice hospital up there. They can take a look at you.'

He was right. It was beautiful! We walked through woods of beautiful beech and pine. We passed quaint old half-timbered buildings with ancient painting and Gothic writing on their spotless walls and beams. Most had bright red and white geraniums in window-boxes. It was a Hansel and Gretel setting. The contrast between ancient and modern was striking. Scharff proudly pointed out the large towers and metal discs on top of the Taunus hills which were part of a pre-war telephone-television system, which he said was the first in the world.

Then he pointed to where the ruins of the castle of Kronberg rose above the town.

'There's also the castle of the Princes of Hessen in Kronberg. It was the home of Friedrich and his wife, Princess Victoria, the eldest daughter of Queen Victoria of England.'

'Yes,' I said. 'Friedrich's father, Kaiser Wilhelm I, didn't give up the throne till he died at the age of ninety-three, by which time Friedrich was dying of cancer. Friedrich was an Anglophile, and he and Victoria had a dream of bringing England and Germany together to guarantee the peace of Europe. It's interesting to think that if Wilhelm had died at a normal age, or even if Friedrich had had a normal lifespan, there would probably never have been a First World War, and, therefore probably no Second World War either. No millions of dead on the Western Front then; no millions of dead on the battlefields and in the cities now; and all that hanging on happenstance.'

Scharff looked at me in amazement. Europeans were always surprised when Americans showed a knowledge of history.

'Maybe you don't agree with that. Maybe you are of the Gibbons' belief that history is governed by economic and social forces rather than the Macaulay theory that great men and their deeds mould the fate of nations.' I was showing off now, but Scharff seemed genuinely intrigued.

'The Nazi philosophy is that great men and great nations shape the future,' he said. 'The Führer and the great German nation will rule the destinies of nations for years to come.'

'And of course you, as a fervent Nazi, believe that too.'

'Of course!' he said.

'Of course!' I said.

I looked him in the eyes and smiled. It took a moment or two, then he smiled back.

'Well, you have to admit that Hitler has accomplished great things and revolutionized Germany!' he said.

'He was smart enough, or lucky enough to epitomize the ambitions and desires of the German people. He was voted into power, and even now I'm sure he has the vast majority of Germans behind him. If he hadn't been in the right place at the right time, saying what the Germans wanted to hear, he would still be an unknown house painter. Social and economic forces made him, and social and economic forces will break him!'

I waited for a reaction from Hanns. I waited in vain.

'You don't agree,' I said.

'Are you interviewing me or am I interviewing you?'

'You don't ask me any questions,' I said. 'So I'm just making conversation.'

'The trouble is, I know all about the Fourth, and all I need to know about the details of your air force career. I even know how much you know; so I know that you don't know anything that I don't already know.'

I believed him. 'So when do I leave you and move on to POW camp?'

'What's your hurry? Don't you like it here? Believe me, it's more pleasant here. I enjoy talking to you, and I had hoped you liked talking to me.'

'Of course I do. And I'm in no hurry at all to leave this lovely spot. In fact, if the Princes of Hessen have excess room in their *Schloss*, I'm available.'

'Well, I could try to arrange for you to visit the castle, but it might be difficult.'

'Don't put yourself out, Hanns. I'll come back after the war and spend some time in Schloss Kronberg.' I was quite serious. Very often I have said to myself, one day I'll do this, one day I'll live there and so on; and no matter how remote or unlikely the prediction at that time, in many cases, it actually came true. I liked to think it was a question of setting one's sights on something and dedicating onself to achieving it, but it might be nothing but sheer chance. Anyway, in this case, after the war, when my friend Pertram had persuaded the Princes of Hessen to convert their castle into a hotel, I spent many a night there, overlooking the magnificent trees sent from all over the world as wedding presents to the ill-fated Royal couple; chatting with my friend Westrich, the great and charming lawyer, who lived next door; and even sleeping in the room which had been left unchanged since Queen Victoria slept there.

Scharff looked at me quizzically.

'Yes,' he said. 'I believe you might just do that!'

Finally, we reached the small hospital of 'Hohe-Mark'. It was a lovely old building. Typical of the solid mansions of the Taunus, almost like a church, with its clock tower and pointed roof. It was nestled among the great trees of the Taunus, and had its own peaceful little park.

Most of the patients were Allied airmen from Oberursel, and it was obvious they were being extremely well treated, and had great respect and affection for all the staff, from Dr Ittershagen, the chief surgeon, on down.

I understood why when I was the object of their tender mercies. Some of the flak which had shot me down had come up through the floor of the cockpit, peppering the undersides of my legs, and wounding my knee. The treatment at the hospital was excellent, if sometimes undignified. I remember being bent over and hearing the clink of the pieces of shrapnel, as they were dug out of my flesh, and dropped into the metal enamel bowl.

It was all part of the unreal world of Oberursel, in which you had to keep reminding yourself that you were in the hands of the enemy. We were made to feel that we were among friends. We were taken on walks into the Taunus, up to the hospital, even into Frankfurt to the swimming pool. We met German pilots and talked flying in the same way as we did among ourselves. There was a famous cognac party in Scharff's office, when a group of pilots from 334 Squadron of the Fourth Group were invited to greet (Duane) 'Bee' Beeson, their CO, when he arrived at Oberursel. 'Bee', always inclined to be more correctly military than most of the wild ones of the Fourth, froze as he stepped into Scharff's office to be greeted by 'Blacksnake' Peterson, 'Van' Van Epps, 'Clod' Clotfelder, 'Hank' Mills and 'Bud' Care, all waving glasses and yelling their welcome. Major Duane Beeson maintained a straight face, and a rigid brace. 'I don't know these gentlemen', he said, determined not to fall into what he figured had to be a trap; but that only lasted a minute, and soon the Boise Bee was relaxing with his boys. Later, when he learned that Scharff, and, indeed, the whole of the Luftwaffe, knew all about the Fourth, and their red-nosed planes, Bee sent the famous postcard back to Blakeslee in Debden: 'The red-noses are known and respected here. Paint them all red!'

The atmosphere at Oberursel was even more amazing against the background of Gestapo atrocities and the Concentration Camps. Hanns Scharff has been credited with the introduction of this revolutionary, humane, and undoubtedly, effective approach to interrogation, and he was obviously the instigator. Nevertheless, as he himself admitted, he couldn't have got away with it if he hadn't had the backing of his boss, Horst Barth and CO Oberstleutnant Killinger, and he, in turn, must have had the approval, at least tacit, of Göring. There were Gestapo officers at Oberursel, but they were kept well in the background. To me, it was another example of the schizophrenia of war-time Germany. There was the Germany of the ordinary German civilian, of the Luftwaffe, Navy and regular army; decent people with principles. Then there was the darker side, which no one dared admit existed: the Germany of the gas chambers, the Gestapo, the political arm of the SS and all the other horrors of Naziism.

Scharff's world was the innocent world of pre-war values. Before the war he had spent much of his youth in South Africa where he had married the daughter of Lieutanant-Colonel Claude

Stokes of the Royal Flying Corps, who had been shot down and killed by von Richthofen in 1917. I'm sure that these international influences in no way diminished Scharff's patriotic loyalty, but it was a loyalty to the old Germany of strong principles and fair play. For this he was prepared to fight injustice, even on the part of the powerful Gestapo forces of that other Germany.

This was well demonstrated by Scharff's fair and impartial defence of Walter Beckham, a leading ace with eighteen destroyed, who arrived in Oberursel at the same time as an official accusation from Poladen where he was shot down, that he had strafed civilians in a small village before he crashed.

Scharff also put his own career on the line with his tireless work in the affair of the Greifswald Seven. Greifswald, a small university town on the Baltic, suddenly found itself attacked by low flying, strafing P-38 Lightnings and P-51 Mustangs. The pilots involved were relatively inexperienced, a fact underlined by the loss of twelve planes in the Mustang Group alone. Five of the pilots were killed; seven were taken prisoner, and arrived at Oberursel. German propaganda wanted fuel for their *Luftgangster* programme, and Göring in his 'holier than thou' role of the World War I ace demanded a personal report. It took a lot of courage for Obergefreiter (Private 1st Class) Scharff to take the unpopular course of proving, by brilliant interviewing and conscientious study of evidence, including gun-camera film, that the prisoners were innocent, and that any wilful attack on civilians had been made by the pilots who had either returned to their base, or had been killed.

Scharff was deeply concerned about incorrect behaviour on the part of Allied airmen. He told me the story of a B-17 of the 100th Group which was badly shot up by German fighters. The pilot lowered his wheels and flap as the accepted signal of surrender, but, when a Luftwaffe fighter pulled up alongside to escort them to the nearest airport, the rear gunner of the Fortress opened up and killed him. Ever since, said Scharff, the Luftwaffe picked out the distinguishing markings of the 100th Group for their most aggressive attacks. It was certainly true the 100th took a terrible beating, and even had the dubious distinction of being the one group that lost every plane on a single mission; no one got back.

Scharff didn't get much change out of me with this story.

'I've never heard of dropping wheels and flaps as an official sign of surrender. It's more likely to mean that the hydraulic system's been shot out, or that the pilot's slowing down the plane to make it easier for the crew to bail out. In any case, the poor rear-gunner probably wouldn't know what was going on, and any crew would be concerned with bailing out, not getting fighter escort to a German airfield.'

Scharff also told me that USAAF top commanders had instructed pilots to shoot German pilots in their parachutes. 'Well,' I said, 'they never told me, or anyone in my group, and I don't believe any pilots do it.'

Scharff kept it up, saying they had camera film to prove improper conduct on the part of the US Air Force. If this aim was to annoy me, he was successful.

'If you're so anxious to find atrocities, you don't have to go so far afield. Why don't you drop in on your Gestapo friends and study their methods, or interrogate some of Germany's Jewish families, if you can find any.'

That seemed to be the end of any close relationship we had. Shortly afterwards I left Oberursel.

There was one final visit to Scharff's office. He told me he had enjoyed meeting me, and wished me well.

'Thanks!' I said. 'It has been very interesting here; but, since your interrogation of me is over, may I ask you a question?'

'Of course.'

'You have amassed a great deal of detailed information about the airmen in the various groups, and everyone is amazed when you go into your act. That undoubtedly enables you to get more of this type of detail, so that not a single POW has given you only his name, rank and serial number, as he swore to do when he came in. I'm sure your methods are far more effective, and, of course, more civilised than those of the Gestapo. But surely the problem is that the pilots you interview don't know anything that you don't already know. It's great that your file on me contains information, and even photographs, which you couldn't even get from *The Stars and Stripes* forces newspaper; but what good does that do you when it comes to fighting the war? You

showed me the line-up of my squadron for a recent mission, but
what does it matter whether Smith, Jones or Jackson is flying
in a given position, and is Hitler really going to change his tactics
because you can tell him the barmaid's name in the Crackers
Club? Don't you sometimes feel you're wasting your talents?'

Scharff was a little taken back. 'No,' he said. 'We have assembled
a lot of very useful information, and we have been successful in
supplying our superiors with the information they have requested.
Pilots know more than they realise themselves. Nevertheless, I
admit that there is a lot in the area of new secret technology
where you combat officers can't help us. Take a look at this,
for instance.'

He unrolled a blue-print on his desk. 'This is a Rolls-Royce jet
engine. You see it's a photocopy of an original.' He pointed to
the Rolls-Royce name down in the corner.

'Do you know how a jet engine works?'

I shook my head.

Scharff explained the principle of jet propulsion, using the
Rolls-Royce drawing.

'Now, these ducts on this turbo are what interest us. These
turbos rotate at speeds up to 25,000 rpm. At those speeds, these
little ducts are inclined to fly off, and this could cause imbalances
which could result in the whole thing disintegrating. We believe
the British have an alloy which handles this problem, and we'd like
the formula. Of course, we know you pilots don't know anything
about things, but that doesn't mean we don't learn a lot from
you.'

'And what have you learned from me?' I asked.

He smiled. 'That we have a worthy adversary,' he said.

As I lay in bed in the cooler on my last night in Oberursel, I
pondered the enigma of Hanns Scharff. I felt that there was a
phoneyness about his friendly, almost pally, approach to those
who were for him, after all, enemy officers from whom his job
was to extract information which they were not allowed to give
him.

There was no doubt about his efficiency in his job. I was sure
his methods got better results than torture or other means of
putting on pressure. The system was simple. A tired, worried

POW, probably suffering from some degree of shock, fearing the worst, suddenly found himself, not facing physical or mental torture from Nazi thugs, but being greeted by a charming and sympathetic young man, who not only spoke his language, but knew all about him, his squadron and his buddies. No wonder Scharff could boast that none of the POW's he interviewed limited their conversation to 'name, rank, and serial number'. However, I still feel that very little of the information gathered by Scharff was of enormous help to the Germans.

Even long after the war, when the excellent book, *The Interrogator* on which Scharff collaborated with Colonel Ray Tolliver appeared, there were no dramatic disclosures. Indeed, most of Scharff's work helped the Allies more than Germany. This was particularly true of his investigations into cases in which American pilots were accused of attacking civilians or Luftwaffe pilots who had bailed out. His findings were strictly correct and fair. He found evidence of misconduct, but usually on the part of young, inexperienced pilots in new squadrons with few combat missions behind them. As for POW's like Beckham and the Greifswald Seven, Scharff defended them successfully, at considerable risk to himself and his career.

Nevertheless, his holier-than-thou attitude on this subject annoyed me. While it was true that the Luftwaffe pilots had high standards of chivalry, Scharff must have known about the atrocities of the SS and Gestapo, the concentration camps, and other Nazi atrocities. Against this background, his play-acting at Oberursel was as unrealistic as Oscar Wilde's Victorian comedy being played at the outset of the war.

But the more I considered Scharff's position and background, and the more I learned about Nazi Germany, the more I realised that he was perfectly sincere and honest according to his lights. Scharff's schizophrenia was the schizophrenia of Germany. The decent people tried to uphold the old traditions of decency and honour. If they knew about Nazi atrocities, they put them out of their minds. If the facts intruded so strongly that they could not be denied, Scharff would probably have argued: 'If others break the code of honour, then all the more reason for me to uphold it'. But the facts seldom did intrude. People knew that political enemies of the Third Reich were put in concentration camps, which were obviously no more comfortable than other prisons. That people died in them were rumours, not facts, and everyone will believe what he wants to believe, and not believe what he cannot bring himself to believe. Albert Speer gave the most honest reply for all decent Germans at his trial in Nuremberg: 'No, I didn't know, but I could have known, and I should have known. Therefore, I plead guilty.'

I now look on Hanns Scharff as a decent, honourable, outstanding man, who defended the right and held to his own high principles of honour while serving his country faithfully and extremely capably. In his position in Nazi Germany in 1944, that was no mean feat!

When we left for prison camp, Scharff was at the railway station to say goodbye to us.

'Well', he said to me, 'what do you think of our interrogation methods? Not too bad, eh?'

'Personally,' I replied, 'I was very disappointed in you.'

His smile disappeared. 'What do you mean?' His voice was angry.

'You never asked me for my name, rank and serial number!'

'Dammit! I always forget something!' The charming smile was back.

Postscript

After the war, there weren't many of us left, and those of us who were still around were not too good at reunions. We knew what we'd been through together could never be relived.

I heard that Johnnie Godfrey had married a beautiful girl, had two fine boys, and had become a highly successful businessman, with his own private planes, and a string of race horses for good measure. But I didn't get in touch with him until I heard that his amazing luck had finally run out. He had contracted multiple sclerosis.

At first he refused to accept it, and fought it with his usual energy. He organised an international group of fellow sufferers, he contacted every expert in the world, but the crippling disease continued its inexorable fatal course.

The last time I saw him, he was in a clinic in Germany. He was lying helpless in bed, and it was difficult for me to hide the shock when I saw how the handsome face and six foot two frame had deteriorated. Only the piercing black eyes were recognisable.

'How you doing, Johnnie?' My question was stupid, but what else could I say?

'I'm dying, Goody.' He had trouble mouthing the words. The muscles in his face had gone.

'Well, I guess we're all dying.'

He shook his head. 'It's OK, Goody. I've had a good run for my money. I've hit the highs, and the lows, and it's all been good.

'I've done a lot of thinking while I've been lying in bed — waiting; and think I've learned a lot about life — and death. I don't mean I understand the meaning of life, no one can; but I think I know what life is for: life is for living; living to the full. If you've done that, death isn't so sad. And, by God, we've lived life to the full. I did it all a little faster than most people; but I did it. Death is only sad for people who have never lived — whatever age they die at.'

'Funny,' I said, 'I came to the same conclusion when I spent a night thinking I was going to be shot. It's like a game. It's only good if you throw yourself into it and play it to the hilt, and enjoy it. Then it's good.'

'And it's not only the high spots that are good. You need the lows too. Even prison camp was good for me. I was a spoiled kid when I went back for the hero's treatment; being a POW made me human again. You know what I'm thinking of now? Not the successes and the ballyhoo and the glory. I'm back in the Mess in Debden. Mac's banging the piano and those crazy wonderful characters . . . Don, Millie, Hank, Red Dog, Deacon, Jim, Bud . . .'

'Yeah! We were crazy — and naive — and corny —'

'And great!' he added.

After a pause he said, 'Do you remember that poem you had put up in the Mess? You knew the guy that wrote it, he was an American in the RCAF, and got killed early on.'

'Sure,' I said, 'John Magee. He called it "High Flight".'

'How did it go?'

I recited it for him.

Oh, I have slipped the surly bonds of earth
And danced the skies on laughter-silvered wings;
Sunward I've climbed, and joined the tumbling mirth
Of sun-split clouds — and done a hundred things
You have not dreamed of — wheeled and soared and swung
High in the sunlit silence. Hov'ring there
I've chased the shouting wind along, and flung
My eager craft through footless halls of air.
Up, up the long, delirious, burning blue
I've topped the windswept heights with easy grace
Where never lark, or even eagle flew —
And, while with silent, lifting mind I've trod
The high untrespassed sanctity of space,
Put out my hand, and touched the face of God.

Appendix
and Index

Appendix

ACES OF THE FOURTH FIGHTER GROUP

The official US Air Force definition of an 'Ace', is a pilot who has destroyed a minimum of five enemy aircraft.

There are conflicting lists of top-scoring aces. Some take into consideration planes claimed on the last mission which were not confirmed by cine camera film or independent eye witnesses; others list only aerial victories. We have simply taken the list that is officially confirmed by the War Department.

Maj John T. Godfrey	36	Lt Col Jack Oberhansley	9
Maj James A. Goodson	32	1st Lt Grover C. Siems	9
Maj Don S. Gentile	30	1st Lt Van E. Chandler	9
1st Lt Ralph K. Hofer	27	Capt William B. Smith	9
Maj Duane W. Beeson	25	1st Lt James W. Ayers	8
Maj Fred W. Glover	24	Capt Carl R. Alfred	8
Lt Col Claiborne H. Kinnard	20	1st Lt Joe H. Joiner	7
Capt Nicholas Megura	19	Col Chesley G. Peterson	7
Maj Pierce W. McKennon	19	Capt Raymond C. Care	7
Maj George Carpenter	18	1st Lt William O. Antonides	7
Capt Charles F. Anderson	18	Maj Henry L. Mills	6
Col Donald J.M. Blakeslee	17	Capt Kenneth G. Smith	6
Maj Gerald E. Montgomery	17	Maj Winslow M. Sobanski	6
Lt Col James A. Clark	16	Maj Michael G.H. McPharlin	6
Maj Louis L. Norley	16	1st Lt Clemens A. Fiedler	6
Capt Willard W. Millikan	15	Capt Archie W. Chatterly	6
Maj Howard (Deacon) Hively	15	1st Lt Robert F. Nelson	6
Capt Albert L. Schlegel	15	1st Lt Frank E. Speer	6
1st Lt H. Thomas Biel	13	1st Lt Douglas P. Pederson	6
Capt Joseph L. Lang	12	1st Lt Arthur R. Bowers	6
Lt Col Sidney S. Woods	12	Capt Carl G. Payne	5
1st Lt Paul S. Riley	11	1st Lt Gilert L. Kesler	5
Capt Kendall E. Carlson	11	Capt Thomas P. Bell	5
Capt Shelton W. Monroe	11	1st Lt Loton D. Jennings	5
Col Everett W. Stewart	10	Lt Col Roy W. Evans	5
Capt Frank C. Jones	10	1st Lt Spiros N. Pissanos	5
Capt Donald M. Malmsten	10	Maj Gerald C. Brown	5
Capt Ted E. Lines	10	1st Lt Alex Rafalovich	5
Capt Victor J. France	10	Capt Vasseure H. Wynn	5
Capt Donald R. Emerson	10	1st Lt Jack D. McFaddan	5
Maj James R. Happel	10	Capt Robert D. Hobert	5
Capt Joseph H. Bennett	9	Capt Nelson M. Dickey	5
Capt Bernard L. McGrattan	9	1st Lt Kenneth G. Helfrecht	5
Lt Vermont Garrison	9	1st Lt Gordon A. Denson	5
Capt David W. Howe	9	F/O Donald P. Baugh	5

Pilots of the Eagle Squadrons at the time of transfer to the Fourth Fighter Group, of the Eighth Air Force in September, 1942.

71st EAGLE SQUADRON

Maj Gus Daymond,
　commander, Burbank, Calif.
Capt Oscar H. Coen, Carbondale, Ill.
Capt R.S. Sprague, San Diego, Calif.
Lt M.G. McPharlin, Hastings, Mich.
Capt S.A. Maureillo, Astoria, N.Y.
Lt T.J. Andrews, Costa Mesa, Calif.
Lt W.T. O'Regan, Los Angeles, Calif.
Lt H.H. Strickland, Washington, D.C.
Lt R.D. McMinn,
　Salt Lake City, Utah
Lt W.J. Hollander, Raleigh, N.C.
Lt H.L. Stewart, Raleigh, N.C.
Lt James A. Clark, Jr., Westbury, L.I.
Lt W.C. Brite, Evansville, Ind.
Lt G.C. Ross, Albuquerque, N.M.
Lt. A.H. (Hoppy)
　Hopson, Dallas, Tex.
Lt Robert (Junior)
　Priser, Tucson, Ariz.
Lt G.H. Witlow, Denver, Colo.
Lt J.F. Lutz, Fulton, Mo.
Lt Howard (Deacon)
　Hively, Athens, O.
Lt S.M. Anderson, Indianapolis, Ind.
Lt M.S. Vosberg, Azusa, Calif.
Lt H.L. (Hank) Mills, Leonia, N.J.
Lt Duane W. Beeson, Boise, Idaho.
Lt R.C. (Bud) Care, Angola, Ind.
Lt R.A. Boock, Springfield, Ill.
Lt J.C. Harrington, Buffalo, N.Y.
Lt A.J. Seaman, Greenville, N.C.
Lt Victor J. France,
　Oklahoma City, Okla.
Lt Vernon A. Boehle,
　Indianapolis, Ind.
Lt W.B. Morgan, Honolulu, T.H.

121st EAGLE SQUADRON

Maj W.J. Daley,
　commander, Amarillo, Tex.
Capt Selden R. Edner,
　San Jose, Calif.
Lt Gilbert (Gunner)

121st EAGLE *(cont.)*

　Halsey, Chickasha, Okla.
Lt G.B. Fetrow Upland, Calif.
Lt Frank R. Boyles, Mt. Vernon, N.Y.
Lt E.D. Beattie, Albany, Ga.
Lt F.O. Smith, Foard City, Tex.
Lt A.D. Young, Buffalo, Kan.
Lt B.A. Taylor, Salem, Ore.
Lt J.M. Osborne, Washington, D.C.
Lt Cadman V. Padgett, Bethseda, Md.
Lt Frank M. Fink,
　Philadelphia, Penn.
Lt D.K. Willis, Leavenworth, Ind.
Lt R.G. Patterson, Los Angeles, Calif.
Lt K.G. Smith, Boise, Idaho.
Lt J.G. Matthews, Wallington, N.J.
Lt C.A. Hardin, Harrodsbury, Ky.
Lt George Carpenter, Oil City, Pa.
Lt Paul M. Ellington, Tulsa, Okla.
Lt Leon M. Blanding, Sumter, S.C.
Lt R.J. Fox, Larchmont, N.Y.
Lt Jimmie Happel, Paulsboro, N.J.
Lt Roy Evans, San Bernardino, Calif.
Lt W.P. Kelly, Saratoga, N.Y.
Lt J.M. Saunders, Nashville, Tenn.
Lt J.T. Slater, Waverly, N.Y.
Lt Thomas Wallace, Pasadena, Calif.

133rd EAGLE SQUADRON

Maj C.W. McColpin,
　commander, Buffalo, N.Y.
Capt M.E. Jackson,
　Corpus Christi, Tex.
Capt C.A. Cook, Jr.,
　Alhambra, Calif.
Lt W.H. Baker, Temple, Tex.
Lt G.B. Sperry, Alhambra, Calif.
Lt R.M. Beaty, Rye, N.Y.
Lt L.T. Ryerson, Whitinsville, Mass.
Lt Don S. Gentile, Piqua, O.
Lt D.D. Smith, Orlando, Fla.
Lt G.G. Wright, Wilkes Barre, Pa.
Lt G.H. Middletown, Visilia, Calif.
Lt E.L. Miller, Oakland, Calif.
Lt R.E. Smith, Washington, D.C.

133rd EAGLE (cont.)

Lt G.P. Neville,
    Oklahoma City, Okla.
Lt Leroy Gover, San Carlos, Calif.
Lt D.E. Lambert, Exeter, Calif.
Lt Carl H. Miley, Toledo, O.
Lt Don D. Nee, Long Beach, Calif.
Lt G.J. Smart, Solan, Kans.
Lt H.L. Ayres, Indianapolis, Ind.
Lt R.L. Alexander, Aylmer, Ontario
Lt W.C. Slade, Jr., Brama, Okla.
Lt C.H. Patterson, Fort Worth, Tex.
Lt Joe L. Bennett, Tusumcari, N.M.
Lt J. Mitchelweis, Jr., Rockford, Ill.
Lt J. Goodson, New York, N.Y.
Lt Raymond Fuchs, St. Louis, Mo.

*Top Scorers of other Eighth
Air Force Fighter Groups*

(20 and above)

Aces of the 55th Fighter Group

Lt Col Elwyn G. Righetti   33

Aces of the 56th Fighter Group

Capt Fred J. Christenson   21
Lt Col Francis S. Gabreski*   33
Capt Robert S. Johnson   28
Col Dave C. Schilling   32
Col Hobert Zemke   28

*Lt Col Gabreski scored 6 more
victories in the Korean war

Aces of the 78th Fighter Group

Col John D. Landers   28

Aces of the 339th Fighter Group

Lt Col Joseph L. Thury   28

Aces of the 352nd Fighter Group

Capt Edwin L. Heller   22
Capt Raymond H. Littge   23
Lt Col John C. Meyer   37
Maj George E. Preddy   30

Aces of the 353rd Fighter Group

Col Glenn E. Duncan   26

Aces of the 355th Fighter Group

Capt Henry W. Brown   31
Lt William J. Cullerton   27
Lt Col John L. Elder   21
Col Claiborne H. Kinnard   25

Aces of the 357th Fighter Group

Maj Leonard K. Carson   22
Maj Robert W. Foy   20
Lt Col John D. Landers   28

Aces of the 359th Fighter Group

Maj Ray S. Wetmore   24

Aces of the 479th Fighter Group

Maj Robin Olds   23

*

NB: Wing Commander W. Urban-
owitz, Polish but now an American
citizen, scored 20 victories, of which
17 were with the RAF in Europe
and 3 with the USAAF.

Index

GREAT BATTLES OF HISTORY
FROM ST. MARTIN'S PAPERBACKS

MEN AT WAR
The battles. The blood.
The way it was.